SHARPENING STRATEGIC INTELLIGENCE

This book critically examines the weaknesses of U.S. intelligence led by the Central Intelligence Agency in informing presidential decision making on issues of war and peace. It evaluates the CIA's strategic intelligence performance during the Cold War and post–Cold War periods as a foundation for examining the root causes of intelligence failures surrounding the 11 September 2001 attacks and assessments of Iraq's weapons of mass destruction programs in the run-up to the Iraq War. The book probes the root causes of these intelligence failures, which lie in the CIA's poor human intelligence collection and analysis practices. The book argues that none of the post-9/11 intelligence reforms have squarely addressed these root causes of strategic intelligence failure, and it recommends measures for redressing these dangerous vulnerabilities in American security.

Richard L. Russell is professor of national security affairs at the National Defense University's Near East and South Asia Center for Strategic Studies. He also holds academic appointments as adjunct associate professor in the Security Studies Program at Georgetown University and research associate in the Institute for the Study of Diplomacy at Georgetown University. Russell is the author of *Weapons Proliferation and War in the Greater Middle East: Strategic Contest* and *George F. Kennan's Strategic Thought: The Making of an American Political Realist.* He served seventeen years as a political-military analyst at the Central Intelligence Agency where he analyzed security issues in the Middle East and Europe. He received numerous CIA Exceptional Performance Awards, two of which were for his work during the Gulf War and the Kosovo War. Russell has been interviewed on National Public Radio, ABC News, and CNN, and his analyses have appeared in leading publications including the *Los Angeles Times, New York Times, Wall Street Journal, Washington Post, New Republic, Weekly Standard, USA Today,* and *U.S. News and World Report.* He holds a Ph.D. in foreign affairs from the University of Virginia and is a member of the International Institute for Strategic Studies.

Sharpening Strategic Intelligence

WHY THE CIA GETS IT WRONG, AND WHAT NEEDS TO BE DONE TO GET IT RIGHT

Richard L. Russell

Professor of National Security Affairs,
Near East and South Asia Center for Strategic Studies,
National Defense University

CAMBRIDGE
UNIVERSITY PRESS

CAMBRIDGE UNIVERSITY PRESS
Cambridge, New York, Melbourne, Madrid, Cape Town, Singapore, São Paulo

Cambridge University Press
32 Avenue of the Americas, New York, NY 10013-2473, USA

www.cambridge.org
Information on this title: www.cambridge.org/9780521878159

First published 2007

Printed in the United States of America

A catalog record for this publication is available from the British Library.

Library of Congress Cataloging in Publication Data

Russell, Richard L., 1961–
Sharpening strategic intelligence : why the CIA gets it wrong, and what needs to
be done to get it right / Richard L. Russell.
   p.   cm.
Includes bibliographical references and index.
ISBN 978-0-521-87815-9 hardback – ISBN 978-0-521-70237-9 paperback
1. United States. Central Intelligence Agency.   2. Intelligence service – United
States.   3. Terrorism – Government policy – United States.   I. Title.
JK468.I6R87   2007
327.1273 – dc22   2007000003

ISBN   978-0-521-87815-9 (hardback)
ISBN   978-0-521-70237-9 (paperback)

For Richard F. Russell, Jr., and Leavitt E. Moulton,
gentlemen who are deeply missed.

You shall know the truth, and the truth will make you free.

– St. John 8: 31–32

Many intelligence reports in war are contradictory; even more are false, and most are uncertain.

– Carl von Clausewitz, *On War*

Contents

Acknowledgments

The art of intelligence has occupied more than a fair share of my professional life for more than twenty years. I resigned from the Central Intelligence Agency after a seventeen-year stint as a political-military analyst in July 2001, just months before the 9/11 attacks. I will show "my cards" or biases up front and tell the reader that the principal reason I resigned from the CIA was that I had come to the conclusion that working life in the Agency simply prevented me from honing expertise in international security affairs. This reason may strike the reader as odd given a public perception that the CIA is loaded with "experts," but, as I detail in this book's pages, nothing could be farther from the truth.

Unshackled from the oppressive bureaucratic environment at the CIA, I have immensely enjoyed my second career as a university professor. It has given me a wonderful opportunity to think more strategically about the nexus of international security and intelligence. Strategic thought is a rare commodity in the CIA because analysts as well as their managers have allowed themselves to be consumed by the constant flood of classified cable traffic coming from a variety of sources. These sources of information more often than not are tactical minutia or blades of grass in the forest of contemporary international security. They consume most of the attention of CIA analysts and managers who do not have the time, discipline, inclination, or bureaucratic responsibility to take a step back to survey the forest and look at "big picture" strategic issues. The CIA's systemic failure to consistently and reliably do strategic intelligence was exposed to the American and international public with the intelligence debacles surrounding the 11 September 2001 al-Qaeda attacks and the abysmal assessments of Iraq's weapons of mass destruction programs in the run-up to the 2003 war.

The reader, in the interests of fair disclosure, should be aware that this book was submitted to pre-publication reviews at the CIA and the Department of Defense. The reviews were conducted to ensure that I had not inadvertently disclosed any classified information gained during my former career at the CIA or in my current position as a professor at the National Defense University. The CIA Publications Review Board requires that I publish the following disclaimer: "All statements of fact, opinion, or analysis expressed are those of the author and do not reflect the official positions or views of the CIA or any other U.S. Government agency. Nothing in the contents should be construed as asserting or imply-ing U.S. Government authentication of information or Agency endorse-ment of the author's views. The material has been reviewed by the CIA to prevent the disclosure of classified information." Not to be outdone, the National Defense University insists that I print this disclaimer: "The views expressed in this book are the author's alone and do not reflect the position or policy of the National Defense University, the Department of Defense, or the U.S. Government." The author can only apologize to readers for subjecting them to this fit of bureaucratic excess.

With that bit of unpleasantness out of the way, I take great pleasure in thanking a variety of distinguished journal editors who have given me the opportunity over the past several years to commit to paper some of the ideas about intelligence banging around inside my head and to share them with their readerships. I was pleased that one of the leading experts on intelligence, Loch Johnson, found my article "A Weak Pillar for Ameri-can National Security: CIA's Dismal Performance against WMD Threats" worthy of publication in his journal *Intelligence and National Security* (Fall 2005). Demetrios James Caraley graciously published "CIA's Strategic Intelligence in Iraq" in the *Political Science Quarterly* (Summer 2002). Tod Lindberg kindly published "Intelligence Failures: The Wrong Model for the War on Terror" in the Hoover Institution's journal *Policy Review* (February & March 2004). Nikolas Gvosdev generously published "Spies Like Them" in *The National Interest* (Fall 2004). None of these articles are reprinted in this book, but bits and pieces of their analyses and assessments are sprinkled throughout.

The use of my professional experience and academic scholarship as intellectual building blocks for the construction of the more comprehensive and in-depth analysis of what ails American strategic intelligence found in this book would not have been possible without support from the Earhart Foundation. I wish to thank the Trustees of the Earhart Foundation, President Ingrid Gregg, and Secretary and Director of Programs Bruce Frohnen for a fellowship research grant that enabled me to research and write this book. I especially appreciated the Earhart Foundation's recognition of the importance of strategic intelligence for American security as well as its confidence that I could get the project done.

The book greatly benefited from my discussions and debates with expert colleagues and friends. I wish to thank James Wirtz and Richard Shultz, whose work on intelligence I have long studied and learned from, for their help on this book. They, as well as Loch Johnson, graciously gave their time, attention, and expertise to review my research proposal for the Earhart Foundation. Heartfelt thanks go to Kenneth Thompson, my intellectual mentor and friend since I started my doctorial studies at the University of Virginia in 1993. Mr. Thompson was a pillar of support for this project just as he had been for my two previous books. Joseph DeSutter, Herman Meyer, and Thomas Blau were good colleagues who kindly invited me to teach a course on intelligence for the National Defense University's School for National Security Executive Education, which prompted me to read and think more systematically about intelligence. I am also indebted to the research assistance of Jessica Harris and Ryan Taugher, who both ably and cheerfully provided fast "Dominoes-like" delivery service to feed my intellectual cravings for the latest articles and books in a rapidly growing body of literature on intelligence. Those who tolerated my arguments and thoughts in these pages and offered wise corrections and refinements are Daniel Byman, Roger George, Robert Jervis, Paul Pillar, and Michael Yaffe. The book undoubtedly remains flawed due to my own intellectual frailties, but it was not for lack of help from these people who gave generously of their time and talents.

I would be seriously remiss if I failed to mention the invaluable help I received from my publisher, Cambridge University Press. Senior Editor John Berger was a guiding intellectual light who, in the earliest stages of work, encouraged me to make a balanced and scholarly study of intelligence and policy to distinguish it from the bulk of intelligence literature that has flooded the book market in the aftermath of 9/11, which often steers away from scholarship and into exposé. I kept John's wise counsel in mind throughout the research and writing of this book. Armed with the helpful, constructive, and thoughtful critiques and suggestions from Cambridge University Press's three superb and efficient anonymous reviewers, I hope that I have stayed solidly in the realm of scholarship and sober and balanced critical analysis. Barbara Walthall, the project manager for Aptara, Inc., and copyeditor Elizabeth Budd also were extremely efficient in ushering this book, as well as its author, into print.

On the home front, I owe my wife Lilian a thank you for her understanding and tolerance of my practice – born years ago of necessity to finish a dissertation while working full-time – of waking in the wee hours of weekend mornings to pound my laptop keys on the kitchen table in order to be close to the coffeepot. And to our young and energetic boys, Daniel and Ryan, I owe my apologies for being less than a cheerful father on weekend mornings for most of the past several years when they refused to sleep late and instead leapt down the stairs to look for breakfast. If only I could have somehow tapped a tiny fraction of their energies, I could have finished this book in much less time!

SHARPENING STRATEGIC INTELLIGENCE

1 Strategic Intelligence and American Statecraft

THE U.S. INTELLIGENCE COMMUNITY SUFFERED FROM TWO of the greatest intelligence debacles in its sixty-year history with the 11 September 2001 ("9/11") al-Qaeda attacks and the assessment of Iraq's weapons of mass destruction (WMD) programs in the run-up to the war launched in 2003 against Saddam Hussein's regime. Although the intelligence community is made up of some sixteen intelligence agencies with varying responsibilities and functions, the lion's share of the burden of these failures falls squarely on the shoulders of the Central Intelligence Agency (CIA), which had been the lead agency for providing strategic intelligence to the president in his role as commander in chief.

Taxpayers now pay about $44 billion per year on intelligence to support the president of the United States in defending U.S. interests.[1] This is a steep increase from the 1998 intelligence community budget of some $27 billion.[2] The U.S. intelligence community budget, moreover, is a sum that dwarfs the entire defense expenditures of most countries. All of the sixteen intelligence organizations that comprise the intelligence community have about 100,000 people working for them.[3] Although the CIA consumes only a small portion of the total intelligence community budget, it still has a workforce of some 17,000 people, by the account of former Director of Central Intelligence (DCI) George Tenet.[4]

Yet that large annual investment and sizable manpower did not spare the United States its two most devastating intelligence failures since the inception of the U.S. intelligence community in 1947. United States intelligence in general and the CIA in particular failed to warn with sufficient clarity and specificity of the 11 September 2001 conspiracy that caused the deaths of nearly 3,000 civilians in the American homeland. That intelligence debacle was quickly followed by miserably inaccurate CIA intelligence assessments in 2002 that Saddam Hussein's Iraq was reconstituting its nuclear weapons program and restocking his chemical and biological weapons when, in fact, its WMD programs had been largely mothballed since the mid-1990s.

American policy makers, members of Congress, and the general public have a right to ask, "Why don't our tax dollars produce better intelligence for the president to safeguard our country and national interests?" The key to answering this question lies in probing the weaknesses of the CIA, which has long served as the "first among equals" in a sprawling intelligence community. The CIA, with its Directorate of Operations (DO) charged with conducting espionage against U.S. adversaries and its Directorate of Intelligence (DI) responsible for conducting intelligence analysis, had long enjoyed unparalleled access to the president.

Much attention has hailed the creation of the new director of national intelligence (DNI) as the cure for U.S. intelligence. The DNI position was a key recommendation of the 9/11 Commission that examined the failure of the intelligence community to provide the intelligence needed to disrupt the al-Qaeda plot.[5] The 9/11 Commission managed to parlay the understandable emotional appeals made by the families of victims into a venerable political steamroller to flatten President George W. Bush's initial resistance to the creation of the DNI. The Bush administration, however, mistakenly caved in to the pressure and lukewarmly supported the new position. As Judge Richard Posner, who has extensively studied the *9/11 Commission Report,* rightly comments, "allowing several thousand emotionally traumatized people to drive major public policy in a nation of almost 300 million is a perversion of the democratic process."[6]

The American public mistakenly believes that our intelligence problems have been fixed, when the reality is probably that we have created even more problems with the reforms that have been implemented. About 65 percent of Americans believe that the reforming of the intelligence community is the best way to strengthen U.S. security, and about 40 percent of Americans give the government an A or a B for already "making the changes needed to improve U.S. intelligence and spying."[7] Despite the political fanfare and public support for the restructuring changes, the DNI's responsibilities are little more than rehashed responsibilities that had traditionally been exercised by the DCI who had overseen the entire intelligence community as well as headed the CIA.

The creation of the DNI position in and of itself will do nothing to correct the fundamental and root cause of the CIA's intelligence failures – to include many others before 9/11 and the Iraq War begun in 2003 – which is the systemic failure to deliver first-rate human intelligence and analysis to the commander in chief. Stolen human secrets and strategic analysis are critical components for deciphering for the president the innermost thinking of U.S. adversaries such as North Korea, Iran, and other states that are on the cusp of acquiring WMDs, as well as terrorist groups such as al-Qaeda and Hezbollah that want to get their hands on such weapons.

This book takes a step back from the mad rush in the public debate to diagnose the problems of the CIA by examining only the events surrounding 9/11 and the Iraq War. It aims to make a strategic assessment of U.S. intelligence performance throughout the Cold War, post–Cold War, and post–9/11 periods. Only such a broad assessment provides the necessary framework for diagnosing the real systemic causes of U.S. strategic intelligence failures.

Understanding Strategic Intelligence

A great deal can be read of espionage exploits and covert action, but comparatively little research examines the use of intelligence in policy making.[8] Retired or resigned CIA case officers, commonly referred to as "spies," write many of the books in the intelligence literature market. To read only these exposés, a reader might conclude that the U.S. government recruits, trains, and sends these people abroad to live out their personal "James Bond" fantasies at taxpayers' expense. Readers might also get the mistaken impression that U.S. intelligence and the CIA are ends in and of themselves and not instruments for U.S. power in the world.

Much of the debate and discourse on intelligence does not appreciate or even understand the nature of strategic intelligence. Strategic intelligence and its use in armed conflict has been a mainstay of international relations for thousands of years. Military historian John Keegan reminds us that statesmen and military leaders such as the duke of Marlborough and George Washington placed a high priority on strategic intelligence and that "From the earliest of times, military leaders have always sought information of the enemy, his strengths, his weaknesses, his intentions, his dispositions."[9] But the history of strategic intelligence stretches back even further. In the Bible, the Old Testament books of Numbers and Joshua, respectively, tell of Moses sending a reconnaissance team to the Promised Land and of Joshua dispatching spies to reconnoiter Jericho.[10]

To be fair, scholars have not done a lot of research to help the public, or policy makers for that matter, to understand the full dimensions of strategic intelligence. Sherman Kent, a scholar whose service in the intelligence community as head of national intelligence estimates in the wake of World War II, started the spade work in his landmark book *Strategic Intelligence for American World Policy*. Kent defines strategic intelligence as "the knowledge which our highly placed civilians and military men must have to safeguard the national welfare."[11] Scholar Adda Bozeman picks up where Kent left off, writing that strategic intelligence should "facilitate the steady pursuit of long-range policy objectives even as it also provides guidance in the choice of tactically adroit ad hoc responses to particular occurrences in foreign affairs."[12] Since Kent and Bozeman, the scholarly attention to strategic intelligence has dropped off considerably. On top of that, Michael Herman rightly observes that "Intelligence power has not yet received anything like the prolonged attention given to military power, or to the diplomacy with which intelligence is connected."[13]

Perhaps the pendulum will swing toward a renewed interest in strategic intelligence in light of the grave consequences of recent shoddy strategic intelligence to U.S. policy makers. As potentially illustrative of a move in this direction, Loch Johnson and James Wirtz recently edited an important book in which they define strategic intelligence as that which "contributes to the processes, products, and organizations used by senior officials to create and implement national foreign and defense policies. Strategic intelligence thus provides warning of immediate threats to vital national security interests and assesses long-term trends of interest to senior government officials. Strategic intelligence is of political importance because it can shape the course and conduct of U.S. policy."[14]

Strategic intelligence is contrasted with lesser-order information that is more germane to the demands of operational and tactical levels of the military. Tactical intelligence collected and analyzed for military commanders is generally not pertinent to presidential interests. A battalion commander, for example, would undoubtedly want to know the nature of fortifications and enemy strength at a hilltop he has been ordered to capture, but the president normally need not be briefed on such tactical military affairs. It is an important caveat to this generalization that, in some cases, tactical engagements might have consequences that could ripple up the chain of command with operational and strategic consequences for the president and his key policy lieutenants, but these would be exceptions rather than the rule. Bruce Berkowitz and Allan Goodman rightly point out that "Strategic intelligence is designed to provide officials with the 'big picture' and long-range forecasts they need in order to plan for the future."[15]

In this book, strategic intelligence is information and analysis that is most germane to the interests and responsibilities of the president as commander in chief to protect the nation. Information obtained via clandestine means is an important but not an exclusive component of strategic intelligence. In the information-technology era, an enormous amount of information about world affairs is available publicly and instantaneously via the Internet. Clandestinely collected information supplements the massive amount of public information but will rarely be sufficient in and of itself for understanding the complexities of contemporary strategic issues.

In essence, strategic intelligence is information – both from public and clandestine sources – combined with analysis that is pertinent to presidential decision making in gauging threats of force and violence against U.S. interests as well as in guiding the commander in chief's use of force against adversaries. The president bears unique responsibility as commander in chief for orchestrating strategy that occupies a zone between setting political objectives and wielding the threat, use, and management of U.S. force to achieve political objectives.[16] Strategic intelligence accordingly often entails assessing the capabilities, intentions, and threats of adversaries to U.S. interests and citizens.

Another way of putting it is this: Strategic intelligence is the use of information, whether clandestinely or publicly acquired, that is synthesized into analysis and read by the senior-most policy makers charged with setting the objectives of grand strategy and ensuring that military force is exercised for purposes of achieving national interests. As Loch Johnson puts it, "intelligence is *information*, a tangible product collected and interpreted in order to achieve a sharper image of political and military conditions worldwide."[17] Strategic intelligence is the analytic synthesis of information from a variety of clandestine sources – to include human spies, diplomats, defense attachés, intercepted communications, satellite imagery, and electronic emissions – as well as open-source information such as newspapers, Internet, radio, and television – that, when packaged together, is of relevance to the roles and responsibilities of the president and his key national security lieutenants charged with setting and implementing policies to achieve the country's strategic objectives.

Strategic intelligence is not the same as "military intelligence," much of which is produced by the Defense Intelligence Agency (DIA) and the intelligence arms of the U.S. Army, Air Force, Navy, and Marine Corps. Most of the intelligence products from these components of the U.S. intelligence community are funneled and blended into the operational and tactical views of the service chiefs and operational military commanders. It makes its way up to the senior-most rungs of the government in briefing books for the chairman of the Joint Chiefs of Staff and the secretary of defense who are sitting in the Oval Office helping the president exercise his powers as commander in chief. The secretary of state comes prepared for Oval Office meetings with intelligence analyses provided by the Department of State's small but able Bureau of Intelligence and Research. The CIA, however, has traditionally been unique among intelligence components in having its director at the table to bring political-military intelligence and analysis directly to the president as he weighed threats of force against the United States and managed the use of U.S. force against adversaries.

This book focuses on the problems of strategic intelligence that occupy the space between the realms of politics and force. Although the DIA and service intelligence organizations produce an enormous amount of military-related intelligence on the operational side, they do not routinely marry military analysis to the political and policy-relevant dimensions attuned to presidential responsibilities to the same extent as the CIA. To be sure, the CIA produces a great array of intelligence on a variety of topics other than those in the strategic realm, such as demographics and global disease, but rarely, if ever, have intelligence mistakes on such topics had the dramatic impact on U.S. national security that mistakes on strategic intelligence revolving around issues of war and peace have had.

A core challenge for strategic intelligence is the acquisition of "secrets" and the analysis of "mysteries," which are useful distinctions made by keen observers and practitioners in the intelligence business, such as Gregory Treverton and Joseph Nye.[18] Berkowitz and Goodman also make this distinction: "Secrets provide the analyst with information about issues, situations, and processes that are intended by foreign governments or groups not to be known."[19] Secrets are knowable facts that can be captured by satellite photographs analyzed by the National Geospatial Intelligence Agency or communications intercepted by the National Security Agency or stolen by agents and passed on to their CIA case officers. Examples of secrets susceptible to theft by the CIA are military order-of-battle information, such as the numbers of tanks, soldiers, and aircraft and their organizational structure and deployment areas as well as military contingency plans.

Mysteries, on the other hand, fall in the realm of analysis and conjecture about the future in strategic affairs. According to Berkowitz and Goodman, "Mysteries are just that: questions or issues that no amount of intelligence analysis or collection of secret information will reveal."[20] Mysteries cannot be answered by a spy stealing a document. Even foreign leaders and adversaries do not know the answers to mysteries. Examples of mysteries are questions such as "Is Iran primed for revolution?" or "When is the Soviet Union going to collapse?" As a general statement, secrets are the realm of CIA case officers, and mysteries are the challenge for analysts.

The CIA's strategic intelligence in the past has helped as well as hindered presidents in carrying out U.S. statecraft. These days, statecraft is unfortunately rarely studied in the academy and in the security studies field, which must be considered a glaring hole in intellectual inquiry. As Carnes Lord astutely observes, "Although far from absent in the language of contemporary political discourse, the concept of statecraft is rarely analyzed carefully or brought into relationship with the idea of leadership. Even its basic meaning is not especially clear. The term is now used almost exclusively to refer to diplomacy or the conduct of foreign policy in a broad sense."[21] The use of the concept of statecraft in this book is pegged to Lord's view that "statecraft is an art of coping with an adversarial environment in which actions generate reactions in unpredictable ways and chance and uncertainty rule. Like strategy, too, statecraft is also an art of relating means to ends. If, in Clausewitz's formulation, strategy is the art of using battles to achieve the objectives of the war, statecraft is the art of using wars and other instruments available to political leaders to attain national goals."[22]

Strategic intelligence produced by the CIA is one of the critical instruments of national power for the president exercising his authorities as commander in chief. Scholar and strategist Richard Betts points out that "If capacity for informed strategic analysis – integrating political, economic, and military judgment – is not preserved and applied, decisions on the use of force will be uninformed and, therefore, irresponsible."[23] Good strategic intelligence can magnify the power and influence of other instruments of national power. By the same token, poor strategic intelligence can weigh down and diminish the influence of other instruments of statecraft. As a Council on Foreign Relations task force assessed, "Accurate intelligence significantly improves the effectiveness of diplomatic and military undertakings; while good intelligence cannot guarantee good policy, poor intelligence frequently contributes to policy failure."[24]

Distracted by the Mystique of the CIA's Covert Action and Special Activities

A sustained and sober assessment of the CIA's strategic intelligence performance and the origins of its failures has been distracted by public fascination with the "sexier and exciting" aspects of the CIA's mission in carrying out covert action and special activities at the president's behest. Much ink has been spilt on the controversies surrounding covert actions, which are designed to influence affairs abroad while hiding the hand of the United States and includes such activities as planting newspaper articles abroad to supporting politicians and political parties. Special activities, on the other hand, can range from the provision of training and technical expertise to foreign military, security, and intelligence services to support for paramilitary operations.[25]

Both covert action and special activities have taken on an importance in public policy debate in the post–9/11 environment with controversies swirling around the accusations that the United States planted newspaper stories favorable to it in budding Iraqi media as well as CIA-orchestrated renditions or covert spiriting away from the streets of suspected al-Qaeda members to a series of clandestine prisons reported to be in the Middle East and Eastern Europe.[26] The CIA's support to paramilitary operations reached an apex with the deployment of small paramilitary CIA teams into Afghanistan to pave the way for the insertion of U.S. Special Forces in the impressive 2001 military campaign that ousted the despicable Taliban regime in Afghanistan.[27]

Reaching back into the history of the CIA's formative years, the United States successfully used covert action to advance U.S. policy interests throughout the globe. It spent some $75 million over twenty years in Italy, as a former senior CIA official and scholar Ray Cline recalled, "to help save it from impending disaster in 1948 and to support the 'opening-to-the-left' in the mid 1960s, the United States for reasons of political prudence and economy discontinued subsidies to Italian political parties."[28] The CIA's covert action that returned the shah of Iran to power in 1953 is still heralded as a high-water mark for the agency's myth of covert action capabilities.[29] In Latin America, the CIA levied covert action in Chile, Guatemala, and against Fidel Castro's Cuba in the 1950s, 1960s, and 1970s. These operations, as historian John Lewis Gaddis rightly observes, gave the CIA "an almost mythic reputation throughout Latin America and the Middle East as an instrument with which the United States could depose governments it disliked, whenever it wished to do so."[30] This reputation, largely unfounded, has had a long life and persists today among elites and publics alike, especially in the Middle East, where many are still more willing to believe that the CIA, not al-Qaeda, was behind the 9/11 attacks.

One of the largest covert action programs in the CIA's history was the military backing of the insurgency against the Soviet Union's occupation of Afghanistan during the Cold War. The CIA spent millions of dollars and provided tons of military arms and equipment to the Afghan insurgents over a period of years to increase substantially the costs of Soviet occupation and contributed to the Soviet decision to withdraw militarily from Afghanistan. This less-than-secret war is heralded by CIA veterans as an exemplar of covert action that contributed to ending the Cold War. Other commentators are not so sanguine and argue that the CIA covert action program gave military training, expertise, and battlefield experience to militant Islamic extremists, who later went on to found al-Qaeda. The truth probably lies somewhere in between, but it is important to note that the United States never dealt directly with bin Laden during the Afghan war. Bin Laden's direct sponsors and benefactors were intelligence services of Saudi Arabia and Pakistan.[31]

More recently, the CIA has had a hand in special activities to support U.S. policy in the Middle East. Former Israeli Mossad chief Efraim Halevy writes that the CIA played a mediating role between Palestinian and Israeli forces in their conflict, and the CIA "assumed a role of coordinating the training of Palestinian security forces and ran training courses for them with the participation of Egyptian and Jordanian instructors."[32]

Covert action has taken on an increasingly important role in the war on terrorism, which the public gets glimpses of through leaks. Covert actions such as the ones carried out in Afghanistan are carried out by the CIA and need to be authorized by a presidential order called a "Finding," which must be shared with and approved by the House and Senate Intelligence Oversight Committees to be legal in the U.S. judicial system. Traditionally, the U.S. presidents have banned American assassination of foreign leaders under executive orders, a practice that has been perpetuated since President Gerald Ford's Executive Order 12333, which prohibited assassinations, a move to stem the tide of public criticisms against the CIA and the intelligence community during a tumultuous period of history in U.S. intelligence.[33] Former CIA Director Porter Goss recently told Congress in public testimony that the ban on assassinations by U.S. intelligence is still in force but that it does not prohibit the CIA from killing terrorists.[34]

The CIA appears to be effectively using armed unmanned aerial vehicles (UAVs) to kill al-Qaeda operatives. The CIA has used armed UAVs to kill al-Qaeda operatives in Yemen and Pakistan as well as in Iraq. According to the *Los Angeles Times*, "Several U.S. officials confirmed that at least 19 occasions since Sept. 11 on which Predators successfully fired Hellfire missiles on terrorist suspects overseas, including 10 in Iraq in one month last year [2005]. The Predator strikes have killed at least four senior Al Qaeda leaders, but also many civilians, and it is not known how many times they missed their targets."[35]

Some CIA critics have faulted the agency for failing to use the armed UAVs to target bin Laden or mount covert paramilitary operations to capture him before 9/11. The CIA's DO chief in 1998, for example, did not want to use his funds to sponsor a paramilitary operation to grab bin Laden from his farm in Afghanistan and "expressed concern that people might get killed" and that "the operation had at least a slight flavor of a plan for an assassination. Moreover, he calculated that it would cost several million dollars. He was not prepared to take the money 'out of hide,' and he did not want to go to all the necessary congressional committees to get special money."[36] Although civilians tragically have been killed in paramilitary operations, military strikes, and UAV attacks since 9/11, the strikes probably still are legitimate instruments of war as long as there is a reasonable chance of killing al-Qaeda operatives and leaders who are sworn to kill as many U.S. civilians and soldiers as they can as long as they live.

The CIA also is using covert teams to locate suspected al-Qaeda operatives abroad – in countries where UAV attacks would not be politically viable options such as in Europe – and in raids called "renditions" to sweep them off the streets and bring them to other countries for detention and interrogations. These operations have been embroiled in controversy. Italy, for example, experienced a political uproar because a team took an individual off Italian soil, according to the *New York Times*.[37] Other European and Asia countries are in an uproar over the purported existence of a string of clandestine CIA detention facilities on their soil. The CIA also has been publicly condemned for blatant violations of the Geneva Conventions with the use of techniques that are commonly considered to be torture in its interrogations undertaken in U.S. military detention facilities in Afghanistan, Iraq, and Guantanomo Bay, Cuba.[38]

These accusations include charges that the CIA is using a technique called "water-boarding," which makes detainees believe they are drowning. Not only is this technique morally unacceptable, many professional interrogates judge that the technique produces bad intelligence because prisoners will say or make up anything to get interrogators to stop the water-boarding.[39] The United States may have already fallen victim to this intelligence pitfall. James Risen reports that some information the CIA received from debriefing one high-level al-Qaeda operational commander was fabricated because he wanted to stop water-boarding.[40] Another individual, who was reportedly tortured after he was turned over to Egyptian officials, fabricated information on Iraq's links to al-Qaeda in the run-up to the 2003 Iraq War, the *New York Times* reports.[41]

Notwithstanding the public fascination and controversies surrounding covert action and special activities, the lion's share of the intelligence community and the CIA's budget is devoted to the collection and analysis of intelligence. According to former DCI Robert Gates, "over 95 percent of the national intelligence budget is devoted to the collection and analysis of information. Only about three percent of the CIA's people are involved in covert action."[42] That figure undoubtedly has changed over the years, but the broad point remains valid.

Reflecting on the CIA's Strategic Intelligence for U.S. Statecraft

The foundation for the intelligence community was part of the National Security Act of 1947. The legislation created the CIA to be a central point for the collection and analysis of intelligence gathered throughout various agencies and departments, including the U.S. Army, Air Force, and Navy, as well as the Departments of State and Defense. The CIA was by design a "first among equals" headed by the DCI, who served as the head of both the CIA and the entire intelligence community and as the president's principal advisor on intelligence. The CIA was wisely given the central role in the intelligence community as a means to correct the intelligence deficiencies that the United States experienced in World War II, during which parts of the U.S. government, including the Department of State and the army and navy each had snippets of intelligence but not the entire intelligence picture of Japanese plans and preparations to attack Pearl Harbor in 1941.[43] There had been no central intelligence clearinghouse that could have brought the raw intelligence in the form of military attaché and diplomatic reports and intercepted communications and drawn the analytic assessment to warn the president of the impending Japanese attack on Pearl Harbor.

The CIA's bureaucratic autonomy from the policy community had given it a better chance than other intelligence community components to produce strategic intelligence that is divorced from policy equities. At the CIA's inception in 1947, the Truman administration wisely sought to create a largely civilian institution that was not bureaucratically embedded in another designed to implement U.S. policy. The worry was that intelligence shops in the Departments of State and Defense under pressure from their bosses charged with devising and carrying out policy would put either implicit or explicit pressure on intelligence analysts and collectors to produce intelligence that conformed to or supported policy. The CIA also stood aside from the intense budgetary and operational pressures inside the military to produce intelligence assessments to justify larger shares of the country's defense budget and produce positive news, especially during wartime when the military is prone to emphasize successes and underplay the shortcomings of performances in battle.

Although the CIA's principal customer is the president, its relationship with Congress, which controls the Agency's purse strings, also gave the CIA some cushion from potential pressures from the executive branch to produce intelligence that supported White House policy interests. As former DCI Gates captured the relationship, the CIA over the years had moved to an area nearly equidistant between the White House and Capitol Hill.[44] The House and Senate Intelligence Oversight Committees received most of the finished intelligence published by the intelligence community.[45] Notwithstanding growing links to Congress over the years, the CIA continued to see the president as the principal customer because of the commander in chief's larger responsibilities for governing U.S. statecraft on a day-to-day basis whereas Congress had a secondary oversight role in national security.

The CIA traditionally had had the unique responsibility for getting intelligence from human sources, especially from states hostile to the United States. The CIA has been responsible for sending intelligence officers abroad, primarily under official cover, to spot, assess, develop, and recruit agents or spies to provide information to the CIA and the U.S. government. The primary task of these covert officers, called case officers, has been to seduce and manage foreign diplomats, intelligence officers, soldiers, and politicians of other countries who are committing treason by providing, or, to put it more bluntly, stealing secrets for the United States. The CIA's DO had long held as its core mission the stealing of foreign secrets to reveal for the president and other key U.S. policy makers the plans and intentions of foreign adversaries.

The CIA complemented its human intelligence collection operations with the analysis of information collected from throughout the U.S. intelligence community. After all, individual and separate human reports seldom make strategic sense in and of themselves. As Treverton rightly points out, in an age of the information revolution and globalization, "the business of intelligence is no longer just to provide secrets; rather, its business is to produce high-quality understanding of the world using all sources."[46] The CIA's DI had long been charged with the crafting of a variety of "finished" intelligence products that were often based on a wide variety of clandestine and classified sources of information as well as publicly available information. These analyses were published in a variety of formats and publications, from longer research reports to shorter and more time-sensitive current intelligence products for key policy makers.

The CIA's senior management, including both the DO and DI components, for years had considered the Presidential Daily Brief (PDB) to be the primary means for the CIA to have access to and to serve the president with strategic intelligence. The PDB is a short document of no more than twenty pages treating current intelligence topics judged by the CIA management to be of presidential interest. The CIA typically dispatched a team of briefing officers from the CIA's headquarters in Langley, Virginia, located just outside Washington, D.C., downtown almost daily to deliver the PDB to the president and the key advisors whom he designated to receive the PDB. These policy makers typically included the vice president, the president's chief of staff and national security advisor, the secretaries of defense and state, and the chairman and vice chairman of the Joint Chiefs of Staff. On some occasions, the DCI led the president's briefing team, although under George Tenet's directorship, he very often led the briefing for the president – arguably too often because it distracted Tenet from his other responsibilities for managing the CIA and the intelligence community. The president and his key national security lieutenants typically would read the PDB in the presence of the CIA briefer, who would sit ready to answer any questions as well as to take back to CIA headquarters any questions or requests for follow-on or new intelligence analysis or collection.

The PDB in essence was the vehicle for the CIA to nurture a running strategic dialogue with the commander in chief. As Michael Herman observes, the CIA did not expect the PDB to "lead regularly to immediate action, any more than newspapers expect to change the world with every issue. Of all the contents of daily and weekly high-level intelligence summaries only a minute proportion feed directly into decisions."[47] Herman continues that "Consequently the role of most intelligence is not driving decisions in any short term, specific way, but contributing to decision-takers' general enlightenment; intelligence producers are in the business of educating their masters."[48]

The CIA did not always enjoy steady and ready access to the president, however. Rather, this access waxed and waned from administration to administration. The CIA's access to the president was strongest under George H. W. Bush and his son George W. Bush, who both received the PDB directly and routinely from the CIA briefers, in many instances accompanied by the DCI himself. As George H. W. Bush recalled his days in the Oval Office, "I made it a point from day one to read the PDB in the presence of a CIA briefer and either Brent [Scowcroft, Bush's national security advisor] or his deputy. That way I could task the briefers to bring in more information on a certain matter or, when the reading would bring to mind policy matters, ask Brent to follow up on an item of interest. The

CIA officers would write down my questions; in a day or so, I would get an answer or an elaboration."[49] The agency's access to the president under Ronald Reagan, Jimmy Carter, and Richard Nixon was profoundly less intimate because the CIA briefers delivered the PDB via the national security advisors for each of these presidents. Robert Gates recalls, for instance, that "The views of the Central Intelligence Agency counted for little as the Nixon administration developed policy strategies for Vietnam, Europe, arms control, defense, the Soviet Union, and China – the issues that would dominate Nixon's first term" and that the president paid little attention to the PDB.[50]

The CIA began to attach so much importance to access to the president that it pushed and encouraged the establishment of relationships with presidential contenders and president-elects. The practice of the CIA briefing presidential contenders began under President Harry Truman, who "in 1952 authorized the CIA to brief Gen. Dwight Eisenhower and Governor Adlai Stevenson so that the successful candidate would be as well informed as possible on the world situation when he took office."[51] The CIA had wanted to establish a relationship early, and incumbent presidents have generally overlooked partisan issues to grant their challengers access to CIA intelligence briefing for the sake of larger national interests. The process, however, had not always produced the result for which the CIA's senior management had hoped. The CIA, for example, had nurtured a close briefing relationship with president-elect Bill Clinton, who welcomed CIA briefings. After Clinton assumed the Oval Office, however, the CIA's direct access was cut off, and CIA PDB briefers were relegated to delivering the PDB to Clinton's national security advisor. "Despite the secrecy and exclusivity of the PDB, Clinton would often complain that most days the document contained much that he had already read elsewhere," intelligence expert James Bamford reports.[52]

The 9/11 and Iraq War Watersheds

The ultimate aim of the CIA's case officers and analysts is to provide strategic intelligence to the country's top national security officials to help reduce the ambiguity of international security issues. Perfect clarity is rarely, if ever, achievable given the complexity of human affairs. Predicting the future is the task of prophets, not intelligence officers. Recognizing the inability of human beings to predict the future readily and consistently, some observers, most eloquently and persuasively Richard Betts, argue that intelligence failures are inevitable.[53]

Intelligence failures may well be inevitable, but accepting the proposition as an empirical reality too readily becomes a master escape clause for intelligence officials to rationalize away major strategic intelligence failures. Eliot Cohen and John Gooch draw an important observation from their expert study of war that there are "failures to learn," "failures to anticipate," and "failures to adapt," and "When all three kinds of failure occur together, catastrophe results."[54] It is argued in this book that the CIA has systemically, throughout its sixty-year history as an intelligence organization, suffered from all three types of failures; the catastrophic results of this are all too clear after the 9/11 attacks and the Iraq WMD debacle.

The CIA was designed to do what today is commonly referred to as "connect the dots." Yet it failed to penetrate sufficiently with human intelligence agents or to fathom analytically with sufficient clarity the al-Qaeda 9/11 conspiracy that lead to the slaughter of some 3,000 individuals on U.S. soil. The national security debacle of that day exceeded that of 7 December 1941, which gave birth to the modern U.S. intelligence community. The Japanese attack on Pearl Harbor was directed against a military target and resulted in the deaths of about 2,000 people, primarily soldiers and sailors, and Hawaii was still a world away from the continental United States. The attacks of 11 September were of even greater magnitude and calamity for U.S. national security because they were targeted against civilians in the continental United States. Not since the War of 1812 when the British sacked Washington, D.C., had the United States come under such a direct attack, and not since the battle of Antietam in the American Civil War had the United States suffered the loss of so many of its citizens on its own soil.

The nature and magnitude of the intelligence failure on 11 September had not yet been fully absorbed by U.S. policy makers and citizens when the CIA suffered another huge debacle. The agency had assessed for President Bush that Saddam Hussein's regime was aggressively rebuilding its chemical, biological, and nuclear weapons programs in violation of the United Nations Security Council resolutions that led to the cease fire of the 1990–1 Gulf War. The CIA's assessment directly contributed to a powerful strategic rationale for the 2003 U.S. and British invasion of Iraq and the ousting of Saddam's regime. After the invasion, extensive weapons inspections found that Iraq had no militarily significant WMD stocks and that its WMD programs were largely dilapidated, contrary to the CIA's prewar assessments.

The CIA's bureaucratic autonomy increased the odds that intelligence would be freer from policy or military bias, but it by no means ensured that the CIA always made the right intelligence calls. The CIA, as is examined in subsequent chapters, has made many bad strategic intelligence calls throughout its history. These failures or blunders more often than not were the result of poor human intelligence collection and shoddy analysis, not a reflection of pandering to policy masters to deliver intelligence to please them. The epigraph of St. John in this book, "Seek the truth and it will set you free," as well as a motto (commonly attributed to former Secretary of State George Marshall), "Speak truth to power," had been inculcated over the years as the professional loadstars for the CIA's case officers and analysts, even if they often failed to achieve these lofty goals – as all human beings are wont to do. Jami Miscik, head of the CIA's analytic corps in 2001, boasted that "We truly are speaking truth to power."[55]

An institutional arrogance was an unseemly and unfortunate side effect of the CIA's secretiveness and separateness from the policy side of the U.S. national security apparatus. As intelligence expert Gregory Treverton astutely observed from his stint serving on the National Intelligence Council, an advisory board to the DCI, "Intelligence analysts thought of their calling as one apart, with whiffs of superiority and condescension in their view … that said we're in the business of speaking truth, and if those policy types downtown don't listen, the hell with them."[56] The CIA indeed was the best bureaucratically situated organization to "call them as you see them," but that autonomy did not mean that the CIA was always right, as the recent intelligence failures surrounding 9/11 and Iraq painfully attest. These failures struck at the pride and arrogance of many inside the CIA and fueled leaks to the press critical of Bush administration policy, which further undermined the relevance and potential contribution of the CIA's strategic intelligence to the commander in chief.

The public outcry over the dismal performance of U.S. intelligence and the CIA led to a series of investigations to probe the sources of these failures, most notably the 9/11 Commission. The Bush administration bowed to political pressure and accepted the 9/11 Commission's recommendation to create the DNI post to oversee the entire intelligence community, including the CIA, and to serve as the president's chief intelligence advisor. The move represented the CIA's demotion from its traditional position since 1947 as the "first among equals" in the intelligence community to a "one of many." The DCI position went to the ash heap of history to be replaced by the director of the CIA. Perhaps most significantly, the CIA lost its traditional and unique access to the president.

The intelligence blunders of 11 September and the Iraq War in many respects were a culmination of the CIA's incompetence, which had finally caught up with it because the magnitude of the failures could no longer be hidden behind a cloak of secrecy. The CIA's inability to competently carry out its core missions of stealing human intelligence from our adversaries and analyzing intelligence information had been made plain to the public, as well as to the executive and legislative branches of government. To put it simply, the CIA's demotion was the well-deserved result of its own incompetence. And although it might be a slight overstatement to say the CIA has rightfully met its "demise," because it probably will stagger on as most bureaucracies do, it is fair to say the CIA's traditional stature and influence both within the intelligence community and among policy makers and the public has indeed come to an end.

The CIA's demise is nowhere more evident than in the loss of its unique and privileged institutional access to the president. The DNI, Ambassador John Negroponte, has taken over the former DCI's responsibility to brief the president daily. The DNI, moreover, no longer delivers a CIA-produced PDB but a collection of intelligence reports produced from agencies throughout the intelligence community.[57] In Washington, D.C., where access to the president is power, the CIA has clearly been benched to second string and is no longer the premium intelligence service for the president. The CIA's loss of nearly exclusive presidential briefing privileges is a "smoking gun" piece of evidence that the CIA's once-exalted position in the intelligence community is a thing of the past.

Diagnosing the Origins of Strategic Intelligence Failures

What went wrong with U.S. strategic intelligence? Why did we fail to stop the al-Qaeda 9/11 attacks? Why were we so wrong about Iraq's WMD programs? Have all the post–9/11 reforms fixed all that ails U.S. intelligence? Or, in the political rush to tape the emotions of 9/11 victims' families, has the United States misdiagnosed the sources of the CIA's failures? Might the reforms even further downgrade the performance of the nation's strategic intelligence?

To answer these questions, one must take a step back from the daily news headlines and understand that the role of strategic intelligence in the foreign-policy decision-making process at the highest echelons of government is a neglected field of study. Much of the scholarly literature on intelligence is written from the perspective of intelligence officers, whereas significantly less is written from the perspective of policy makers. As Gates observes, "A search of presidential memoirs and those of principal assistants over the past 30 years or so turns up remarkably little discussion or perspective on the role played by directors of central intelligence or intelligence information in presidential decision making on foreign affairs," and "in intelligence memoir literature, although one can read a great deal about covert operations and technical achievements, one finds little on the role of intelligence in presidential decision making."[58] We need in the study of intelligence to give more attention to the policy maker's perspective if it is to yield a more robust understanding of the strengths and weaknesses of strategic intelligence and to focus attention on areas where intelligence collection and analysis needs improvement.

Apologists for the CIA's strategic intelligence performances are fond of retorting to critics that whereas intelligence failures become public, the CIA's intelligence successes must remain secret. The defense has become cliché, but it does not hold up very well against the public record. In fact, a great deal of public information is available on the CIA's successes as well as its failures. A jaded observer might even argue that one of the most innovative reforms that the CIA ever undertook under DCI George Tenet was to revamp the CIA's Office of Public Affairs to ensure that word of the CIA's successes leaked to the press from unattributed sources.

What is lacking in the public debate is not information on strategic intelligence successes and failures but rigorous, scholarly, and systematic analyses that make sense of this body of evidence. What is especially lacking are examinations of what impact or influence strategic intelligence, or the paucity of strategic intelligence, had on presidential decision making. Too much of the growing body of intelligence literature restricts itself to the inside workings of the intelligence process as if intelligence was an end in and of itself and ignores the role of intelligence in informing presidential decision making, which is the ultimate end of strategic intelligence. Far too many critical assessments of American intelligence examine only one case of intelligence failure and then extrapolate reform recommendations based on only that one case. A grave shortcoming of the 9/11 Commission's report, for example, is that it examined only one case of intelligence failure – the attacks on 9/11 – and made sweeping recommendations for reforming intelligence as if al-Qaeda is the only threat that the United States is likely to face in the coming decades. Likewise, the Senate Select Committee on Intelligence uses only the case of the Iraq War WMD failures to make its recommendations for reform.[59] The

Silberman–Robb Commission on WMD takes a broader look at strategic issues,[60] but it too looks at only a slice of potential threats to American national security in coming decades.

What is needed is a substantively broader examination of challenges to American national security over a wide span of history and against a greater variety of threats to get a more comprehensive or strategic perspective of the strengths and weaknesses of American intelligence. This book aims to fill this intellectual and public-policy black hole. A strategic study of the CIA needs to focus on the performance of its core tasks of stealing secrets with its case officers in the DO and fathoming the answers to mysteries by analysts in the DI over the Cold War, the post-Cold War, and the 9/11 periods. Such a study is what is missing from the intelligence debate and reforms contemplated or underway.

"We won the Cold War" is a constant, and borderline annoying, refrain heard from the lips of CIA case officers and analysts who labored in the prime of their careers during the international competition for power between the United States and the Soviet Union. The claim is made so often that it escapes a critical examination of how well it fits reality. Chapter 2, "Debunking Cold War Myths," makes a critical appraisal of the CIA's strategic intelligence performance during the Cold War. The CIA had some significant strategic intelligence successes during the Cold War, especially in the Polish crisis and in a "war scare" during the Reagan administration, but it had more than a fair share of performances that are best characterized as failures, including the running of numerous human agents who were working for adversarial governments and the loss of its entire stable of human agents inside the Soviet Union. These performances undermine the myth of a "golden or stellar" Cold War era of CIA performances against a traditional nation-state threat in the Soviet Union.

For lack of a better characterization, the period after the fall of the Berlin Wall and the collapse of the Soviet Union up until 11 September 2001 is generally called the "post–Cold War period." Whether or not the CIA adequately warned the president of the collapse of the Soviet Union is debatable, but other CIA strategic intelligence performances in the 1990s are more readily and easily identified as failures. Chapter 3, "Stumbling after the Cold War," takes a broader look at the CIA's intelligence failings in the collection and analysis of critical issues confronting three American Presidents – George H. W. Bush, Bill Clinton, and George W. Bush – since the end of the Cold War. It examines the CIA's inability to recruit spies inside Iraq close to Saddam Hussein before his 1990 invasion of Kuwait; penetrate al-Qaeda to confidently locate Osama bin-Laden for military attack in the aftermath of his orchestration of terrorist attacks against American embassies in Africa and the USS *Cole* in Yemen; warn of India's nuclear weapons testing in 1998 that launched South Asia into a strategic arms race; detect early on the Pakistan-A. Q. Khan network that was establishing nuclear weapons programs in Libya and Iran; and make an accurate assessment of nuclear weapons programs in South Africa and North Korea.

The CIA followed in the footsteps of these intelligence failures with two more of even greater magnitude because of the direct and negative consequences to American national security. Chapter 4, "Blundering in the 'War on Terrorism,'" makes a deeper examination than media coverage of the root causes of the CIA's failure to sufficiently penetrate al-Qaeda to disrupt the 9/11 plot. To be fair, the CIA did indeed provide strategic warning to the president of the impending al-Qaeda attacks, but it failed to marshal the resources to work against al-Qaeda that were commensurate with the threat. The CIA probably would have been able to give a better strategic threat assessment to the president had it had access to information related to the al-Qaeda plot that the Federal Bureau of Investigation (FBI) had collected but failed to share with the CIA and the intelligence community. On the other hand, the CIA's strategic intelligence performance in assessing Iraq's WMD programs was a major debacle. It failed miserably in giving the commander in chief an accurate strategic assessment of the status of Saddam Hussein's WMD programs by the CIA's own incompetencies in the collection of human intelligence and analysis, not by way of any undue political pressure to have the CIA's assessments dovetail with policy-maker prejudices.

Taking a step back from the dismal history of the CIA's strategic intelligence performances during the Cold War, post–Cold War, and 9/11 periods, Chapter 5, "Spies Who Do Not Deliver," makes a critical assessment of the CIA's human intelligence collection operations. Although the recruiting and running of spies to steal secrets from foreign governments has always been a core mission of the CIA to help narrow the range of ambiguity for the president in his policy deliberations, the CIA has systematically failed to deliver the spies needed to reveal the plans and intentions of American adversaries. Chapter 5 diagnoses the key root causes of the CIA's human intelligence collection performances that lie at the heart of most, if not all, of the CIA's strategic intelligence failures. This chapter takes critical look at the human intelligence collected by the CIA's case officers and argues that despite their tales of adventure and bravado catalogued in their memoirs, they have collectively done a poor job of serving the president and American national interests. It argues that the business of getting spies for the United States must be dramatically reformed if the president is to gain access to the plans and intentions of adversaries – whether nation-states armed with WMD or terrorist groups – to counter them before they strike American citizens, property, liberty, and interests.

The CIA's failings in the collection of human intelligence have been compounded by inconsistent and shoddy intelligence analysis. Chapter 6, "Analysts Who Are Not Experts," explains how the CIA has traditionally and institutionally failed to recruit, train, retain, and reward high-caliber political and military analysts who are essential for answering the "mysteries" of strategic affairs for the president and his national security lieutenants. The CIA has a public reputation of being a "think tank" or "government university," but Chapter 6 debunks that myth. It shows why the CIA's analytic shop excels at producing bureaucrats but fails miserably at nurturing nationally much less internationally recognized experts needed to tackle strategic intelligence mysteries for the president.

Given the depth and width of the CIA's strategic intelligence failures and blunders due to poor human intelligence collection and shoddy analysis over the entire course of the Agency's history, which cascaded into the debacles of 9/11 and Iraq, Chapter 7, "Facing Future Intelligence Challenges," critically examines the post–9/11 reforms of the American intelligence community. The creation of the DNI position has been publicly hailed by the Bush administration and the Congress as the answer to all our strategic intelligence problems. The reality, however, is that the creation of the DNI in and of itself does nothing to correct the root causes of the recent intelligence debacles that lie in the shortcomings of human intelligence and analysis. On the contrary, the creation of the DNI runs the risk of generating a false sense of accomplishment that Washington has "fixed the problem" and defusing the government's and public's sense of urgency for making profound changes in the way the United States produces strategic intelligence. Chapter 7 makes a series of recommendations for the DNI to shore up our deficit intelligence capabilities. The implementation of real reforms needs to take place from the top to the grass roots of the new intelligence infrastructure if the American president – whether Republican or Democrat – is to have top-quality strategic intelligence to guide American statecraft.

Only by examining the wider swath of cases in this book will policy makers, congressmen, and citizens be able to understand the root causes of the United States' massive intelligence failures in the past several years. In fact, the review of American strategic intelligence performance reveals that the failures of 9/11 and Iraq were simply the latest and greatest of a decades-long string of failures due to systematically dismal human intelligence collection and shoddy intelligence analysis that characterized the CIA's performance throughout the Cold War, the post–Cold war, and the war on terrorism periods. The systematic failures of American strategic intelligence and the CIA since its inception have been obscured by the political and emotional impulse to examine each and every incident of intelligence failure in isolation and not to put them together into a larger context with other intelligence failures that shared the same root causes. In other words, scholars, policy makers, congressmen, and citizens have been examining each intelligence failure as a blade of grass and no one has sought higher ground to survey the forest of strategic intelligence failures, a task taken up in these pages.

2 Debunking Cold War Myths

A REFRAIN FREQUENTLY HEARD FROM SENIOR CIA OFFICIALS in defense, if not denial, of the intelligence debacles of 9/11 and the Iraq War is that the public must remember the CIA "won the Cold War" against the Soviet Union. Never mind the fact that the Cold War ended about half a generation ago, these CIA apologists would have the public, the Congress, and the White House tread lightly in current criticisms out of deference to the CIA's purported decisive role in "winning the Cold War." The implicit defense is that the CIA in a "golden era" during the Cold War was a well-honed instrument to support the commander in chief against a formidable nation-state adversary. The argument, though, reflects more than a fair share of hubris on the part of those CIA officials who spent the lion's share of their careers in the Cold War. It fails to recognize that intelligence is merely one of many tools, including diplomatic, military, and economic strength, that the presidents wielded to contain the Soviet Union until the weight of its own internal inconsistencies brought the Soviet empire crashing down.

A comprehensive diagnosis of what hampers the CIA's ability to craft and deliver strategic intelligence for the commander in chief requires an analysis of its performance during the Cold War. Recent investigations of intelligence failures by congressional committees and presidentially appointed commissions have had only a narrow investigative scope of events surrounding 9/11 and the Iraq War. An examination of the CIA's Cold War strategic intelligence performance exposes the origins of the

CIA's habitual failing – the same ones that caused the 9/11 and Iraq debacles. These systemic problems all too likely will cause future intelligence
debacles because they have remained undiagnosed by recent reviews and
have been left untreated by the reforms that the president has imposed
on the intelligence community.

What follows is a critical look at the CIA's performance in carrying
out its core mission to obtain and deliver strategic intelligence to the
president during key crises and episodes that involved a looming and
large military dimension during the Cold War. Historians will bristle that
too much history is covered in the span of one chapter, whereas political
scientists will object that the chapter lacks a theoretical or methodological
approach, which they argue is the hallmark of social science. But such a
broad and sweeping analysis of the CIA's performance is needed if the
public, Congress, and the executive branch of government are to form
a strategic assessment of the origins of its intelligence failures, past and
present, to prevent more of the same in the future.

The brief case studies in this chapter unpack the cluster of challenges involving "secrets" and "military hardware" versus "mysteries"
and "plans and intentions" in key international Cold War crises in which
the president had to contemplate, threaten, or use force against an adversary or in which an adversary threatened or used force against U.S.
national security interests. Historian and intelligence expert Ernest May
judges that "The net performance of the U.S. intelligence community in
dealing with major cold war threats probably merits a grade somewhere
between B and C."[1] This chapter shows that Professor May is being too
gentlemanly in his grading. The review of major political-military crises
and episodes in the Cold War reveals that the CIA on balance did a poor
job – and probably merited a D grade – of gauging the intentions and plans
of U.S. adversaries and in making strategic intelligence assessments. The
CIA consistently failed to deliver strategic intelligence to the president on
the Soviet Union as well as against smaller Soviet client states that directly
threatened U.S. national interests. The CIA in essence had no better handle on enemy plans and intentions of the Soviet Union, North Korea, and

North Vietnam during the Cold War than it did against al-Qaeda and Iraq in more recent years.

Warning Failures: The Korean War and Chinese Intervention

One of the primary reasons for establishing the CIA in the National Security Act of 1947 was to have a central clearinghouse to analyze information coming from the various U.S. intelligence organizations and to synthesize strategic assessments for the president. The intent behind the CIA's creation was to avoid strategic warning failures, the likes of which the United States suffered in 1941 in which no U.S. intelligence organization sufficiently warned President Franklin D. Roosevelt of the Japanese attack on Pearl Harbor.

But only three years after its creation, the CIA failed to perform its principal warning mission. It failed to warn President Harry Truman of North Korea's June 1950 invasion of South Korea. The agency first suffered a major blow to its reputation when it failed to predict clearly the outbreak of the Korean War. As John Ranelagh, the author of a fine history of the CIA, recounts, "it was a situation too reminiscent of Pearl Harbor: an 'enemy' had massed its forces and launched a successful surprise attack without the United States being prepared. The CIA's overriding purpose was to prevent another Pearl Harbor, and the North Korean attack on South Korea on June 25, 1950, was too close a parallel to pass without changes being made."[2]

The CIA added insult to injury by failing to warn President Truman of the dangers of Chinese military intervention in the conflict. After Truman dispatched U.S. forces to South Korea to reverse the on-the-ground gains made by North Korean forces, the commander of U.S. forces operating under United Nations (UN) auspices, General Douglas MacArthur, argued for going beyond establishing the status quo ante and militarily pushing north to oust the North Korean regime. President Truman went along with MacArthur's recommendation, a decision that was informed by analysis from the CIA. United States and other forces operating under the auspices of the United Nations were subsequently surprised when they crossed the Yalu River and were attacked by Chinese forces that had moved into North Korea. Eliot Cohen observes that in a paper prepared for President Truman shortly before the Chinese intervention, "CIA analysts concluded that the Chinese could intervene effectively, but not necessarily decisively, in the Korean conflict. Believing the time for successful intervention had passed, and that such an intervention would only occur in the context of a global war unleashed by the Soviet Union, the CIA concluded that the Chinese would continue to give only covert aid to the North Koreans."[3] In November 1950, when the U.S. Eighth Army pushed north of the Yalu River, the Chinese intervened with a massive force of some thirty divisions, bludgeoned American forces, and sent them back south on the Korean Peninsula.

The CIA failed to both steal human intelligence secrets and fathom analytically the strategic mysteries in the Korean War. Despite the Agency's mission to steal human intelligence secrets to reveal adversaries' plans and intentions, it had no human agents inside the upper rungs of regimes in either North Korea or China who could have revealed the enemies' perceptions or plans. This left CIA analysts, as well as the president and policy makers, to guess at the intentions of both regimes. CIA analysts compensated for the lack of raw human intelligence and "mirror imaged" in their analysis – that is, they assumed the Chinese would act as Americans would if put in the same position. CIA analysts had assumed that the Chinese would not directly intervene in the conflict to avoid sparking a direct conflict with the United States and turning the Korean conflict into a major war. CIA analysts also failed to appreciate that the Chinese viewed U.S. forces north of the Yalu River as a direct threat to the territorial integrity of China.

These intelligence failures had major consequences for U.S. national security. As former senior intelligence official Harold Ford judges, "The price of these intelligence failures was a terrible one: thousands of needless casualties among U.S.–UN forces, and an abetting of the enemy's ability to overrun much of South Korea twice (in June–July, and again beginning in November 1950)."[4]

The Dark Underside of the Cuban Missile Crisis

The CIA's performance in the service of President John F. Kennedy in the October 1962 Cuban missile crisis goes down as a high-water mark in the annals of strategic intelligence. Using U-2 aircraft reconnaissance photography, the agency detected the Soviet Union's deployment of strategic ballistic missiles in Cuba. The CIA ably warned Kennedy and gave him invaluable time to convene a tightly knit policy deliberation body to map out U.S. policy for dealing with the Soviet Union's bold move to challenge American hegemony in the Western Hemisphere and to threaten the continental United States. The CIA's strategic intelligence from the U-2 was dramatically revealed by President Kennedy in an address to the nation as well as to the United Nations Security Council in the face of Soviet denials.

But the CIA's dramatic role in providing strategic intelligence during the October 1962 crisis overshadows the CIA's intelligence collection and analysis failures in the run-up to the crisis. A National Intelligence Estimate (NIE) on Cuba published in September 1962, which conveyed the consensus of the CIA and the rest of the intelligence community to the president and his key policy makers, judged that the "Soviets would not introduce offensive weapons in Cuba."[5] Although the Director of Central Intelligence (DCI) John McCone personally disagreed with the NIE's assessment and warned in August 1962 of the possibility of Soviet strategic missiles in Cuba, he came to that assessment on the assumption that the Soviet deployment of SA-2 air defense missiles to Cuba portended the deployment of strategic missiles.[6] The linkage is a false one, however; the Soviets used SA-2 missiles to provide air defenses for territories whether or not they had strategic missiles deployed in an area. In other words, McCone got the right answer but for the wrong reasons.

Lacking human intelligence penetration of the decision-making circles in the regimes in Havana and Moscow, reminiscent of the CIA's lack of human agents in the Korean War, CIA analysts fell back again on the analytic device of mirror imaging and projecting American perceptions onto that of the Soviet leadership. There was a commonly held view in the intelligence community and in the CIA that "So bold a Russian move apparently was considered to be too radical a departure from normal Soviet behavior to be regarded as anything but improbable."[7] CIA analysts concluded that the Soviets would not dare to risk a direct military confrontation with the United States – much as they had judged of the Chinese intervention in the Korean War – by the deployment of nuclear missiles in its client state in Cuba.

Although the CIA lacked human intelligence penetration of the strategic decision-making circles in Cuba and the Soviet Union, it did manage to gain access into the information in Soviet military intelligence channels. This human intelligence access was useful for illuminating the technical and military capabilities of the Soviet missiles. Former DCI Richard Helms recalled that a Soviet military intelligence officer "supplied CIA and the British Secret Intelligence Service more than five thousand pages of highly classified Soviet missile data, war plans, and military and political intelligence. This information was without question a fundamental part of the data that permitted President Kennedy [during the Cuban missile crisis] to make the decisions that avoided the possibility of a nuclear showdown and perhaps war."[8]

Perhaps even more damning of the CIA's strategic intelligence performance is that the Soviet Union managed to slip nuclear warheads into Cuba without the CIA detecting them. John Lewis Gaddis observes that the Soviets had even given their commander in Cuba preauthorization to use nuclear weapons in the event of a U.S. invasion of Cuba and the disruption of communications with Moscow, although Khrushchev had rescinded the order after the Americans detected the Soviet missiles in Cuba.[9] The CIA's human collection and analysis missed this strategic facet of the crisis, a fact that put the United States and the Soviet Union closer to the precipice of nuclear war than either side recognized at the time.

Blind Spot on North Vietnam's Plans and Intentions

The CIA's analysis for President Lyndon Johnson on the strategic course of the Vietnam War was fairly good. Throughout the conflict, the CIA was relatively consistent in assessments to the president that the situation in South Vietnam was deteriorating, notwithstanding the increasing numbers of U.S. forces in the country. The CIA largely stood its ground, was true to its unofficial motto to "speak truth to power," and withstood the voiced frustrations of policy makers, especially President Johnson, over the agency's bleak assessments of the war. The CIA took a dismal view of a host of policy-sensitive issues to include the prospects for political survival of the South Vietnamese regime, the U.S.-led counterinsurgency campaign in South Vietnam, the bombing interdiction campaign against North Vietnamese supply routes through Laos and Cambodia, and the effects of bombing against North Vietnam.[10] In short, as former CIA Deputy Director for Intelligence Ray Cline recalled, "The CIA's estimates and other analytic papers in the entire Kennedy-Johnson era were more sober and less optimistic than those of the Department of Defense, particularly those of Secretary of Defense McNamara."[11]

The CIA's bureaucratic autonomy from policy interests increased the odds of objective analysis, but it did not guarantee fault-free or perfectly accurate intelligence. CIA analyses at the operational level of the Vietnam War at times were inferior to those produced by defense intelligence services and agencies. The CIA, for example, grossly overestimated the numbers of irregular Vietcong and regular North Vietnamese forces operating inside South Vietnam. As James Wirtz points out, a key CIA analyst responsible for order-of-battle estimates during the Vietnam War estimated that the troop strength of the Vietcong in South Vietnam was about 600,000 in 1967, more than twice the size of the estimate produced by the Military Assistance Command, Vietnam (MACV).[12]

The CIA stumbled in warning of the magnitude and sophistication of the 1968 Tet Offensive mounted by North Vietnamese regular forces and Vietcong forces operating in South Vietnam. As Wirtz recounts elsewhere, "The Tet attacks failed on the battlefield, but U.S. forces did not anticipate fully the scope, intensity, targets, and timing of the offensive. The allies suffered a failure of intelligence during Tet, a failure that set the stage for changes in U.S. strategy."[13] Although the American military and South Vietnamese forces levied substantial losses on the Vietcong and North Vietnamese forces in the Tet Offensive, the scope and coordination of the offensive that engulfed thirty-nine of forty-four South Vietnamese provinces with some 85,000 North Vietnamese troops was politically devastating for the U.S. public, which had come to believe President Johnson's positive appraisals about the course of the war.[14] The Tet Offensive is largely seen as a watershed event that led to the eventual withdrawal of U.S. forces from the conflict under the Nixon administration, the subsequent collapse of the South Vietnamese government, and the outright invasion by North Vietnamese regular military forces to unify Vietnam under a communist government.

The importance of having an intelligence organization that is bureaucratically divorced from policy or military operational equities was demonstrated in the Vietnam War. Although CIA analyses were bleak on the overall course of the war, the military was producing intelligence that was more positive, in no small measure because of pressure from senior military officers to have intelligence produced by subordinates reflect "good news" for the military's chain of command and the commander in chief. Wirtz astutely observes one of the most important lessons to be learned from the analytic disputes between the CIA and the military's intelligence services during the Vietnam War and the factors that contributed to the differing assessments: "MACV analysts focused on battlefield events, while CIA analysts tended to integrate political, economic, and social developments into their judgments about the conflict. Analysts working at CIA headquarters also enjoyed a degree of detachment that was not available in Saigon. CIA analysts had the luxury of focusing on the big picture, while analysts working at MACV concentrated on supporting the day-to-day conduct of military operations. In addition, it was less onerous for CIA analysts to identify weaknesses in the American war effort: the U.S. military and not the intelligence community was largely responsible for the implementation of U.S. policy in Vietnam."[15]

The CIA's analyses during the Vietnam War were pieced together from a variety of sources but did not benefit from high-level human intelligence penetration of the North Vietnamese regime. Much as in the case of the Korean War, the CIA failed to deliver any high-level human agents who revealed the plans and intentions of the North Vietnamese regime for the president and his key national security lieutenants.

Counted Soviet Military Hardware but Missed the Biological Warfare Threat

The CIA did an enormous amount of collection and analysis on Soviet strategic nuclear forces during the Cold War. The United States' technical intelligence collection, primarily satellite imagery, enabled the CIA to have a fairly good handle on the quantities of Soviet strategic forces deployed in bombers, submarines, and intercontinental ballistic missiles. The CIA's intelligence was an invaluable crutch for U.S. policy makers throughout the Cold War as they negotiated arms-control initiatives with their Soviet counterparts.[16] Nevertheless, after an exhaustive review of declassified NIEs, Soviet expert Raymond Garthoff judged that "Overall, the record of NIE assessments of Soviet intentions shows a tendency in the late 1940s and 1950s, and again in the last half of the 1970s and first half of the 1980s, to overstate a Soviet propensity to rely on military power and its offensive applications."[17]

The Cold War witnessed major strategic intelligence controversies over the perceived inferiority of U.S. strategic nuclear forces vis-à-vis Soviet strategic bomber and missile forces, the so-called bomber and missile gaps. In these controversies, which are hallmarks in much of the Cold War intelligence literature, U.S. military intelligence, principally from the air force, substantially overestimated the number of Soviet bombers and missiles and gave Moscow the quantitative lead when measured against the U.S. inventories of bombers and missiles. In the early 1950s, the air force estimated that the Soviet Union would have a bomber force of more than 1,000 aircraft within a decade, an inventory far beyond that of the United States. The CIA disagreed and argued that the Soviet industrial base was not sufficient to support such a high rate of production. In 1956, U-2 photography confirmed the CIA's hunch and showed that the

Soviets did not have a large bomber fleet. By 1957, the CIA was confident that the Soviet strategic bomber force was actually much smaller,
estimating it between 90 to 150 aircraft.[18]

During his presidential bid in 1960, John F. Kennedy made a political
issue out of the "missile gap," which heightened public concerns that the
Soviets were racing ahead of the United States technologically, a fear
that was sparked by the Soviet launching of the Sputnik satellite in 1957.
President Eisenhower knew from CIA analysis of U-2 photography that
these fears were overblown, but he refused to jeopardize his intelligence
by releasing it publicly to calm fears. The air force, however, tried to use
the "missile gap" just as it had tried to use the "bomber gap" to obtain
larger defense budget appropriations.[19]

The CIA's assessments of Soviet missile forces were bolstered by
human intelligence provided by a Soviet spy, the same one whose intelligence was mentioned earlier in the discussion of the Cuban Missile Crisis. As Rhodri Jeffreys-Jones recalls, "From April 1961, Oleg Penkovsky
further assisted CIA's analysts. A colonel in Soviet military intelligence
(GRU), Penkovsky served as a 'defector in place.' Before his arrest in the
fall of 1962 and execution by firing squad, he supplied Western powers
with thousands of pages of secret strategic documents, some of which contained information that could be usefully collated with satellite evidence.
The combined picture destroyed the 'missile gap' theory."[20]

Once again, the CIA's bureaucratic autonomy gave it a comparative
advantage over military intelligence services for gauging an adversary's
capabilities. The air force had a vested interest in inflated estimates to justify greater defense spending on its bomber and missile forces to redress
the perceived gap with Soviet forces.[21] The CIA, on the other hand, had
no vested interest in the estimates, and its civilian analysts had more
accurately estimated the number of Soviet bombers and missiles to give
Presidents Eisenhower and Kennedy sounder bases for evaluating the
needed investments in the U.S. strategic posture.

On the downside of its Cold War performance against Soviet strategic
forces, the agency suffered from shortcomings in gauging Soviet intentions

for their strategic nuclear forces. The CIA analysts had largely assumed that the Soviets intended to use their nuclear forces as a deterrent, whereas scholars and observers outside of the agency were not so sanguine and worried that the Soviets planned to use nuclear weapons for fighting a war with the United States. Then-DCI George Bush authorized what became know as the Team A and Team B exercise in 1976 during Gerald Ford's presidency. In the analytic exercise, CIA analysts in Team A squared off against outside experts in Team B who had reputations for being defense "hawks" and analyzed the same intelligence on Soviet strategic forces. The exercise became engulfed in political controversy, but it was a useful means for competitive analysis to find holes or weaknesses in prevailing intelligence assessments. As Lawrence Freedman assesses from an extensive examination of the controversy, "Team B raised important questions on Soviet doctrine and objectives but did not provide an answer with any sophistication."[22] Perhaps the broader and more lasting legacy of the Team A and Team B experiment was that the CIA would later shriek against such competitive exercises. But they probably should have become the norm rather than an exception because the CIA analysts grew more isolated and needed outside light exposed to their classified assessments.

In a colossal and infrequently examined intelligence failure that bridged the Cold War and post–Cold War periods, the CIA failed to detect the Soviet Union's massive biological warfare program that Russia also tried to hide from the international community after the fall of the Berlin Wall. The CIA only had suspicions of a Soviet biological warfare program in violation of Moscow's commitment to ban such a program under the terms of the 1972 Biological and Toxin Weapons Convention. Two Soviet scientists who defected to the West in 1989 and 1992, respectively, were the means by which the CIA learned that the Soviets maintained a massive biological warfare program that "dwarfed anything American experts have ever imagined."[23] The CIA had failed to detect for about two decades the massive biological warfare program that consisted of about 60,000 personnel and more than 100 facilities that stockpiled plague, smallpox, anthrax, and other agents.[24]

Flatfooted on Europe, the Middle East, and Southwest Asia

The CIA suffered several major intelligence failures during the Cold War in the Middle East and Southwest Asia, regions in which the United States and the Soviet Union waged their rivalry with the use of surrogates. To name just the highlights, the agency failed to warn President Richard Nixon adequately of the Egyptian invasion of the Sinai in the 1973 war and President Jimmy Carter of the Soviet invasion of Afghanistan in 1979. Likewise, it failed to alert President Ronald Reagan that the Soviets were committed to withdrawing forces from Afghanistan in 1988.

The CIA's strategic warnings to U.S. presidents of war in the Middle East were of mixed performances during the Cold War. The CIA failed to warn of the 1956 war in the Sinai Peninsula and President Eisenhower was outraged at the extent of the French-Israeli-British plot to take back the Suez Canal from Egypt through military force.[25] On the other hand, the CIA provided a fairly solid warning to President Johnson of the prospects for the 1967 Arab-Israeli War, in historian David Robarge's assessment.[26] But the CIA failed to provide strategic warning of the 1973 war to President Nixon. His National Security Advisor Henry Kissinger recalls in his memoirs that the CIA in September 1973 – just days before the outbreak of war when the Egyptian military pushed into the Sinai Peninsula – that Egypt was not preparing for war with Israel. In Kissinger's words, "The CIA reassured us on September 30 that the whole thrust of President Sadat's activities since the spring had been in the direction of bringing moral, political, and economic force to bear on Israel in tacit acknowledgment of Arab unreadiness to make war."[27] Egypt obviously did not conform to the CIA's mirrored image of "rational behavior" and launched its attack on 6 October 1973. The war brought President Sadat enormous geopolitical strategic gains, which he would later parlay into a negotiated peace settlement with Israel. In the final analysis, Sadat was a statesman with strategic vision, qualities that no analyst at the CIA shared.

The CIA again had egg on its face, and former DCI Robert Gates captured some of the Agency's embarrassment at being caught unawares by the 1973 war. Gates was then an intelligence advisor to the U.S. arms control delegation in Geneva and on the morning of 6 October, he brought the morning intelligence summary to Paul Nitze, the lead negotiator. As Gates recalls, "The cable version of the CIA's National Intelligence Daily that morning reported on the developments in the Middle East but again suggested that there was not likely to be a conflict. Nitze read that, looked up at me from his desk, and asked if I spoke French and listened to the radio. I replied 'No' twice and Nitze proceeded to inform me that had I answered 'Yes' I would have known that war had already broken out – because he had found out from the radio news."[28]

The CIA, by and large, also failed to warn President Carter of the Soviet invasion of Afghanistan. In 1979, satellite imagery revealed that the Soviets were building up forces along the border with Afghanistan. Former senior CIA official Douglas MacEachin in a retrospective analysis of the CIA's strategic intelligence performance found that "The military intervention the Soviets carried out in the last week of December 1979 – particularly its timing and scope – came as a surprise to the US intelligence community at large and to US policy officials in general. . . . There were, at most, only a few exceptions to the consensus that Soviet introduction of military forces would continue to be in small increments to augment security for Soviet personnel and to help the Kabul regime maintain its authority."[29] The CIA again had no high-level human intelligence penetrations inside the Kremlin, and CIA analysts were unable to gauge the plans and intentions of the Soviet leadership to invade Afghanistan.

CIA analysts fell victim to a failure to challenge conventional wisdom and lapsed again into the mirror-imaging problem. As MacEachin details, analysts had concluded early on in the buildup of Soviet forces along the Afghan border that major military intervention was unlikely: "One key intelligence assessment, in fact, specifically identified it as an operation Moscow would *not* be willing to undertake."[30] In the absence of human sources inside the Kremlin to report on political intentions behind the military buildup, CIA analysts projected the U.S. view onto the Soviets that the political costs of direct and massive military intervention in Afghanistan would be too much for the Soviet leadership on the global stage to justify it as a rational move. But, alas, the Soviet leadership refused to conform to the CIA's mirrored image.

Years later, the CIA failed to anticipate that the Soviet Union was preparing to pull its forces out of Afghanistan. Secretary of State George Shultz was especially dismayed at the CIA's performance on this score. Soviet Foreign Minister Eduard Shevardnadze told Shultz privately in September 1987 that the Soviets would soon leave Afghanistan, and Shultz was convinced that it would occur.[31] The CIA thought that was political deception, but that if a Soviet pullout occurred, the Soviet-backed regime in Kabul would collapse in short order. In February 1988, Mikhail Gorbachev publicly announced that Soviet forces would start withdrawing from Afghanistan, and by May they had completed the withdrawal in less than a year.[32] To add insult to injury, the CIA's prediction that the regime would fall turned out to be wrong.[33]

The CIA apparently suffered from the same package of shortcomings a decade before the Soviet invasion of Afghanistan. In the summer of 1968, U.S. intelligence had detected the mobilization of military forces with some 300,000 troops in the Soviet Union and Warsaw Pact allies surrounding Czechoslovakia. At the time, a new Czech government was leading an aggressive reform movement that challenged Soviet political domination in Eastern and Central Europe.[34] Despite the intelligence detection of mobilization and activation of reserves, as MacEachin recalls, the "official records of a meeting in the White House on the evening of August 20, convened shortly after these forces launched their invasion of Czechoslovakia, the president and all of his top national security cabinet officials expressed surprise that the invasion had taken place."[35] The dominate presumption that prevailed among the CIA's analytic minds was that Moscow was using the military buildup to bluff an invasion and coerce Prague to comply with the Soviet line and that Moscow would not jeopardize the growing trend toward détente in Europe with military intervention.[36] This was another instance in which Moscow had been unwilling to conform to the CIA's mirrored image.

On the other hand, to be fair to CIA analysts who were involved in the intelligence warning failures in the 1968 Soviet invasion of Czechoslovakia and the 1979 Soviet intervention in Afghanistan, calls for challenging conventional wisdom are easier said than put into practice. As MacEachin ably sums up the dilemma for intelligence analysts in these crises, "In every case the 'alternative scenario' did not have to be constructed – it was manifest. But it was considered a dumb move and analysts and policy officials alike concluded that the governments in question would not do something dumb. When some analysts did try to make the case for the dumb move, they were also categorized as dumb."[37] To compound the problem further is that often the "conventional wisdom" is correct. As historian Ernest May judges of analysts from his study of intelligence in the early twentieth century, "Their ability to interpret other peoples' politics is always limited. Their easiest course is to assume that another government will do tomorrow what it did yesterday, and ninety times out of a hundred events justify such an assumption."[38]

President Carter was blindsided by the 1979 revolution in Iran, a development that cut against the grain of the CIA's conventional wisdom on the Iranian regime's stability. The CIA judged in a study titled "Iran in the 1980s," its most comprehensive analysis of Iran published in August 1977, that "the shah will be an active participant in Iranian life well into the 1980s" and that "there will be no radical change in Iranian political behavior in the near future."[39] But here again, the CIA had no human intelligence on the plans, intentions, and influences of Iranian opposition to credibly gauge the threat posed to the shah's regime. As Barry Rubin points out, "CIA operatives in Iran concentrated on gathering material about the Soviets and since they were careful not to offend the shah, the United States was almost completely dependent on SAVAK [the shah's intelligence service] for intelligence on developments in Iran itself."[40]

Policy makers share some of the burden for the intelligence failure on Iran. They were too close to the shah and his intelligence service and had forbidden the CIA from going outside of the relationship with the shah to collect "unilateral" intelligence against Iranian opposition. By the same token, the shah's intelligence service grossly underestimated the power and public appeal of the opposition among the lower classes as well as the rising frustrations with the inequities of the shah's rule and passed along these inadequate assessments to the CIA. CIA analysts consequently had a poor empirical intelligence base on which to answer the mystery of the stability of the Iranian regime.

The White House was disgusted by the lack of CIA human intelligence on Iran. The National Security Council official responsible for Iran, Gary Sick, wrote a memo to his boss, National Security Advisor Zbigniew Brzezinski, in the run-up to the revolution noting that "the most fundamental problem at the moment is the astonishing lack of hard information we are getting about developments in Iran."[41] He elaborated that "this has been an intelligence disaster of the first order. Our information has been extremely meager, our resources were not positioned to report accurately on the activities of the opposition forces, on external penetration, the strike demands, the political organization of the strikers or the basic objectives and political orientation of the demonstrators."[42]

Brzezinski's criticism of the CIA's strategic intelligence on Iran was even more scathing. He recorded the following in his journal: "I was really appalled by how inept and vague Stan Turner's [the DCI] comments on the crisis in Iran were. This reinforces my strong view that we need much better political intelligence."[43] Further, William Daugherty, a CIA case officer who was a hostage in Iran in the aftermath of the revolution, concludes in a retrospective and insightful analysis of the Iran crisis that "The intelligence community did not serve the President well. As such, it constitutes a failure of serious magnitude."[44] Brzezinski, in turn, prompted President Carter in November 1978 to write a broader criticism of the CIA's global performance to DCI Turner that "I am not satisfied with the quality of our political intelligence. Assess our assets and, as soon as possible, give me a report concerning our abilities in the most important areas of the world."[45]

The analytical side of the CIA also shared responsibility for the Iranian revolution intelligence failure. In the years before the Iranian revolution, Rubin points out that "Analysts were not encouraged to challenge conventional wisdom, which many accepted anyway, either out of habit or out of conviction. Dissenting views were weeded out as briefings and position papers wended their way up the chain of command."[46] The CIA's analytic corps also was desperately short of substantive experts on Iran. Michael Ledeen and William Lewis noted that "there was a surprising paucity of experts at CIA. Throughout most of the crisis there were at most two analysts working full time on Iran, and for much of that period there was only one individual following and analyzing events at the agency.... For those one or two individuals working on Iran in 1977–78, there was little time for serious research, since they were forced to cope with a mounting pile of paper coming in from all directions, and with the necessity of contacting the few experts in the United States with knowledge of Iran."[47] The lazy acceptance of conventional wisdom and the lack of serious expertise and long-term research were perennial problems with the CIA's strategic analysis that would rear their ugly heads many times in the intervening years between the failure to warn of the Iranian revolution and the failure to assess accurately Iraq's weapons of mass destruction programs in the run-up to the Iraq War that began in 2003.

Two Lonely Bright Spots: The Polish Crisis and the "War Scare"

The lack of human intelligence was at the core of most of the CIA's strategic intelligence failures during the Cold War. But two Cold War strategic intelligence successes, both of which escape much attention from the public and the intelligence literature, were possible because the CIA had first-rate human intelligence sources. Both of these human sources in the Polish crisis in the early 1980s and the 1983 "war scare" volunteered their services to the CIA. They were not spotted, assessed, developed, and recruited by CIA case officers, the process through which the CIA's directorate of operations folklore holds as the best means for obtaining human agents.

The Soviet client state in Poland was beset with internal strife from the Solidarity labor movement in the early 1980s. The regime was threatened

with public unrest of a magnitude that brought direct Soviet military intervention into Soviet bloc countries of Hungary in 1956 and Czechoslovakia
in 1968. The CIA in the Polish crisis was able to provide President Carter
with plans and intentions of the Soviet leadership and military because a
brave colonel serving in the Polish General Staff had volunteered to spy
for the CIA. Former DCI Robert Gates pays tribute to the Polish General
Staff Colonel Ryszard Kuklinski's contribution to the annals of U.S. intelligence until November 1981, when he was compromised and the CIA
helped him escape from Poland: "He had been one of the most important CIA sources of information on the Soviet military of the Cold War
period. Faithful always to his beloved Poland, he provided us with more
than thirty thousand Soviet documents over a ten-year period, including Warsaw Pact contingency plans for war in Europe, details on large
numbers of Soviet weapons systems, planning for electronic warfare, and
much more. His efforts, I am convinced, allowed the United States and
its allies to help deter a Soviet invasion of Poland in December 1980 and
allowed us to forewarn and then expose the Soviet role in Jaruzelski's
declaration of martial law a year later."[48] Gates continues that because
of Kuklinski, "we knew what was going on between the leaders of Poland
and the Soviet Union and between their military high commands. We were
able to speak out strongly at key moments and emphasize to the Soviet
leadership the extraordinary costs of intervention. The United States had
limited power to affect the course of events in Poland. In retrospect, our
government under two Presidents made maximum effective use of that
power. And the Soviets' decision not to intervene would have enormous
historical consequences."[49] The Polish case was a strategic intelligence
success exemplar based on superb human intelligence that acted as an
invaluable power magnifier for U.S. statecraft.

Another intelligence controversy in the Cold War swirled around
Poland. The assassination attempt in May 1981 against Pope John Paul
II, a Pole who was instrumental in giving political backing to the Polish
Solidarity movement, prompted speculation that the Soviet intelligence
services had sponsored the assassination attempt against the pontiff. The

CIA's Office of Soviet Analysis (SOVA) had assessed that the assassin had no ties to the Kremlin, but DCI William Casey was not convinced. His then-Deputy Robert Gates tasked SOVA to do a competitive analysis and work backward from the conclusion that the Soviets had had a hand in the assassination attempt. Gates, from his standpoint, had ordered just another analysis that employed a different methodology to see whether the evidence on hand would support the hypothesis that the KGB backed the plot. The SOVA analysts balked and claimed that Gates was trying to "politicize" intelligence and compel SOVA analysts to reach a conclusion with which the DCI agreed. In retrospect, the methodology proposed by Gates was a legitimate devil's-advocate approach to analysis designed to identify weaknesses in conventional wisdom. Post–Cold War information, moreover, has brought to light the fact that the KGB was lending a far greater hand to international terrorists, especially through their East German and Hungarian satellite intelligence services, than SOVA analysts had appreciated during the Cold War.[50]

The question of Soviet sponsorship of the assassination attempt against John Paul II is still an open one. A former senior KGB officer who defected to the West reported that about half of his former KGB colleagues "were convinced that the KGB would no longer contemplate a 'wet affair' of this kind even indirectly through the Bulgarians," whereas another half suspected that a special operations KGB directorate had been involved.[51] Perhaps the most incriminating evidence against the Soviet Union and its client Eastern bloc intelligence service is that no one has satisfactorily explained how the pope's would-be assassin, Mehmet Ali Agca, a man from a poor family and no personal wealth, was able to escape from a Turkish prison and roam the world traveling on holidays in Europe and the Middle East and perhaps the Soviet Union for more than one year before his attempt on the pope's life.[52] In light of this mystery, the view that Soviet intelligence or its Bulgarian client intelligence service had lent a financial and logistic helping hand to Agca is more than plausible.

Although the Polish crisis was plain for all to see, a later crisis during the Cold War was hidden from the public view. In 1981, the Soviet

Union's leadership had become in essence a prisoner of its own myopic and paranoid worldview that profoundly distorted its perception of reality. The Soviet leadership had become convinced that President Ronald Reagan was firmly intent on attacking the Soviet Union. It ordered its intelligence services, in an operation dubbed RYAN, to monitor for indications and warnings that the United States was preparing to launch an attack on the Soviet Union. Fortunately for the sake of international stability, the KGB's chief officer in the United Kingdom, Oleg Gordievsky, had volunteered to spy for British intelligence. He provided unique and invaluable reports revealing that the Kremlin had ordered its intelligence apparatus to look for indications of a surprise U.S. attack against the Soviet Union. Gordievsky especially warned the British that the Soviets were concerned that a NATO exercise in 1983, called Able Archer, was a cover for an attack against Moscow. [53]

British intelligence shared Gordievsky's intelligence with the CIA. The agency passed the information to National Security Advisor Robert McFarlane, who briefed President Ronald Reagan. Reagan was taken aback that the Soviets had so wrongly gauged U.S. intentions and subsequently sought out Soviet leadership to put Sino-American relations on more stable footings.[54] In a retrospective analysis, Christopher Andrew and Oleg Gordievsky commented that "The world did not quite reach the edge of the nuclear abyss during Operation RYAN. But during Able Archer 83 it had, without realizing it, come frighteningly close – certainly closer than at any time since the Cuban missile crisis of 1962."[55]

Missing the End of the Cold War?

The CIA received much public criticism for failing to predict the collapse of the Soviet Union and "missing the end" of the Cold War. One of the most eloquent and vocal critics of the agency's performance on this score was the late and distinguished senator from New York, Daniel Patrick Moynihan. His criticisms were especially pointed and carried a great deal of weight because Moynihan was one of the most scholarly members of the Senate and had extensive experience with intelligence after serving for many years as vice chair on the Senate Select Committee on Intelligence for which he oversaw intelligence operations. Moynihan argued that the CIA should be abolished because it failed to predict the Soviet Union's demise, a prediction that he was able to make given a close study of publicly available information.[56]

The question of the stability of the Soviet Union was clearly a mystery in that there was no piece of paper or plan that could have been stolen by human spies to answer it. Moynihan's point about the CIA's myopic focus on classified information to the neglect of publicly available information was ahead of its time. With today's explosion of information available at a couple of computer key strokes on the World Wide Web, Moynihan's criticism is more on the mark today than it was during the Cold War when public information was less readily available.

A review of declassified CIA assessments of the Soviet Union, however, belies criticisms that the agency miserably failed to predict the collapse of the Soviet Union. Intelligence experts Bruce Berkowitz and Jeffrey Richelson, after an extensive review of an enormous body of now-declassified CIA assessments from the Cold War, conclude that "throughout the 1980s the intelligence community warned of the weakening of the Soviet economy, and, later, of the impending fall of Gorbachev and the breakup of the Soviet Union."[57] A senior CIA analyst even personally briefed President Reagan, six years before the Soviet Union's collapse, on an estimate of "Domestic Stresses on the Soviet System"; the document described the alcohol and drug abuse, crime, and loss of popular confidence, nationalism, and corruption in the Soviet Union.[58] The CIA might not have baldly predicted the outright collapse of the Soviet Union but neither did the mastermind of Soviet reform Gorbachev anticipate that his actions would set in motion the chain reaction that would end with the Soviet empire's collapse.

The CIA had painted so bleak a picture of the Soviet Union that President George H. W. Bush set up a small shop inside his National Security Council staff to make contingency plans for the collapse of the Soviet

Union. As Robert Gates recalls from his time as deputy national security advisor in the Bush administration, "Thanks to analysis and warning from CIA, we at the White House began in the summer of 1989 to think about and prepare for a Soviet collapse."[59] Gates elaborated that in September 1989 the NSC established a group of people and in secrecy worked on contingency plans for dealing with the potential collapse of the Soviet Union.[60]

The team's deliberations served as the foundation for U.S. policy immediately after Gorbachev was ousted in a short-lived coup in August 1991. The CIA, to its credit, had assessed for President Bush that the coup was not a competent one and that its prospects for success were not good. "Once the coup was underway, the intelligence community quickly determined that, precisely because the signs of adequate preparation were missing, the plotters had little chance of success."[61] That critical assessment led President Bush to hold off recognizing the coup plotters, a move that denied them international political legitimacy and contributed to the coup's ultimate failure.

A Balance Sheet for the CIA's Cold War Performance

This survey is hardly exhaustive of all intelligence issues during the Cold War, but it touches on salient and important geopolitical and strategic issues that were of critical importance to the presidents. The review concentrated on strategic issues that crowded the policy plates of presidents, issues that involved the threat, use, or management of force in international crises. The review shows that the list of the CIA's Cold War strategic intelligence successes is shorter than the list of failures in contrast to the public mythology perpetuated by CIA apologists today.

On the positive side of the ledger, Penkovsky's intelligence on Soviet missile forces showed the potentially invaluable contribution that first-rate human intelligence can make to the quality of strategic intelligence analysis. To its credit, the CIA fulfilled its core mission of stealing hostile government plans and intentions against the Soviet Union in the Polish crisis and the "war scare" of the early 1980s. These episodes are models of human intelligence performance. They were achieved because a courageous Soviet military intelligence officer, a brave Polish military officer, and a Soviet KGB officer all volunteered their services to the CIA. No CIA case officer spotted, assessed, developed, and recruited these individuals as CIA folklore and business practices would have it. Regrettably, these stellar human intelligence performances were the rare exceptions rather than the standard rule in the Cold War.

The CIA was also successful in analytically warning the president of the increasing odds of the Soviet Union's failure than is publicly recognized. Its analysis sufficiently illuminated a key strategic mystery to warn President Bush of the chances of a Soviet collapse. This episode, like the Polish crisis and the war scare, is a model of strategic intelligence performance.

On the negative side of the ledger, the CIA's utter failure to detect the massive Soviet biological warfare program until the defection of two Soviet scientists at the closing of the Cold War portended a similar failure to detect Saddam Hussein's substantial biological warfare program in the run-up to the 1990 war as well as the imagining of the reconstitution of an even more ambitious biological weapons program in the run-up to the 2003 war. The lack of human spies contributed to the CIA's failure to gauge Iranian opposition to the shah in the run-up to the 1979 Iranian revolution and failure to warn the commander in chief of military invasions of South Korea, the Sinai Peninsula, Czechoslovakia, and Afghanistan.

The most damning CIA strategic intelligence failure was the lack of a deep penetration of the top Soviet political-military decision-making hierarchy. For all the resources devoted by the CIA to spot, assess, develop, and recruit Soviet human agents, the CIA for the entire course of the Cold War failed to get a spy deep inside the Kremlin. As Robert Gates has objectively reflected on the CIA's human intelligence performance, "We never recruited a spy who gave us unique political information from inside the Kremlin, and we too often failed to penetrate the inner circle of Soviet surrogate leaders."[62] The most successful spies that the CIA managed to run, moreover, were at the periphery, not the center, of Soviet decision making, depriving U.S. commanders in chief access to the innermost strategic calculations of their most formidable adversary throughout the history of the Cold War.

3 Stumbling after the Cold War

T HE CIA, MUCH LIKE THE REST OF THE U.S. NATIONAL SECU-rity apparatus, had lost its bearings and stumbled while searching to regain a central focus during the post–Cold War period. The term "post–Cold War" awkwardly describes the period between the collapse of the Soviet Union and the attacks of 11 September 2001. The CIA's senior management was bewildered by the evaporation of the Cold War rivalry that had shaped the worldviews nurtured throughout their careers.

The CIA's Directorate of Operations (DO) managers were especially befuddled and, at least initially, had wanted to continue to place a priority on spotting, assessing, developing, and recruiting Russian agents even though these DO business practices had produced less-than-stellar human intelligence results during the Cold War. The DO's perpetuation of these failed practices produced even less impressive results in the post–Cold War period. As a former senior DO official, Milt Bearden, who had a justifiable hallway reputation in Langley as a free-wheeling and aggressive case officer, lamented of the difficulty the DO had in the transition from Cold War to the post–Cold War period, "Too much of the CIA's clandestine collection effort had too little relevance in the fast-moving new world. Landing a Soviet defector had been our bread and butter in the old days, but now we found ourselves simply in the resettlement game, with no real evidence that we were getting much of anything useful in return."[1]

The Directorate of Intelligence (DI) senior management too was profoundly disoriented by the post–Cold War period. Most of the DI's senior managers had risen up through the analytic ranks as political or economic analysts and few had any expertise on political-military affairs. The DI's senior managers all too easily and naively fell into the cliché and philosophically liberal worldview that in the post–Cold War, military issues were not to be as important as political-economic issues because democracy had triumphed over communism.[2] The course of events in the 1990s would belie the notion that the world was on the cusp of a democratic and utopian peace.

The DI's senior managers were a hardheaded bunch, however. Iraq's 1990 invasion of Kuwait, the Balkan wars, and the opening stages of the war with al-Qaeda throughout the 1990s were not enough to cause DI managers to put adequate resources into military analysis, which as an analytic discipline withered on the vine as the DI recruited and trained fewer and fewer military analysts. And the minority of the DI analytic workforce that did have expertise in military affairs was increasingly exhausted from working one crisis after another, focused on current intelligence to the detriment of longer-term strategic research to warn policy makers of crises that laid over the horizon. It would not be until well after the 9/11 attacks, the 2001 war in Afghanistan, and the Iraq War beginning in 2003 that the DI management woke up to international realities and began to recruit military analysts to replenish ranks that it had allowed to atrophy and decay in the 1990s. But that would be too late, and the president and his key national security lieutenants would not have the benefit of expert CIA military analysis for the opening of the "War on Terror."

A survey of the most important strategic intelligence challenges in the post–Cold War 1990s reveals that expertise in political-military affairs was a more important factor in the quality of intelligence than rungs of management in an intelligence bureaucracy. The CIA's DI managers traditionally argue that the analyses produced by the directorate are "corporate products" that reflect the views of the agency, not individual analysts. That DI view, much like the DO's folklore that it won the Cold War, bears no resemblance to reality. The review of strategic intelligence during the post–Cold war period in this chapter clearly shows that the intellectual caliber of individual analysts matters significantly. In other words, the CIA's bureaucracy does not produce strategic intelligence, analysts do. No amount of management scrubbing or massaging of analyses or rewiring of the bureaucratic organization will reliably transform third-rate into first-rate strategic analysis for the president.

These states of mind in the DO and DI set the stage for examining the CIA's strategic intelligence performance during the post–Cold War period. This chapter evaluates the CIA's provision of strategic intelligence to the commander in chief during the 1990–1 war with Iraq, during civil war and the use of U.S. force in the Balkans, and in al-Qaeda's attacks against the United States in Africa. Although the CIA's strategic intelligence performance scored some notable successes, its overall performance was lackluster. Many of the shortcomings during the post–Cold War decade foreshadowed the systemic strategic intelligence failings that would give rise to the 9/11 and Iraq War debacles.

The First Iraq War

The CIA's performance during the 1990–1 Gulf War was mixed. On the positive side of the ledger, CIA analysts warned the president in July 1990 that Iraq was building up military forces opposite its border with Kuwait. On the eve of Iraq's 2 August invasion of Kuwait, the CIA had assessed that Saddam Hussein was likely trying to pressure the Kuwaitis to bow to his desired oil-production levels to boost the price of oil. The CIA judged that Saddam was likely to use limited force to cross the Iraq-Kuwait border over a contested oil field but that he would only conduct a limited cross-border operation. Although the CIA failed to warn of an all-out Iraqi invasion of Kuwait, its analysis of the likelihood of a cross-border operation was more accurate than that of many Arab leaders in the region, most notably Egypt's President

Hosni Mubarak and Jordan's King Hussein, who assessed that Saddam was merely using his military buildup along the border to pressure Kuwait politically.[3]

The CIA lacked human sources inside Saddam's regime who could have had access to Saddam's plans and intentions or at least give some pointers as to Saddam's thinking toward an all-out invasion of Kuwait. Secretary of State James Baker and commander of the coalition force General Norman Schwarzkopf both criticized the CIA in their memoirs for the agency's lack of good human sources inside Saddam's Iraq. As Schwarzkopf observed after the war, "our human intelligence was poor."[4] Secretary Baker recalled that U.S. "intelligence assets on the ground were virtually nonexistent."[5] He elaborated on the consequences for senior policy makers of the lack of human sources inside Baghdad: "it was extremely difficult to determine the extent to which Saddam was making strategic shifts or mere tactical changes."[6]

The CIA played a constructive role in challenging U.S. military intelligence assessments during the war, much as it had during the Cold War, even if the help was not appreciated by the commander in chief. Saddam Hussein fired tens of ballistic missiles at the Arab Gulf states and at Israel, which were politically motivated to draw the Israeli military into the fray and to disrupt Arab participation in the coalition arrayed against Iraq. Military intelligence, especially from U.S. Central Command, (CENTCOM) had assessed that coalition forces were destroying Saddam's ballistic missiles and their launchers with airpower in the run-up to the coalition ground force invasion. The CIA, on other hand, with the benefit of a small cadre of expert analysts in the Office of Imagery Analysis (OIA), assessed that the coalition was destroying Iraqi decoys but not actual missiles or launchers, contrary to the military intelligence assessments that Schwarzkopf was publicly touting. Postwar investigation confirmed the CIA's assessment and found no evidence to confirm that the coalition aircraft destroyed any Iraqi ballistic missiles or launchers during the war.[7]

The CIA also challenged military intelligence's "battle damage assessment." General Schwarzkopf had advised President Bush that the commencement of ground invasion would be possible after the air campaign had attrited 50 percent of Iraqi forces. In January 1991, CENTCOM had assessed that 50 percent of Iraq's tanks, armored personnel carriers, and artillery tubes inside the Kuwaiti theater of operations had been destroyed. The CIA, on the other hand, wrote a Presidential Daily Brief (PDB) for the president in which it assessed that coalition forces had not yet destroyed this percentage of Iraqi tanks, armored personnel carriers, and artillery tubes.[8] Again, the assessment was driven by a handful of expert imagery analysts in the CIA. Schwarzkopf was furious at what he saw as the CIA's attempt to undermine his authority as the regional commander in chief. The president's national security advisor eventually accepted CENTCOM's assessment over the CIA's assessment in large measure to avoid upsetting the military.[9]

The CIA was trying not to undermine Schwarzkopf but merely to give the president an honest assessment using the criterion that the general had established. Here again, postwar assessments confirmed that the CIA's analysis was largely correct and that CENTCOM had grossly overestimated its battle damage assessments.[10] In the final analysis, Iraqi forces were still too weak to oppose rigorously coalition ground force operations to retake Kuwait, but they were not attritted the 50-percent level as Schwarzkopf had claimed.

The final upshot of the controversy was that the CIA lost responsibility for battle damage assessments as a feature of its strategic intelligence responsibilities for the commander in chief. Then-chairman of the Joint Chiefs of Staff, Colin Powell, insisted that the CIA never again conduct battle damage assessments, which he argued was the purview of the military alone.[11]

The CIA's performance in the heat of battle was marked by other controversy. The CIA identified an Iraqi command and control bunker, for example, at al-Firdos, which was a legitimate military command and control site. Unfortunately, unknown to the CIA at the time, Iraqi regime officials used the bunker to house their families, and the U.S. aircraft bombing of the site tragically caused hundreds of innocent Iraqi civilian deaths.[12] The strike caused a public uproar and the CIA's management subsequently added a bureaucratic layer of senior official review, ostensibly to stop a similar event in the future.[13]

The Gulf War ended in a ceasefire, but not a formal treaty, and Saddam was compelled to exist under international economic sanctions until the United Nations certified that Baghdad had fully accounted for its weapons of mass destruction and ballistic missile programs. The CIA had done a reasonable job of assessing Iraq's ballistic missile and chemical weapons capabilities for U.S. policy makers before the war. The CIA had watched Iraq closely during its eight-year war from 1980 to 1988 with Iran in which Saddam made widespread use of chemical weapons and ballistic missiles. On the other hand, the CIA had a poor prewar understanding of Iraq's biological and nuclear weapons programs. The CIA knew virtually nothing about Iraq's biological warfare program going into the war. The UN weapons inspections teams that operated inside Iraq from 1991 to 1998 had discovered that Iraq had a massive biological warfare program and had even loaded twenty-five ballistic missiles with biological warfare agents and was prepared to use them against the coalition forces unbeknownst to the CIA.[14] Saddam apparently did not order the firings of these missiles because the coalition never marched on Baghdad to threaten his hold on power.[15]

The UN inspections also discovered that Iraq had a massive nuclear weapons program, most of which had gone undetected by the CIA before the war. The Gulf War Airpower Survey assessed that Iraq's nuclear weapons program was closer to fielding a nuclear weapon than U.S. intelligence realized before the war. The target list in the run-up to the war contained two nuclear-related targets, but after the war, UN inspectors uncovered more than twenty sites involved in the nuclear weapons program, sixteen of which were described as "main facilities."[16] In retrospect, Saddam's greatest strategic folly was his decision to go to war without nuclear weapons. Had he waited and acquired even a handful of nuclear weapons, the U.S. decision to reverse his invasion of Kuwait would have been an even more difficult one for the president to make given the graver dangers that would have faced American and coalition forces.

War in the Balkans

Perhaps one of the greatest unheralded successes of the CIA figuring out a difficult intelligence "mystery" was in assessing the prospects for civil war in the Balkans after the end of the Cold War and the collapse of the Soviet Union. The CIA's analysts had based their assessment on study of the history, politics, and trends. No human source or sources could have stolen any secret to "answer" this mystery.

Agency analysts had assessed in a National Intelligence Estimate (NIE) that the prospects for Yugoslavia erupting into civil war were high. As Gregory Treverton, former vice chair of the National Intelligence Council that produces NIEs, assesses, "In the autumn of 1990, my prede-cessors at the National Intelligence Council (NIC) predicted Yugoslavia's tragedy with a prescience that is awe inspiring. The national intelligence estimate, or NIE, concluded that Yugoslavia's breakup was inevitable. The breakup would be violent, and the conflict might expand to spill into adjacent regions."[17] The recent declassification of the NIE shows that it was on the mark on the breakup of Yugoslavia: "within two years Yugoslavia will probably have dissolved as a state."[18] The NIE also was on target in predicting violence in Kosovo: "It is likely that Serbian repres-sion in Kosovo will result in an armed uprising by the majority Albanian population."[19] One would be hard-pressed to find as prophetic an analysis of political-military events elsewhere in NIE history annals, an achieve-ment that must be attributed to a handful of superb analysts working on Yugoslavia, not the bureaucratic wiring diagram of the CIA or its human intelligence operations in the Balkans.

The George H. W. Bush administration made the policy decision not to intervene into the Balkans, calculating that the region held no major American national interests that warranted direct U.S. military interven-tion to derail the Balkan drive to civil war. President Bush's National Security Advisor Brent Scowcroft recalled that the Yugoslavs "would have been better off if they had stayed together, but their collapse was not central to U.S. interests as long as it could be contained."[20] That was indeed a legitimate policy decision, but at least policy makers had the benefit of an accurate and foresighted NIE on the strategic situation in the Balkans.

The Kosovo War

The United States eventually was drawn into the Balkan violence in the mid- to late 1990s to try to help cement the Dayton Peace Accords, which led to the stabilization of the situation. The ruthless Serb campaign against insurgent forces in Serbia's Kosovo province in 1999 brought the United States deeper into the Balkans. The United States, along with its North Atlantic Treaty Organization (NATO) security partners, mounted the largest combat mission in the alliance's history to stop Serb forces from committing military onslaughts against the Kosovars.

NATO had initially planned for an air campaign of a handful of days, but Serbia leader Slobodan Milošević refused to cave in to NATO's political demands in such a short time span. Pressure built on the alliance to move from targeting political, military, and economic infrastructure in Serbia to attacking Serb forces inside Kosovo, a more difficult mission because NATO pilots had to fly lower and increase their vulnerability to Serb ground fire. The air campaign eventually lasted more than two months as NATO airpower struck Serbia's political, military, and economic infrastructure in Serbia and military formations in Kosovo to coerce Milosevic to stop the ruthless paramilitary counterinsurgency campaign that caused a mass exodus of hundreds of thousands of Kosovars to neighboring states.

The U.S. military, much as it had during the Gulf War at the beginning of the decade, produced exceptionally inaccurate battle damage assessments for the NATO military and political leadership. Military intelligence assessments during the war of the damage inflicted on Serb ground forces was grossly overestimated. According to a leaked postwar U.S. Air Force assessment, NATO airpower failed to destroy most of the Serb ground forces that military intelligence assessments had claimed during the war: "the number of targets verifiably destroyed was a tiny fraction of those claimed: 14 tanks, not 120; 18 armored personnel carriers, not 220; 20 artillery pieces, not 450. Out of the 744 'confirmed' strikes by NATO pilots during the war, the Air Force investigators, who spent weeks combing Kosovo by helicopter and by foot, found evidence of just 58."[21] President Bill Clinton and his key national security lieutenants did not have the benefit of competitive civilian battle damage assessments from the CIA analysts working on the Kosovo War. The CIA's military analysts were prohibited from conducting battle damage assessments as a consequence of the Gulf War assessment controversy. The CIA's DI management prohibited its analysts from getting into what it mistakenly perceived as a "military" responsibility.

The CIA still tried, however, to assist the military campaign against Serbia. Because the air campaign was lasting much longer than anyone had anticipated at the onset of the conflict, NATO military planners were running out of targets in Serbia and Kosovo. The CIA tried to lend a hand and generate targets for NATO commanders, an effort that led to disastrous results. A group inside the CIA's DO responsible for weapons counter-proliferation thought it a brilliant idea to recommend a Serb military production facility that provided equipment to the Serb military as well as to countries of proliferation concern such as Libya. This group generated a target nomination PowerPoint slide identical to that used by the intelligence shop in U.S. military command in Europe responsible for developing targeting lists for NATO operations. The DO counter-proliferation shop passed it up CIA's management chain of command, which included the associate director for military support, an active duty brigadier general.[22] The DCI had designated the general as the final reviewer of target recommendations from the CIA for the military as a "fail-safe" to ensure that the CIA never again poorly designated a target as many had thought it did with the al-Firdos bunker during the Gulf War.[23]

Tragically, no one in the chain of command or in the DO counter-proliferation shop had any expertise or mastery of the facts on the ground in Serbia. What they all had assessed as a Serb military factory was actually the Chinese Embassy in Belgrade. The DO had worked off of old maps to identify the target and ignored pleas to reconsider the target from a more expert imagery analyst who had reservations about nominating the target.[24] The target was accepted by the U.S. European Command (EUCOM), the Chinese Embassy was bombed, and the attack killed two Chinese citizens. The incident, moreover, caused a major diplomatic crisis; Chinese in Beijing destroyed the U.S. Embassy in street protests. China's officials and public widely believed that the Americans, with of all their technology, must have intended to destroy the embassy because of China's diplomatic support to Serbia in the conflict.[25]

Al-Qaeda Wages War on the United States in Africa

While the United States was grappling with issues of war and peace throughout the 1990s in the Balkans, al-Qaeda had declared war on the United States, a reality that went unnoticed by most Americans. In August 1998, al-Qaeda launched nearly simultaneous bombing attacks against the U.S. embassies in Kenya and Tanzania, killing twelve Americans and killing and wounding hundreds of innocent Africans.

The CIA was unable to warn with the specificity needed to derail the al-Qaeda plot to bomb the embassies, which would foreshadow the Agency's failure to do the same in the run-up to the 9/11 attacks. Some evidence has emerged, however, to indicate that the CIA might have missed a golden opportunity to wrap up the embassy bombing plots, but the DO's incompetence threw the opportunity away. Former CIA case officer Melissa Boyle Mahle claims that in early 1998, a "walk-in," or person who volunteered information to the CIA by walking into one of its overseas installations in Africa, told CIA officers of the plot to blow up the U.S. Embassy in Nairobi. The CIA officers, however, assessed the walk-in as a fabricator, and the walk-in subsequently rejoined his al-Qaeda cell and took his revenge on the Americans.[26]

The CIA had relatively quickly linked the bombings to al-Qaeda and informed President Clinton. The CIA fed its human intelligence reports and analysis into Clinton's deliberations on how to best respond to the attacks. The CIA reported that al-Qaeda leaders including Osama bin Laden were meeting in Afghanistan to plan more attacks against the United States, perhaps to include the use of chemical weapons. President Clinton decided to launch retaliatory strikes against the planned meeting in Afghanistan and added a pharmaceutical plant in Sudan to the retaliatory list because the CIA had linked the plant to chemical weapons production with al-Qaeda financial backing. Although the strikes of some seventy cruise missiles in Afghanistan and Sudan were in retaliation for the destruction of the U.S. Embassies and fatalities in Africa, they also were intended as military preemption of future al-Qaeda attacks.[27] National Security Advisor Samuel Berger, for example, argued that the Clinton administration would be rightly pilloried if the United States did not destroy al-Shifa and bin Laden initiated a chemical attack that could have been preempted.[28]

In nominating the Afghan and Sudan targets to policy makers, the CIA counter-terrorism officials might have not passed the proposed targets up the usual chain of command for vetting as was done in the Chinese Embassy fiasco. The Clinton administration had strictly limited the circle of policy makers involved in the decision to a handful. DCI George Tenet might have done the same for inside the Agency to reduce the potential for a damaging public leak of sensitive targeting discussions and deliberations.

The results of the cruise missile strikes were underwhelming. President Clinton was criticized by some for using the attacks to distract from the domestic scandal caused by his affair with a young White House intern, and the Russians, the Chinese, and many Arab states denounced the attacks as U.S. imperialism. The attacks on the camps in Afghanistan, moreover, failed to kill large numbers of the al-Qaeda leadership, who appeared to have mostly departed before the strikes.[29]

The resort to cruise missiles was an easier option for President Clinton than the use of special operations forces, which were difficult to use because they were critically dependent on finely grained intelligence for targeting al-Qaeda leadership. As Richard Shultz has found after an exhaustive study of special operations forces against al-Qaeda before

9/11, the military claims that it never had "actionable intelligence" to target bin Laden.[30] Former White House official Richard Clarke, on the other hand, believes that "There was plenty of intelligence. We had incredibly good intelligence about where bin Laden's facilities were. While we might never have been able to say at any given moment where he was, we knew a dozen places that he moved among. So there was ample opportunity to use Special Forces."[31] Clarke also rails against the CIA's bureaucratic stonewalling of the Clinton administration's presidential authorization to kill bin Laden: "the President's intent was very clear: kill bin Laden. I believe that those who in CIA who claim the authorizations were insufficient or unclear are throwing up that claim as an excuse to cover the fact that they were pathetically unable to accomplish the mission."[32]

The strikes on the Sudanese pharmaceutical plant proved to be the most controversial aspect of the operation. The CIA told President Clinton that a human agent had clandestinely collected samples for the plant's surroundings, which were tested and found to have Empta, a chemical used in the production of nerve agents.[33] On-the-ground inspections of the destroyed plant, however, revealed no evidence that the building was anything more than a pharmaceutical plant, as the Sudanese had claimed. Although the controversy continues today, it is conceivable that the plant might have clandestinely interrupted its normal commercial production of pharmaceuticals for limited production runs of chemical weapons agents, but no solid evidence has come to light. Clinton administration counterterrorism officials still strongly suspect an al-Qaeda link to the pharmaceutical plant because its general manager was living in bin Laden's villa in Khartoum, and an al-Qaeda defector testified in the U.S. court for the bombings of the U.S. Embassies in Africa that al-Qaeda used the plant to manufacture chemical weapons.[34]

Post–Cold War Strategic Intelligence Legacies

The rewards for the CIA's handful of expert imagery analysts in OIA who had the courage to "speak truth to power" and accurately assess

Iraqi ballistic missile and ground force battle damage assessments in the 1991 Gulf War was punishment at the hands of the CIA's weak management. The CIA's management bowed to policy-maker pressure and relieved OIA from the responsibility of making any more battle damage assessments in subsequent wars. The OIA later would be abolished under DCI John Deutch's tenure when in 1996 he moved all intelligence community imagery analysis into the National Imagery and Mapping Agency (NIMA), now named the National Geospatial Intelligence Agency (NGA), which is directly subordinate to the military and designated as a "combat support agency."[35]

Military intelligence analysis by "combat support" organizations proved in both the Gulf War and in the 1999 Kosovo War to be qualitatively inferior to the strategic intelligence produced by a small cadre of civilian imagery experts who had been housed and nurtured for years in the CIA's OIA. Policy makers have the prerogative to reject CIA analyses, but at least with the CIA's OIA they had the benefit of views untainted by the military's operational and battlefield interests as a foundation for policy deliberations and implementation. But today, U.S. policy makers no longer have this important civilian check on military intelligence, and an important facet of civilian control over the military has been eroded.

The CIA's gross underestimation of Saddam's biological and nuclear weapons programs would have a lasting impact on U.S. policy makers. Then-Secretary of Defense Richard Cheney would later become vice president and then-Under Secretary of Defense for Policy Paul Wolfowitz would become Deputy Secretary of Defense under the George W. Bush administration. Both men undoubtedly worried in the run-up to the 2003 war against Iraq that the CIA, without any good human intelligence sources inside Iraq, was again, much like it was in 1990, grossly underestimating Iraq's weapons of mass destruction capabilities.

The Yugoslavia case neatly shows the roles and responsibilities of intelligence officers versus policy makers. The CIA analysts ably discharged their responsibilities to "speak truth to power" and gave a candid and – refreshingly, in this case – an accurate assessment of the situation on the ground and the likely future course of events. Policy makers, on the other hand, exercised their responsibility as officials elected by the U.S. public to read intelligence assessments and measure them against their calculation of national interests.

The tragic bombing of the Chinese Embassy vividly shows that changes to the CIA's bureaucratic wiring diagram did not in and of themselves fix the root causes of intelligence failures. The DCI's bureaucratic fiddling in the aftermath of the al-Firdos bombing in Iraq put yet another layer of management oversight on the intelligence process, but it did not stop the Chinese Embassy bombing. In essence, the CIA imposed layers of bureaucrats to check targeting recommendations in war, but what the CIA needed was more experts, not more bureaucrats, working on targeting issues.

The CIA's strategic intelligence performance in the 1998 al-Qaeda bombings of U.S. Embassies in Africa was mixed. The CIA apparently had no concrete warnings of al-Qaeda plans to attack the embassies and appears to have missed an opportunity to receive an invaluable warning when it turned away an al-Qaeda walk-in who was willing to share information on the plot. The CIA's human intelligence reports on the al-Qaeda leadership meeting in Afghanistan on the eve of the U.S. cruise missile strikes might have been erroneous altogether. If the reports were true, the United States was not able to launch a sufficiently timely attack to catch the meeting in progress. The veracity of the CIA's human intelligence reporting linking the Sudanese pharmaceutical plant to al-Qaeda and its chemical weapons aspirations is still an open question. But the CIA's strategic intelligence shortcomings against al-Qaeda would grow larger in the intervening years from 1998 to 2001.

The CIA's knee-jerk reaction to every intelligence failure seems to be to move and add more bureaucracy, a step that is easy to do and appeases congressional and public demands to "do something," at least until the next intelligence failure occurs to occasion the creation of more bureaucracy as a slight of hand. The real problems, however, lie at the grassroots and the CIA's management has been perpetually derelict in its responsibilities by not nurturing sophisticated analysts at the bottom of the organization. Bureaucracy does not produce first-rate intelligence analyses, smart and wise analysts do. The CIA excels at adding layers to its bureaucratic fat but does nothing to build analytic muscle that would lead over the longer run to better – but never perfect – intelligence and fewer and less catastrophic intelligence failures.

4 Blundering in the "War on Terrorism"

THE UNITED STATES SUFFERED A HUGE INTELLIGENCE FAIL-
ure on 11 September 2001 with the al-Qaeda attacks on the
World Trade Center and the Pentagon and the failed attack
that ended with an airplane crashing in a field in Pennsylvania. The events
took the lives of some 3,000 American citizens. The intelligence community in general and the CIA in particular failed to detect al-Qaeda's intentions with the clarity needed to disrupt the attacks. The attacks set the
United States off on what President Bush calls the "War on Terrorism,"
a government policy that inaccurately lumps together U.S. efforts aimed
at destroying al-Qaeda and the military campaign against the Taliban
regime in Afghanistan with the Iraq War to oust Saddam Hussein's
regime. Al-Qaeda and Iraq had been discrete strategic threats before
9/11 but were blurred together only after the 2003 toppling of Saddam's
regime, which opened a power vacuum that al-Qaeda has sought to exploit
by waging an insurgency in Iraq, much as jihadists had against the Soviet
Union in Afghanistan during the 1980s. Be that as it may, no amount of
debate or discussion is likely to separate the 9/11 events from the Iraq
War, which have been drummed together as the War on Terrorism in the
public's common mind.

The 9/11 attacks were in many ways reminiscent of the surprise attack
on Pearl Harbor in 1941, which was instrumental in giving birth to the
CIA as a central collection and analysis intelligence organization responsible for giving strategic warning of enemy attack to the commander in

chief. The CIA was intended to transcend bureaucratic boundaries in the government such as those among the U.S. Navy, Army, and State Department, which substantially contributed to the failure to warn of a Japanese attack against Pearl Harbor. The 9/11 attacks were an even greater and more devastating intelligence failure and defeat for the United States – an assessment shared even by many World War II veterans – because al-Qaeda, unlike the Japanese, had specifically targeted civilians more than military personnel and the attack was launched against the continental United States rather than "a world away" in Pearl Harbor.

The CIA, at least in the immediate aftermath of the 9/11 attacks, escaped a great deal of public, congressional, and White House criticism, in part because the United States went to war in Afghanistan in October 2001 against the Taliban regime that harbored the central core of al-Qaeda including its top leaders. The CIA's covert paramilitary forces proved to be more readily available and flexible than the military's Special Forces. The CIA was in the vanguard of the military campaign in Afghanistan by sending in covert teams to link up with and bribe Afghani tribal militias opposed to the Taliban to pave the way for the subsequent insertion of larger and more combat capable Special Forces that directed the lion's share of military operations against al-Qaeda and the Taliban. President Bush might have been willing to withhold his administration's criticism of the CIA's failure to warn in detail of 9/11 because it was the instrument trumpeted by Director of Central Intelligence (DCI) George Tenet that allowed the United States to be on the ground in Afghanistan only about a month after 9/11. While the military belabored planning for large-scale operations, President Bush welcomed the CIA's eagerness to get into the fight.[1]

The CIA's respite from criticism was short-lived because the Iraq War would publicly reveal another major intelligence debacle with the gross overestimation of Iraq's weapons of mass destruction (WMD) programs and capabilities. In the run-up to the war in late 2002 and early 2003, the CIA had told President Bush that Iraq was reconstituting its chemical, biological, and nuclear weapons programs and even had stocks of chemical and biological weapons on hand. Postwar investigations revealed that on each of these accounts, the CIA had been wrong. This time, unlike the immediate aftermath of the 9/11 attacks, there was an unleashing of public and congressional criticisms of the CIA. The criticism solidified support for the findings of the 9/11 Commission that investigated the 11 September attacks – which had eclipsed the more insightful Joint House–Senate intelligence committee investigation on the attacks. Likewise, it eclipsed the Senate Select Committee on Intelligence's Investigation on the Iraq debacle and the presidentially appointed commission that investigated the intelligence community's performance against Iraq and against WMD globally.[2]

In the politically charged and psychologically emotional atmosphere, the greatest changes in the bureaucratic structure of the intelligence community since its founding in 1947 were implemented without expert deliberation or analysis commensurate with the proposed changes that were implemented. When the dust settled, the position of the director of national intelligence (DNI) was created, and the director of central intelligence post was eliminated. The CIA fell from a "first among equals" to "one among many" position in the intelligence community, losing its precious and unique access to the commander in chief. No longer would it be considered the premier intelligence agency for strategic intelligence.

The 9/11 Intelligence Failures

The intelligence failure of 9/11 was arguably the greatest debacle in the history of U.S. intelligence. To be fair, the CIA had given the commander in chief strategic warning in his Presidential Daily Brief (PDB) in the summer of 2001 that al-Qaeda was planning a major operation against the United States. The CIA, however, had anticipated that the attack would most likely occur against U.S. assets, property, or citizens abroad. Further, the CIA failed to have access to human intelligence assets who could have penetrated the al-Qaeda conspiracy to allow for U.S. disruption of the plot. The failings of the CIA were substantial but were exceeded by those of the FBI, an observation lost in the public controversy surrounding the 9/11 strategic intelligence failure. Although the CIA had taken the brunt of public criticisms for failing to detect via human intelligence the 9/11 attacks, the FBI has escaped public criticism commensurate with its failures that were even larger and more significant than those of the CIA.

The FBI had a mountain of intelligence on al-Qaeda, but, unlike the CIA and the rest of the intelligence community, it refused to share its intelligence with other intelligence community organizations and key policy makers. Then-DCI James Woolsey, for example, complained of the 1993 al-Qaeda–inspired attack against the World Trade Center that "Any twenty-four-year-old junior agent in the FBI's New York office knew more about the largest-ever terrorist attack on American soil then he did."[3] Daniel Benjamin and Steven Simon, counter-terrorism officials on the Clinton administration's National Security Council staff, have lamented from their policy-making days that "Every day a hundred or more reports from the CIA, DIA [Defense Intelligence Agency], the National Security Agency, and the State Department would be waiting in their computer queues when they got to work. There was never anything from the FBI. The Bureau, despite its wealth of information, contributed nothing to the White House's understanding of al-Qaeda."[4]

The FBI had uncovered specific information on the al-Qaeda 9/11 conspiracy that, had it been recognized and exploited, could have been leveraged to disrupt the attacks. Two FBI field offices had collected information that al-Qaeda members were in the United States training on aircraft. In July 2001, the FBI's field office in Arizona, for example, warned FBI headquarters that "there was a coordinated effort underway by Bin Ladin to send students to the United States for civil aviation–related training" and that the FBI field officer was suspicious that it was part of an "effort to establish a cadre of individuals in civil aviation who would conduct future terrorist activity."[5] A Minnesota agent repeatedly warned FBI superiors in Washington that Zacarias Moussaoui – the only 9/11 conspirator caught before the attacks – was dangerous and that his study of how to fly a Boeing 747-400 seemed to be part of a plot. The FBI agent urged in August 2001 after Moussaoui's arrest that the FBI act quickly because it was not clear "how far advanced Moussaoui's plan is or how many unidentified co-conspirators exist."[6] The FBI had no central analytic unit in Washington capable of linking these related pieces of information together – an activity that has commonly come to be called "connecting the dots" – to determine that al-Qaeda cells inside the United States were training for operations using aircraft. In essence, the FBI had found but had not recognized major threads in the al-Qaeda plot that could have been doggedly pulled to cause the conspiracy's entire fabric to fall apart.

Had the FBI simply shared its field-office threat assessments with larger sets of eyes in the intelligence and policy communities, someone might have recognized the threads and starting pulling. Specifically, had the FBI been more intelligence-oriented and less bureaucratically constipated, it could have shared the field-office reports with other members of the intelligence community such as the CIA's Counterterrorism Center (CTC), whose analysts were warning in the PDB of al-Qaeda plans for a large attack. In turn, the CTC analysts might have connected the dots and ascertained that al-Qaeda was planning to use aircraft inside the United States. The outlines of al-Qaeda's plans for using aircraft as weapons had already been seen in the 1990s in disrupted plans by the cell in the Philippines. Unfortunately, the FBI was bureaucratically ossified and refused to share its information laterally with working levels at the CIA as well as with policy makers on the National Security Council staff, who also might have connected the dots because they were more expert on al-Qaeda than staff at the FBI's headquarters.

The FBI did not have a bureaucratic culture for sharing its data with other members of the intelligence community. The FBI, although formally a member of the intelligence community, culturally viewed itself as a law enforcement agency and perceived that sharing information with other members of the intelligence community or the national security policy-making community would jeopardize criminal prosecutions. Judge

Richard Posner points out, however, that the FBI was overly conservative and that the bureau always had the legal latitude necessary to share its information without jeopardizing criminal cases.[7] Getting the FBI to adapt its institutional culture to support the intelligence mission will be a struggle. Judge Posner illuminates the dimensions of the problem by recalling that "The FBI announced reorganizations of its intelligence operation in 1998, 1999, 2001, and 2002. A further reorganization was decreed by the Intelligence Reform Act in 2004, apparently without effect."[8]

On the other hand, the CIA in fact had given the commander in chief a variety of warnings of a major al-Qaeda attack. It warned the White House in May 2001 that al-Qaeda was planning a "spectacular" attack, although it had assessed that the most likely targets would be overseas, especially in Israel or Saudi Arabia.[9] The CIA, according to Steve Coll, even prepared a briefing paper on 10 July for senior Bush administration officials that read, "Based on a review of all-source reporting over the last five months, we believe [bin Laden] will launch a significant terrorist attack against U.S. and/or Israeli interests in coming weeks. The attack will be spectacular and designed to inflict mass casualties against U.S. facilities or interests. Attack preparations have been made. Attack will occur with little or no warning."[10]

The CIA even directly warned the commander in chief of the possibility of al-Qaeda attacks inside the United States. An article in the PDB on 6 August 2001 was titled "Bin Ladin Determined to Strike in US," and its lead sentence was *"Clandestine, foreign government, and media reports indicate Bin Ladin since 1997 has wanted to conduct terrorist attacks in the U.S."*[11] To be sure, the contents of the article were largely a historical review of al-Qaeda's 1998 attacks against the U.S. Embassies in Africa and the 1999 failed attempt to infiltrate from Canada to attack Los Angeles International Airport; they lacked specific or tactical intelligence on the 9/11 plot. Nevertheless, the article provided a strategic warning to the commander in chief and his national security lieutenants that al-Qaeda had its sights on targets inside the United States. The PDB clearly shows that CIA analysts at the CTC had their antennae up for al-Qaeda attacks inside the United States and would have been receptive to concrete evidence of domestic attacks had the FBI only shared its Arizona and Minnesota field reports on al-Qaeda operatives training on aircraft.

On the negative side of CIA performance, the Directorate of Operations fell down on the job in collecting human intelligence on the al-Qaeda plot. With the benefit of twenty-twenty hindsight, it is apparent that al-Qaeda's operational security to protect its plans was not airtight, and they were vulnerable to human intelligence collection. Even before the August 2001 PDB, the CIA's analysts at the CTC were warning of a major al-Qaeda attack on the horizon. As reporter Steve Coll has uncovered, "In July the CIA's Counterterrorism Center reported that it had interviewed a source who had recently returned from Afghanistan. The source had reported, 'Everyone is talking about an impending attack.' "[12] The source's information suggests that Afghanistan al-Qaeda circles were buzzing with information about the 9/11 attack. The CIA, in other words, simply had to get more access to large bodies of al-Qaeda–affiliated individuals, not the deep penetration of al-Qaeda's high command because al-Qaeda's operational security was not vacuum-tight.

Taking a step back from the details of the 9/11 case, what is striking about the CIA's strategic warning of a major al-Qaeda attack is that it fits neatly into the historical precedents of the victims of surprise attack. However paradoxical, Richard Betts has found in an exhaustive study of surprise attacks that "*All sudden attacks occurred in situations of prolonged tension, during which the victim's state's leaders recognized that war might be on the horizon.*"[13] Betts judges that "*the primary problem in major strategic surprises is not intelligence warning but political disbelief.*"[14] Although Betts was writing of wars between nation-states, the 9/11 surprise attacks by a transnational group conforms to his findings. The commander in chief certainly had ample warning that al-Qaeda had declared war on the United States from the 1998 attacks against U.S. Embassies in Africa, the attack on the USS *Cole* in Yemen in 2000, and even from the failed al-Qaeda–inspired plots to bring down the World Trade Center towers in 1993 and the bid to attack Los Angeles International Airport.

The CIA and intelligence community, notwithstanding the general warning, failed the president and his key national security lieutenants in not formulating a strategic national intelligence estimate on al-Qaeda before 9/11. The 9/11 Commission found that "Despite the availability of information that al Qaeda was a global network, in 1998 policymakers knew little about the organization. The reams of new information that the CIA's Bin Laden unit had been developing since 1996 had not been pulled together and synthesized for the rest of the government. Indeed, analysts in the unit felt that they were viewed as alarmists even within the CIA. A National Intelligence Estimate on terrorism in 1997 had only briefly mentioned Bin Laden, and no subsequent national estimate would authoritatively evaluate the terrorism danger until after 9/11."[15] Terrorism expert Daniel Byman points out that "Indeed, no comprehensive intelligence assessment of al Qaeda was drafted until after September 11."[16]

The CIA's analytic effort, in other words, was almost entirely devoted to providing current intelligence in the PDB to the commander in chief and not broader, more intellectually reflective strategic intelligence assessments based on long-term research. This failure was to be repeated in the run-up to the Iraq War when the CIA and the intelligence community hurriedly produced a strategic national intelligence analysis on Iraq's WMD programs only because of congressional insistence that an National Intelligence Estimate (NIE) be produced.

The Iraq WMD Debacle

United States intelligence performance in assessing Iraq's WMD programs in the run-up to the Iraq War was a catastrophic intelligence failure. Before the war, the CIA gave the commander in chief a horribly incorrect strategic assessment of Iraq's WMD programs. The CIA judged for President Bush in an October 2002 NIE that Saddam's regime was aggressively reconstituting its nuclear weapons program and had active biological and chemical production lines as well as significant biological and chemical weapons stores.[17] In the now-infamous exchange, DCI

George Tenet personally told President Bush that the case against Saddam and his WMD activities is "a slam dunk." What is not publicly touted is President Bush's critical appraisal of the CIA's WMD case on Iraq that triggered Tenet's slam-dunk remark. Bush said to Tenet, "I've been told all this intelligence about having WMD and this is the best we've got?"[18]

Bush administration officials undoubtedly worried that the CIA was only getting glimpses of the tip of the Iraq WMD problem. Key Bush administration officials such as Vice President Cheney and Deputy Secretary of Defense Paul Wolfowitz no doubt remembered well from their experience as Pentagon officials during the 1990–1 Gulf War in which the CIA underestimated Iraq's nuclear, biological, and chemical weapons programs. They probably assumed in the back of their mind that the CIA was again underestimating Saddam's capabilities, and this led them to be somewhat dismissive of CIA analysis.

Despite Bush's reservations about the quality of CIA intelligence on Iraq's suspected WMD capabilities, and although the president used a variety of public justifications for waging war against Saddam's regime such as Baghdad's links to international terrorism, Saddam's active and robust WMD capabilities stood head and shoulders above other justifications for war. The CIA's human intelligence reporting and analysis contained in the October 2002 NIE was funneled into Secretary of State Colin Powell's February 2003 presentation to the UN Security Council in an effort to sway international official and public opinion toward the U.S. strategic objective of ousting Saddam's regime. Secretary Powell masterfully delivered his presentation laying out the U.S. case that Iraq was actively reconstituting its nuclear weapons program as well as producing, weaponizing, and stockpiling chemical and biological weapons in violation of UN Security Council terms for the 1991 war's ceasefire.[19]

What is still more embarrassing about the CIA's performance in this episode was that its staff work on the Iraq WMD issue was so poor, it could not prepare a concise and persuasive presentation for Secretary of

State Powell. The CIA was not sufficiently competent to harness its own human intelligence reporting and analysis into an intelligence portfolio that could be readily used by the secretary of state to marshal the public case against Saddam. Instead, the secretary of state himself had to work like a "staff officer" and devote days to working on the seventh floor of the CIA to prepare his presentation to the UN Security Council.[20] The episode showed a glaring CIA shortcoming that is not appreciated by the public. The Agency's WMD technical analysts often are not able to write in simple and straightforward prose or with the brevity needed for senior policy makers. They are more practiced at dumping bundles of summarized raw intelligence reports sprinkled with analysis on to the desks of senior policy makers and to have them try to make sense of it – an impossible task given the enormous time constraints under which these individuals labor. In exasperation, Powell was forced to do for himself what CIA analysts should have responsibly done.

The post-2003 war investigation on the ground in Iraq revealed a substantially different picture of the status of Saddam's WMD and delivery programs than that painted by the prewar NIE and Secretary Powell's UN presentation. The Iraq Survey Group (ISG) working for DCI Tenet discovered via investigations and debriefings of Iraqi military officers and scientists that Saddam's chemical, biological, and nuclear weapons programs had been abandoned since the mid-1990s in part because of Iraqi fears of detection by the international community.[21]

The reality of Iraq's WMD programs was by and large 180 degrees from the CIA's pre-2003 war assessment. The CIA missed the mark in assessing Saddam's ballistic missiles and chemical weapons capabilities. The ISG found no evidence that Iraq retained Scud-variant missiles, and debriefings of Iraqi officials and some documentation indicate that Iraq did not retain such missiles after 1991.[22] The ISG assessed that "While a small number of old, abandoned chemical munitions have been discovered, ISG judges that Iraq unilaterally destroyed its undeclared chemical weapons stockpile in 1991. There are no credible indications that Baghdad resumed production of chemical weapons thereafter, a policy

ISG attributes to Baghdad's desire to see sanctions lifted, or rendered ineffectual, or its fear of force against it should WMD be discovered."[23]

The CIA also missed the mark in assessing Saddam's biological and nuclear weapons programs. The ISG found "no direct evidence that Iraq, after 1996, had plans for a new BW [biological weapons] program or was conducting BW-specific work for military purposes. Indeed, from the mid-1990s, despite evidence of continuing interest in nuclear and chemical weapons, there appears to be a complete absence of discussion or even interest in BW at the Presidential level."[24] The ISG judged that between 1991 and 1992, "Iraq appears to have destroyed its undeclared stocks of BW weapons and probably destroyed remaining holdings of bulk BW agent."[25] And most damning of the CIA's performance, the ISG determined that "Saddam Husayn ended the nuclear program in 1991 following the Gulf war. ISG found no evidence to suggest concerted efforts to restart the program. Although Saddam clearly assigned a high value to the nuclear progress and talent that had been developed up to the 1991 war, the program ended and the intellectual capital decayed in the succeeding years."[26]

Postwar investigation revealed that the most compelling evidence on Iraq's suspected biological warfare program, used by Secretary Powell in his UN Security Council presentation, came from a sole human intelligence source who was discovered to be a fabricator.[27] The CIA inexcusably based its biological warfare case on one lonely source. No reputable journalist working for a major U.S. newspaper would have ever taken such a foolhardy risk and gone to print without first getting a variety of other sources to corroborate a story.

The CIA had been profoundly wrong in its assessments of Iraq's WMD programs largely because of incompetent human intelligence collection operations that overrelied on few and poor Iraqi defectors coupled with intelligence analysis that leapt to conclusions that went well beyond what intelligence "evidence" supported.[28] As the Senate Select Committee on Intelligence determined, most of the NIE's major key judgments "either overstated, or were not supported by, the underlying intelligence reporting. A series of failures, particularly in analytic tradecraft, led to the mischaracterization of the intelligence."[29]

The sloppy intelligence work in the Iraq WMD NIE reflected the overall poor quality of CIA intelligence for the commander in chief. The CIA has long heralded the PDB as its premier vehicle for providing strategic intelligence to the commander in chief, but an outside group of distinguished individuals evaluated the quality of the PDB and gave it scathing reviews. The Presidential Commission on WMD was granted unique access to the PDB and found it riddled with "attention-grabbing headlines and drumbeat or repetition, left an impression of many corroborating reports where in fact there were very few sources . . . the daily reports seems to be 'selling' intelligence – in order to keep its customers, or at least the First Customer [the president], interested."[30]

The ISG findings exposed to daylight the dark underbelly of failings in CIA intelligence that was hidden before the war. The NIE's little-noticed caveat that "We lack specific information on many key aspects of Iraq's WMD programs" turned out to be a major understatement. The CIA's gross overestimation of Iraq's weapons-related activities probably reflects, in some measure, an analytic overcompensation for the gross underestimation of the scope and progress of Iraq's nuclear and biological weapons programs in the run-up to the 1991 war.[31]

The CIA's poor assessments were fed by inexpert satellite imagery analysis from military intelligence agencies because the CIA had lost its own imagery analysis capabilities as a legacy of the 1991 Gulf War. The Presidential Commission on WMD found that "the NIE's judgment that Iraq had restarted CW [chemical weapons] production was based primarily on imagery intelligence" and that analysts saw a number of "indicators" at numerous sites.[32] The Presidential Commission rightly judged that the intelligence community "relied too heavily on ambiguous imagery indicators at suspect Iraqi facilities for its broad judgment about Iraq's chemical warfare program. In particular, analysts leaned too much on the judgment that the presence of 'Samarra-type' trucks (and related activity) indicated that Iraq had resumed its chemical weapons program."[33]

The poor quality of imagery analysis was in no small measure due to reorganization of imagery analysis in the intelligence community during the 1990s. The CIA had long maintained a small but expert cadre of imagery analysts who ably acted as a civilian quality control on the military's imagery analysis. The CIA's Office of Imagery Analysis (OIA) proved its worth in its objective and accurate assessments during the 1991 Gulf War when it disagreed with military assessments that Iraqi forces had been destroyed by 50 percent in the Kuwaiti theater of operations and when it disagreed with military assessments that numerous Iraqi ballistic missiles and launchers had been destroyed, as discussed in the previous chapter. Notwithstanding these analytic accomplishments, DCI John Deutch, in an effort to consolidate intelligence community components, thought it wise to abolish the CIA's OIA and give total responsibility for imagery analysis to the National Geospatial Intelligence Agency (NGA), a designated combat support agency controlled by the military. Unfortunately, NGA has too many new analysts with little of the long-term research and analytic culture and expertise that was nurtured in the CIA's former OIA. Equally significant, with OIA's abolishment, civilian intelligence officers, principally at the CIA, lost a critical means to keep tabs analytically on military imagery analysis to try to ensure honest, objective assessments untainted by military and operational prerogatives that so often have slanted military intelligence assessments, as was the case in the Vietnam and Kosovo conflicts.

With the benefit of twenty-twenty hindsight, a large pivotal failing of the CIA's strategic intelligence performance of Iraq's WMD was the failure to exploit analytically clues given by a high-level Iraqi defector in the mid-1990s. Hussein Kamil, Saddam Hussein's right-hand man who played a central role in Iraq's WMD programs, defected to Jordan in August 1995 because he feared he was losing a power struggle with Saddam's son Uday. The CIA declassified Kamil's debriefing reports as part of the investigation of Gulf War syndrome, a controversial legacy of the 1991 Gulf War, but these debriefings have been overlooked by all post-2003 Iraq War investigations. Kamil told the CIA in 1995 that Iraq had no Scuds left and was not hiding Scud missile components. The Scuds were launched, unilaterally destroyed, or destroyed by UN weapons inspectors. Kamil also told the CIA that Iraq's centrifuges for enriching uranium were destroyed and that none were left in Iraq. Finally, Kamil reported that no nerve agent or chemical weapons were hidden in Iraq.[34]

CIA analysts dismissed these reports because they did not conform to their view that Saddam was engaged in a massive denial and deception campaign to protect his WMD programs and the belief that Hussein Kamil, a thug and murderer with the moral standing on a par with Saddam Hussein, was lying. Intelligence community suspicions about the quality of Kamil's information were heightened after he abruptly decided to return to Iraq.[35] Apparently, life outside Iraq was not to his liking – a psychological problem for many defectors – and he returned to be promptly killed, along with his brothers, by Saddam's thugs. The biblical image of "Live by the sword, die by the sword" comes to mind. Nevertheless, Kamil provided critical information that could have served as a baseline foundation for a devil's-advocate analysis arguing that Saddam's Iraq no longer had WMD. Such an analysis could have been levied to scrub intelligence previously overlooked or discarded that pointed to confirmation of the devil's advocate, no WMD thesis as well as to task Directorate of Operations (DO) human intelligence collectors for new information that could have opened consideration of the possibility that Saddam had scrapped his WMD programs.

The DO had no sources inside Iraq reporting on WMD in the run-up to the Iraq War and appears to have turned away sources who accurately reported that Saddam had abandoned his WMD programs because it did not fit the CIA's common wisdom. The Presidential Commission on WMD found that "several human sources asserted before the war that Iraq did not retain any WMD. And one source, who may have come closer to the truth than any other, said that Iraq would never admit it did *not* have WMD because it would be tantamount to suicide in the Middle East."[36] The Presidential Commission on WMD found that "Potential sources for alternative views were denigrated or not pursued by collectors,"[37] principally the CIA's DO. Robert Jervis adds that the CIA appears to have made clear to its human agents its bias that Iraq harbored WMD that "may have led its agents and sources to bring in any information, even if insubstantial, and – most importantly – to ignore reports of lack of activity."[38]

Another great tragedy in the Iraqi WMD debacle is the evidence that has emerged indicating that the CIA in the run-up to the war was getting human intelligence from inside Iraq that Baghdad's WMD programs were in complete disarray. The CIA appears to have been getting intelligence via France's intelligence services from Iraq's foreign minister, who in 2002 reported that Iraq had no nuclear weapons and was only "dabbling" with biological weapons but had no "real biological weapons program."[39] Journalist James Risen reports, moreover, that the CIA under maverick senior intelligence officer Charles Allen put into place an innovative and creative human collection program that used Iraqi expatriates living in the United States to contact their relatives still living in Iraq, who the CIA had linked to Iraq's suspected WMD programs. Risen reports that some thirty Iraqi relatives who cooperated with the CIA all reported that Iraq's programs had been abandoned. Inexcusably, "CIA officials ignored the evidence and refused to even disseminate the reports from family members to senior policy makers in the Bush administration. Sources say that the CIA's Directorate of Operations, which was supposed to be in charge of the entire agency's clandestine intelligence operations, was jealous of Allen's incursions into its operational turf and shut down his program and denigrated its results."[40]

There is no concrete evidence that the Bush administration "politicized" the intelligence by dictating to the CIA and the intelligence community the conclusions of the infamous Iraq WMD NIE. The Senate Select Committee on Intelligence study on this intelligence debacle was comprehensive and found no evidence that "intelligence analysts changed their judgments as a result of political pressure, altered or produced intelligence products to conform with Administration policy, or that anyone attempted to coerce, influence or pressure analysts to do so."[41] The Presidential Commission on WMD similarly found that "The analysts who worked Iraqi weapons issues universally agreed that in no instance did political pressure cause them to skew or alter any of their intelligence judgments."[42]

To its credit, the CIA firmly held its ground in opposing the Bush administration's view that Iraq had close ties with al-Qaeda. The Bush administration publicly tried to link the 9/11 al-Qaeda attacks to Iraq, a linkage that is now discredited. The Senate Select Committee on Intelligence investigated the issue and concluded that "Postwar information supports prewar Intelligence Community assessments that there was no credible information that Iraq was complicit in or had foreknowledge of the September 11 attacks or any other al-Qa'ida strike."[43] As Jervis explains, "Intelligence consistently denied that there was significant evidence for Saddam's role in 9/11 or that he might turn over WMD to al Qaeda, holding to this position in the face of frequent administration statements to the contrary, repeated inquiries and challenges that can only be interpreted as pressure, and the formation of a unit in the Defense Department dedicated to finding such a conclusion."[44] On this score, the CIA held to its unofficial motto and "spoke truth to power."

Conspiracy theories that the Iraq WMD NIE was politicized with the White House dictating the conclusions to the intelligence community run wild. But what is missed in the journalistic treatments is the more mundane and more likely explanation of the assertive and definitive nature of the conclusions in the NIE that went beyond the confidence level of more caveated, working-level assessments in the bowels of the CIA. As Bob Woodward recounts, "Stu Cohen, an intelligence professional for 30 years, was acting chairman of the National Intelligence Council when the Iraq assessment of WMD was being prepared. He confided to a colleague that he wanted to avoid equivocation if possible. If the Key Judgments used words such as 'maybe' or 'probably' or 'likely,' the NIE would be 'pabulum,' he said. Ironclad evidence in the intelligence business is scarce and analysts need to be able to make judgments beyond the ironclad,

Cohen felt."[45] As the members of Presidential Commission on WMD discovered in a review of finished intelligence found, "far and away the most damaging tradecraft weaknesses we observed was the failure of analysts to conclude – when appropriate – that there was not enough information available to make a defensible judgment."[46] But the practices of working-level analysts reflects the environment in which they labor. Senior CIA officer insistence on a definitive "answer" is an intellectual arrogance that permeates the CIA's managerial culture.

Assessing Intelligence Performances against WMD Targets

By reaching back even farther behind today's news headlines, a review of the CIA's historical performance against the global WMD challenge reveals a string of serious intelligence failures. The CIA failed, for example, to warn U.S. policy makers in 1998 of India's nuclear weapons tests that led to reciprocal tests by Pakistan, setting South Asia into an overt nuclear weapons race. Retired Admiral David Jeremiah, a former vice chairman of the Joint Chiefs of Staff, was tasked by DCI Tenet to review that intelligence debacle. Jeremiah concluded that the intelligence community's analysts were stretched too thin, satellite collection was vulnerable to simple deception, and human intelligence was seriously limited. The conventional mind-set prevailed that India would not test nuclear weapons and risk negative international reaction. The national intelligence officer for warning, who sat on the National Intelligence Council that produces NIEs, moreover, proved incapable of fulfilling his central task to be an effective devil's advocate to counter prevailing, and profoundly wrong, conventional wisdom at the CIA.[47] And as Ronald Kessler adds, the CIA also hurt its ability to collect intelligence against India because the U.S. ambassador to India "showed top Indian officials photographs from spy satellites that detected preparations for tests in 1995" in an effort to get the Indians not to test their nuclear weapons. Kessler notes that "The photos gave the Indians clues on how they could conceal cables and wires running into the shaft where they conducted the tests."[48]

The CIA also failed in gauging WMD activities surrounding Pakistan's nuclear weapons program. CIA defenders hail the disruption of A. Q. Khan's international nuclear weapons production supply ring as a major intelligence coup that led Libya to admit publicly and surrender its nuclear and chemical weapons programs to the international community. That claim, however, does not hold up under close scrutiny. Khan's network had been operating for decades before it was ostensibly shut down after the United States put diplomatic pressure on Pakistan's President Pervez Musharraf. The network had more than enough time to provide Libya with an infrastructure for building nuclear weapons, including centrifuges for enriching uranium. Khan, in the assessment of nuclear weapons expert David Albright, "with the help of associates on four continents, managed to buy and sell key nuclear weapons capabilities for more than two decades while eluding the world's best intelligence agencies and non-proliferation institutions and organizations . . . as it sold the equipment and expertise needed to produce nuclear weapons to major U.S. enemies including Iran, Libya, and North Korea."[49] Khan's network nimbly managed to evade CIA collection efforts against Libya: "The program was much more advanced than we assessed," according to former National Security Council director for counter-proliferation, Robert Joseph.[50] The $100 million deal included Chinese blueprints once given to Pakistan for a nuclear warhead that could be mounted on a ballistic missile. Further, the CIA also failed to detect that Khan began selling nuclear technology to Iran in the late 1980s.[51]

The Pakistan government, and Musharraf in particular, probably knew that Khan was operating his supply ring despite its public denials. It does not take a great deal of imagination to suspect that Khan was enriching Pakistani military and intelligence service coffers with his nuclear deals in exchange for either turning a blind eye to his activities or even actively facilitating his deals. These suspicions appear more concrete in light of Musharraf's full pardon of Khan and his refusal to grant the United States access to Khan to question him. That refusal should raise alarms that

Khan's network is still in operation and even more deeply hidden and dispersed to avoid future CIA detection.

The CIA also appears to also be falling down in the critical task of identifying which other countries the Khan network might still be supplying with nuclear weapons–related equipment and expertise. Libya's surrender of its nuclear weapons program revealed a clandestine centrifuge construction program in South Africa that apparently was undetected by the CIA. A private company, which included some individuals who had been involved in South Africa's past clandestine nuclear weapons program, was manufacturing a plant designed to operate 1,000 centrifuges for enriching uranium for shipment to Libya. Once assembled in Libya, the plant could have produced enough weapons-grade uranium for several nuclear bombers per year.[52] These uranium-enrichment kits would be ideal for countries such as Algeria, Egypt, Syria, and Saudi Arabia looking for a shortcut from large nuclear energy–related infrastructure to procure fissile material for nuclear weapons.[53]

For about twenty years, a long-running dismal intelligence performance has been underway in Iran, where Tehran's suspected nuclear weapons program went undetected by the CIA.[54] Khan's network appears to have been instrumental in providing critical components to Iran's program, especially centrifuge technology. The massive scope and sophistication of Iran's centrifuge program was revealed in August 2002 by Iranian dissidents and subsequently verified by International Atomic Energy Agency (IAEA) inspections.[55] The IAEA determined that Iran had been violating its obligations under the Non-Proliferation Treaty to notify it of uranium-enrichment capabilities for about twenty years. For all that length of time, the CIA appears to have utterly failed at keeping tabs on Iranian nuclear capabilities, judging – much like Sherlock Holmes's "dog that didn't bark" – from the absence of any public disclosures of such concerns over the past two decades. American intelligence officials have said that they had no evidence during the 1990s that Iran was receiving aid from Pakistan, and one senior intelligence official acknowledged "a fairly major failure, despite the fact that we were watching Iran and Pakistan quite closely."[56]

CIA assessments of North Korea's nuclear weapons program have been of questionable quality. In 2002, the United States was surprised to discover that North Korea had turned to the Khan network for uranium-enrichment capabilities while its plutonium program was ostensibly suspended after being detected in the early 1990s.[57] A scholarly survey of publicly available intelligence assessments of North Korea's nuclear weapons capabilities, moreover, shows that CIA estimates have been erratic and inconsistent. As Asian security expert Jonathan Pollack explains, the CIA in January 2003 told Congress that "North Korea probably has produced enough plutonium for at least one, and possibly two, nuclear weapons," which was less confident than assessments in 2001 and 2002 that Pyongyang already possessed one or two weapons.[58]

The shifting sands of the CIA's assessment of North Korea's nuclear weapons arsenal – whether potential or actual – no doubt led to frustration among policy and law makers. Senator John McCain, for example, who served on a committee appointed by President Bush to examine the intelligence community's performance against WMD targets, publicly commented in late 2004: "We know very little more about North Korea and Iran than we did 10 years ago. This agency [CIA] needs to be reformed."[59] This sad state of affairs has led former ambassador to South Korea, Donald Gregg, to conclude that "North Korea is the longest-running failure in the history of American intelligence."[60] This is a particularly disheartening assessment now that North Korea has openly tested a nuclear weapon.

The hazy intelligence assessment of North Korea's nuclear weapons stockpile is reminiscent of the CIA's foggy assessment of South Africa's past nuclear weapons program. Although the CIA had long suspected that Pretoria harbored a clandestine nuclear weapons program, it was only after South Africa publicly declared in March 1993 that it had secretly built six nuclear weapons during the 1970s and 1980s that the CIA learned South Africa had had a nuclear weapons stockpile.[61] A 1984 NIE on South Africa's nuclear capabilities judged that Pretoria had the capability to produce nuclear weapons on short notice and that it had stockpiled the components for several test devices,[62] but no mention was made of nuclear weapons stocks. The CIA failed to acquire specific intelligence that would have been needed to move militarily against South Africa's nuclear weapons inventory, much as it appears to have failed today to size and locate North Korea's nuclear weapons inventory.

The CIA also missed key efforts to procure and develop ballistic missile delivery systems, potentially for strategic nuclear weapons. The CIA failed to detect Saudi Arabia's secret negotiations and eventual delivery of CSS-2 ballistic missiles from China during the 1980s.[63] The Chinese had sold the Saudis the missiles, which had been operationally deployed with nuclear weapons in the Chinese inventory. Both the Chinese and the Saudis claim that the missiles were armed with conventional munitions when they were transferred to Saudi Arabia, but no outsiders have been allowed to verify these Saudi and Chinese claims.[64]

There is ample public evidence that the CIA's ability to gauge ballistic missile programs is sorely lacking. An outside review of the CIA's performance, ordered by the president, that came to be known as the Rumsfeld Commission concluded that U.S. intelligence agencies did not have the analytic depth or methods to assess the threat accurately. The Rumsfeld Commission found in the case of the missile programs for two unspecified countries that "There were instances in which we didn't know something until two, four, six, eight, twelve, and, in one case, thirteen years after it happened."[65]

The CIA's substantial past intelligence failures and weaknesses in gauging the nuclear weapons programs in Iraq, Iran, India, Pakistan, Libya, North Korea, and South Africa suggest an even greater record of intelligence failures regarding the chemical and biological weapons programs of adversaries, although these failures have yet to come to the public light. Chemical weapons programs, as a rule of thumb, are easier to conceal than nuclear weapons programs because they can more readily be embedded and hidden in civilian economic infrastructure such as pesticide, fertilizer, and pharmaceutical production facilities. Biological weapons programs require little infrastructure compared with nuclear and chemical weapons programs, making them the most difficult to detect via the satellite imagery on which the CIA overly and excessively relies in gauging WMD threats, a fact that the Jeremiah investigation revealed in the aftermath of India's nuclear weapons testing. Detection of chemical and biological warfare programs as well as nuclear weapons programs must in no small measure rely on high-quality human intelligence sources with access to the clandestine programs, as was the case in the much-belated detection of the Soviet Union's biological warfare program. This is precisely the type of intelligence that the CIA has systematically failed to deliver reliably in the past against the WMD targets.

The future of nuclear weapons proliferation poses a daunting challenge to future strategic intelligence. The South African case illustrates how comparatively more difficult the strategic intelligence challenge will be against modern nuclear weapons aspirants in the post–9/11 world compared with the relative ease of following the Soviet Union's nuclear weapons progress in the Cold War. Mitchell Reiss has expertly tracked the South African case. He finds that the South African program during its lifetime employed only about 1,000 people, fewer than ten scientists knew the details of the entire project, and only a handful of government officials were fully privy to the program. The $300 to $600 million price tag for South Africa's nuclear weapons is very affordable for many nation-states, and they achieved a nuclear inventory within a mere eight years.[66] These lessons provide a sobering note and highlight the need for encouraging defections from nuclear programs, especially today in the case of Iran, which now has all of what South Africa had in terms of expertise, money, and infrastructure.

Lessons Learned

In retrospect, many of the problems in human intelligence collection and analysis that caused the 9/11 and Iraq intelligence debacles are the same as those that lay at the core of intelligence failures during the Cold War and post–Cold War periods. These failures, more significantly, were dramatically exposed to the public and not limited to the corridors of the intelligence community, as were many of the Cold War and post–Cold War controversies and shortcomings.

The 9/11 attacks revealed a failed management chain in the CIA. George Tenet in a 1998 memorandum rightly warned that the United States was at war with al-Qaeda and ordered that he wanted no resources spared in this war.[67] That call proved to be more rhetoric than reality. After that memo was disseminated, the CTC still had more layers of management separating the working level from the DCI than it had analysts working against al-Qaeda. The joint House–Senate investigation of 9/11 found that the CIA only had five analysts working on al-Qaeda at the time.[68] At the time of Tenet's war call and until 9/11, the CIA's counter-terrorism effort had more bureaucratic fat than analytic muscle.

Five is hardly a war-fighting force. And with so few analysts working on al-Qaeda, their days were no doubt filled with answering the daily deluge of current intelligence requirements and left no time for thinking or writing strategic intelligence assessments. It is no wonder why on the eve of 11 September the CIA had produced no single strategic intelligence assessment of al-Qaeda. The joint House-Senate investigation found that the CIA had inexperienced analysts – who probably were insufficiently expert to write strategic intelligence – and had not produced a National Intelligence Estimate on the al-Qaeda threat.[69]

A striking feature of the Iraq WMD debacle was that the layers of management that have grown up over the years in the CIA theoretically to excercise quality control over the "corporate product" failed to do so. The CIA's management culture has traditionally maintained that analysts think and write and vet their analyses through numerous layers to produce a product that reflects the agency or "corporate" intelligence assessment, not the personal views of an analyst or group of analysts. But just because CIA management culturally and habitually repeats this mantra does not make it true.

The reality is that analysts, not bureaucracies and bureaucrats, produce intelligence assessments. If an analyst has a third-rate mind – coupled with third-rate human intelligence and other intelligence sources – and writes a third-rate intelligence assessment, no amount of word-tinkering by layers of management bureaucrats is going to transform it into a sterling piece of analysis. The Iraq WMD controversy is a case in point. Lackluster analysts coupled with poor human sources resulted in profoundly wrong intelligence assessments of Iraq's nuclear, biological, and chemical weapons programs, and the CIA's management chain was unable to wield the expertise needed to discover the holes in the evidence and analyses.

On the other hand, unless the management reviewer ranks are filled with intelligent and knowledgeable thinkers, a first-rate analyst could produce iconoclastic and first-rate intelligence assessments only to have them watered down by mediocre managers. The CIA's managers are bureaucratically cultured to think that policy makers are simpletons who need watered-down analyses because they would not understand "complicated" analyses. In reality, it is not uncommon for policy makers to be more expert than most CIA managers and analysts. The largest lesson to be drawn is that excellent analysts produce first-rate intelligence analysis and the intelligence community needs to hire, groom, and retain first-rate minds.

Taking a step back from the contemporary whirlwind of controversy surrounding charges of politicization of intelligence and Iraq WMD and casting eyes backward into history reveals that statesmen are prone to make overstatements – more accurately described as rhetoric in the classical sense – to rally public opinion around war efforts. As distinguished military historian and strategist Lawrence Freedman judges, "In efforts to prepare public opinion for extraordinary exertions and potential sacrifice there is a long tradition of overstatement. In 1947 Senator Arthur Vandenberg explained to President Harry Truman that if he wanted to persuade the American people to take on international communism and re-engage with a war-prone Europe he had to 'scare the hell' out of them.

The adversary must be painted as black as possible, without any shades of grey let alone glimmers of white."[70]

Strategic intelligence assessments such as the Iraq WMD NIE are used to inform policy makers who, by virtue of their elected offices, are representatives of the American people, are responsible for making political decisions of what threats warrant the risks of waging war to protect American national interests. As Richard Betts points out, "A threat consists of capabilities multiplied by intentions; if either one is zero, the threat is zero."[71] Strategic intelligence on a potential adversary's capabilities and intentions are funneled into the threat equation. But, ultimately, the commander in chief with the aid of his national security policy lieutenants must make the calculation and then determine if the American interests at stake warrant war. War is a political endeavor and requires a political decision by officeholders empowered by the people to make decisions of war and peace. Judgments on weighing the high stakes of war and peace are the realm of statesmen, not intelligence officers. The responsibility of the CIA is to deliver its best strategic assessments possible to the commander in chief, but he or she is ultimately responsible for what to do with them, not the CIA, which is the handmaiden, not the master, of policy makers.

5   Spies Who Do Not Deliver

THE CRAFT OF HUMAN INTELLIGENCE OPERATIONS FOR THE public, and even for many inside the halls of government, is shrouded in a glamorous mystique. The CIA's Directorate of Operations (DO) responsible for U.S. human intelligence operations traditionally parlayed that mystique into winning public and congressional support for its budget. Too often, in the face of human intelligence failures, executive and legislative branch overseers as well as the public had given the DO the benefit of the doubt and not raised serious and sustained questions about its performance in stealing secrets to reveal the plans and intentions of U.S. adversaries.

The director of national intelligence (DNI) in 2005 renamed the CIA's DO the National Clandestine Service (NCS), but that move probably is more a bureaucratic show to diffuse outside criticisms than for substantive internal reform. For all intents and purposes, the new NCS remains the old DO. The spate of recent presidential panels and congressional studies centered on the 9/11 and Iraq episodes have touched on human intelligence failures, but these studies still have not probed deeply enough into the DO's human intelligence operations. These studies, moreover, are too narrow in focus because the United States has faced a greater array of national security challenges in the past and will have many others in the future.

Examination of the CIA's human intelligence performance in a broader array of cases from the Cold War, post–Cold War, and 9/11 security environments reveals persistent and systemic shortcomings. As a general observation, the CIA's delivery of strategic intelligence to the president was strong when the CIA had human intelligence penetrations of U.S. adversaries such as in the Polish crisis and the Soviet Union's perceived war scare in the early 1980s. In both of these cases, human agents volunteered their services to U.S. intelligence; it was not gained through the method of agent seduction that the CIA glorifies in its bureaucratic culture. These two crises were sterling examples of the CIA providing invaluable and unique intelligence to the president, which helped him understand the plans, intentions, and perspectives of the Soviet Union in periods of heightened international tension. Unfortunately, these few success stories are dwarfed by a greater number of failures.

The DO – even if it operates today under the cosmetic bureaucratic name change as the NCS – still clings to stealing secrets from states that want to hide them from U.S. policy makers as its raison d'être. But by looking back over the battlegrounds littered with CIA strategic intelligence failures – most of which involved a lack of accurate and reliable human intelligence reports as decisive contributing factors to the failures – it is clear that the DO has performed poorly against its own core mission requirements. It is long past time for outside bodies, whether in the White House under the auspices of the DNI or in Congress, to investigate the origins of the DO's failures and set the organization right. U.S. policy makers and citizens deserve better than the DO has produced.

Why has the CIA's human intelligence operations been so poor? The question is an important one in light of the billions of dollars that U.S. taxpayers have spent on intelligence for the past sixty years. What follows is an examination of how the CIA has traditionally gone about human intelligence operations. An analysis of the weaknesses of the CIA's traditional human intelligence business practices is then presented. Recommendations for strengthening human intelligence operations in the recently revamped U.S. intelligence community under the leadership of the DNI are then put forward.

The Human Intelligence History the DO Wants to Forget

The review of the past sixty years of the CIA's history reveals a stunning array of failures to deliver against its core mission to steal secrets from U.S. adversaries to enlightened presidential decision making, especially in weighing decisions of war and peace. The CIA failed to have high-level human intelligence sources inside the Kremlin's political leadership for the entire period of the Cold War. It failed to have high-level sources inside North Korea to warn of its invasion of South Korea in 1950. It failed to have a high-level source inside the Chinese regime to warn of Chinese military intervention in the Korean War. It failed to deliver high-level human sources inside the North Vietnamese regime when the United States was fighting the Vietnam War in the 1960s and early 1970s. Former Director of Central Intelligence (DCI) Richard Helms admitted that "our failure to penetrate the North Vietnamese government was the single most frustrating aspect of those years. We could not determine what was going on at the highest levels of Ho's government, nor could we learn how policy was made or who was making it."[1]

Despite the common legend of Agency human intelligence brilliance during the Cold War – perpetuated by old-hand CIA case officers – the CIA's performance was less than stellar, perhaps even dismal. All of the CIA's Cuban sources, for example, appear to have been double agents.[2] As Robert Gates eloquently and succinctly assesses the CIA's overall human intelligence performance during the Cold War, "We were duped by double agents in Cuba and East Germany. We were penetrated with devastating effect at least once – Aldrich Ames – by the Soviets, and suffered other counterintelligence and security failures. We never recruited a spy who gave us unique political information from inside the Kremlin, and we too often failed to penetrate the inner circle of Soviet surrogate leaders."[3]

The longtime head of East Germany's foreign intelligence service, Markus Wolf, had little fear of the CIA's human operations during the

Cold War. In his memoirs, Wolf recalls that "spotting CIA operatives in Bonn was ridiculously easy.... For a time in the late 1970s and early 1980s the quality of the American agents was so poor and their work so haphazard that our masters began to ask fearfully whether Washington had stopped taking East Germany seriously."[4] Little wonder then that "By the late 1980s, we [the East Germans] were in the enviable position of knowing that not a single CIA agent had worked in East Germany without having been turned into a double agent or working for us from the start. On our orders they were all delivering carefully selected information and disinformation to the Americans."[5]

The CIA also lost a stable of spies in Iran through incompetence. James Risen reports that in 2004, an incompetent CIA officer mistakenly sent revealing, encrypted, high-speed messages from CIA headquarters to clandestine agents in the field equipped with small, covert, personal communications devices. She sent information to one Iranian agent who was a double agent working for the Iranian regime that was used to identify virtually every spy the CIA had inside Iran.[6]

This was the second time that the CIA's agent stable in Iran had been exposed. In 1988, the Iranians were able to intercept the Agency's communications to its spy network inside Iran, and the Tehran regime arrested at least thirty Iranians, many of whom had been soldiers in the American-trained shah's army, and most of them were believed to have been tortured and executed.[7] Other reports hold that as many as fifty Iranian citizens on the CIA's payroll were arrested after the Iranians intercepted the CIA's agent communication network.[8]

The CIA had no high-level penetrations of the nuclear weapons programs in Pakistan and India, in Iraq during either the Gulf War or the Iraq War begun in 2003, or against al-Qaeda throughout the 1990s and before 9/11. The Joint Inquiry investigating the 9/11 failure determined that "Prior to September 11, 2001, the Intelligence Community did not effectively develop and use human sources to penetrate the al-Qa'ida inner circle. This lack of reliable and knowledgeable human sources significantly limited the Community's ability to acquire intelligence that could be acted upon before the September 11 attacks. In part, at least, the lack of unilateral (i.e., U.S.-recruited) counterterrorism sources was a product of an excessive reliance on foreign liaison services."[9] The dearth of human intelligence (HUMINT) led a frustrated Deputy Secretary of Defense Paul Wolfowitz in 2004 to ask Congress, "How many times do you want to get briefed on al-Qaeda and be reminded we don't have any human sources?"[10] And the over-reliance on foreign liaison services is in no small measure attributable to the dearth of foreign-language skills in the DO.

The DO has consistently failed to deliver what American policy makers need most. That CIA had no spies working inside Iraq on weapons of mass destruction (WMD) since Saddam Hussein unceremoniously threw UN weapons inspectors out of Iraq in 1998 is one of the most damning findings of the Senate Select Committee on Intelligence's (SSCI) report on American intelligence failures in the run-up to the 2003 war.[11] And SSCI, judging from my own seventeen-year career at CIA, has precisely diagnosed the root cause of CIA's failure: "a broken corporate culture and poor management" that "will not be solved by additional funding and personnel."[12]

So what were the CIA's case officers in the DO doing to redress the lack of HUMINT in Saddam's Iraq? The answer is: not much. The Senate discovered that "When UN inspectors departed Iraq, the placement of HUMINT agents and the development of unilateral sources inside Iraq were not top priorities for the Intelligence Community."[13] Apparently, the DO was "whistling past the graveyard" and hoping against the odds that a crisis in Iraq would not emerge again to expose the gaping hole in U.S. HUMINT, a hole that had never been patched after the Gulf War.

Many observers of international relations see the rise of China as a potential challenge to U.S. security, but the CIA appears yet again to be flatfooted. As former DO case officer Reuel Marc Gerecht relates, among case officers still at the CIA to whom he has spoken, "none thinks that the CIA's operational work against Beijing should get high marks. At least one, an attentive Chinese-speaking ops [case] officer who served in

Beijing in the 1990s, believes Langley's Chinese operations are thoroughly penetrated by Chinese counterintelligence."[14] If true, the CIA's China operations today would be much like its utter failures in Cold War human intelligence operations against East Germany and Cuba.

Same Old Tricks: Failed DO Business Practices

The CIA's DO nurtured and developed a business model for human intelligence operations during the Cold War, but that business model failed in the past, fails today, and will fail in the future. The DO's management matured and ascended in the hierarchy wielding these business practices and lacks the critical analysis, initiative, and creativity needed to think beyond the bounds of these business practices. As the House Permanent Select Committee on Intelligence frustratingly assesses, "After years of trying to convince, suggest, urge, entice, cajole, and pressure CIA to make wide-reaching changes to the way it conducts its HUMINT mission, however, CIA, in the Committee's view, continues down a road leading over a proverbial cliff."[15]

The CIA has for too long relied on obsolete means to provide "cover" to its case officers abroad, who mostly are posted to U.S. government facilities. As former CIA case officer Reuel Marc Gerecht assesses, "Today, operational camouflage is usually shredded within weeks of a case officer's arrival at his station, since the manner, method and paperwork of operatives is just too different from real foreign-service officers."[16]

CIA case officers are promoted on the basis of how many recruits he or she makes. The more recruits a case officer makes, the better his or her chances for promotion. The DO's management has placed an undue emphasis on the quantity of recruits and not on the quality of the information that these agents provide. The case officer who recruits several spies who produce third-rate intelligence that is not particularly relevant to U.S. policy-maker interests stands a better chance of getting promoted than the case officer who recruits one spy whose intelligence is extremely relevant and insightful.

For all the time-consuming demands and stress the DO managers place on their case officers to spot, assess, develop, and recruit, the fruits of these business practices are lackluster. More often than not, case officers just pick up the "low-hanging fruit" and recruit agents simply because they can and not because these agents have access to the secrets that the U.S. government, especially the president, actually needs to know. The DO tends to get third-rate intelligence that is not relevant to the most pressing threats to our national security. Former junior case officer Lindsay Moran, for example, recalled that she herself ran a poor intelligence agent "and a number of other second- or third-rate assets, because someone at the CIA thought it was good for my career. Privately, I conjectured what anybody who had lost a loved one in a terrorist attack would think of these pointless exercises."[17] The DO might excel at recruiting diplomats from Third World countries because they are willing to spy to make lucrative money from the CIA, but the information they have most often is not of interest or relevance to the commander in chief.

The DO pumps out this irrelevant HUMINT to both the intelligence and policy communities. In some cases, it slaps classifications on these reports almost as a subconscious attempt to give worthless information an aura of importance and authenticity. While I was at the CIA, I recall that I once stopped by the desk of a friend of mine, Reynard, an analyst working on Africa who was a bright guy and a Stanford University graduate. I asked him why he was laughing hysterically, and he showed me several underlined sentences in a SECRET DO report from Africa. The report struck me as a very reasonable rundown on the economic and political difficulties facing a West African country. I asked him, "So why is this so funny?" He then pulled out a copy of the fine British magazine *The Economist*, where he had underlined the exact passage! Either *The Economist* was plagiarizing from the DO's agent or the other way around; we concluded the latter, given our generally critical views of the quality of DO reporting.

If many of the DO's HUMINT reports were not of much significance to U.S. national security, at least they were sometimes good for a laugh. One day I was taking a cab ride through a posh neighborhood in Washington, D.C., on my way to National Airport for a trip to the Middle East. Along the route, the cab passed by the mansion of the former shah of Iran's exiled son. I made passing comment about the place to my cabbie, who was an Iranian exile himself. For the remainder of the trip, he lectured me about life in Iran under the shah and life under the mullahs. He mentioned how corrupt the clerical regime was and that one of its most powerful players, Rafsanjani, who later became president, had acquired enormous wealth from his family's pistachio nut farms. That comment rang a bell and sounded very familiar to me. I suddenly realized that only the day before I had read a SECRET DO HUMINT report that said exactly the same thing! Now, either I had inadvertently stumbled across the DO's agent or the information was so commonly known in and around Iran that the information really was not a secret. I concluded the latter and had a good laugh imagining that I could be thrown in jail for revealing closely guarded "national security" intelligence that my taxicab driver had shared with me.

In fact, CIA business practices of spotting, assessing, developing, and recruiting even dissuaded potential spies from working with the Americans. Soviet intelligence officers, for example, often said that the best practice for CIA officers to do was to simply give them a business card and contact information and walk away.[18] The procedures for nurturing a personal relationship with Soviets who potentially could work for the CIA only drew the attention of Soviet counter-intelligence officers and prevented an individual from working for the CIA.

The DO's bureaucratic culture nurtures and perpetuates the myth that the winning of human agents is a function of a case officer's ability to seduce recruits. Contrary to this DO folklore, a review of the historical record shows that the best spies the CIA had during the Cold War volunteered their services to the CIA. As Richard Helms recalled, "From 1945 throughout my career in the Agency, defectors from the Soviet and satellite intelligence services continued to give us intimate pictures of the Soviet espionage methods and some of its successful operations. The inside data provided by the defectors helped us develop the means to handle the Soviet and Eastern European volunteers, or 'walk-ins,' as agents in place within their own service."[19]

The CIA's first major penetration of Soviet intelligence was in 1953 when Soviet military intelligence (GRU) Major Pyotr Semyonovich Popov volunteered to spy for the CIA in Vienna. For five years until his detection in 1958, Popov was the CIA's most important agent.[20] Another invaluable Soviet intelligence source also volunteered his services in the early 1960s to the CIA and British intelligence. Soviet military intelligence Colonel Oleg Penkovsky worked for the CIA and British intelligence and provided President Kennedy with important insights into the Soviet Union's policy and the status of its armed forces, making him probably the most important Western penetration agent of the Cold War, according to Christopher Andrew.[21] Another Soviet walk-in to the CIA was a high-level Soviet diplomat posted at the United Nations, Arkady Shevchenko, who defected to the United States in 1978.[22]

The CIA has a long history of turning away walk-ins and defectors; in many cases, these errors were saved by British intelligence, which was not as sloppy or lazy as the CIA. Robert Baer reveals that the CIA turned away "Vasili Mitrokhin, a KGB archivist who then volunteered to British intelligence and provided information that led to the identification of dozens of spies, including a U.S. colonel."[23] Mitrokhin later collaborated with British historian Christopher Andrew to produce invaluable scholarly literature on Soviet intelligence operations.

DO officers are loathe to loudly admit it, but spies, by and large, are not seduced by case officers to commit treason – they volunteer to do so. Former street-savvy case officers who worked important intelligence targets in the Middle East confirm that volunteers, not agents who are seduced, are the best sources of intelligence.[24] One of the most aggressive and accomplished case officers in the Middle East in the 1980s and 1990s was Robert Baer, who revealed in his memoirs that one of the best agents he handled inside the Hezbollah in the late 1980s "walked in" to a U.S. Embassy and asked to see a CIA officer.[25]

An aggressive senior DO official, Duane Clarridge, was responsible for breaking bureaucratic china to collocate DO and DI officers, synergizing collection and analytic capabilities and creating the CIA's Counterterrorism Center (CTC) in the 1980s. In his memoirs, Clarridge mentions casually, almost in passing, of human operations during the Cold War that "The recruitment of Soviets, Chinese, Eastern Europeans, Cubans, Mongolians, North Koreans, and Vietnamese, particularly those with known or suspected intelligence duties, was high priority, not only for what they would know about their local activities but, more importantly, to return eventually to their own countries as intelligence agents reporting secrets. Much effort went into this endeavor, with rather mediocre returns. Individuals of this ilk are often not likely to be the one you believe are vulnerable, and thus you do not pursue them, only to have them 'walk in,' offering their services."[26] Clarridge goes on to make an even more damning assessment of the CIA's operational business practices, "Over time I came to believe that the Clandestine Services wasted a lot of emotional energy trying to recruit Soviets during the Cold War. Historically, those who really wanted to cooperate with the United States have walked in of their own volition and offered their services, usually for money. I know of no significant Soviet recruitment that was spotted, developed, and recruited from scratch by a CIA case officer."[27]

A rare example of a CIA case officer with substantial expertise on China who eventually became the U.S. ambassador to Beijing, James Lilley, attests to the value of walk-in debriefings over the spotting, assessing, developing, and recruitment strategy that dominates the CIA's human operations business practices. Lilley recalled from his experience operating against China during the Cold War that "Using debriefings, I started to gather useful information for the CIA about what was going on in China. Unfortunately, in those days CIA was obsessed with the idea of a resident agent with a radio no matter what the level of his access or his ability to survive. They focused on process over substance."[28] That focus persists today in the DO.

On the other side of the fence, the Americans who have spied for other intelligence services with the most damaging results for U.S. security also self-selected themselves and volunteered to hostile intelligence services. A spy inside the CIA devastated the stable of agents the Americans had managed to establish inside the Soviet Union, although none of these spies had access to political-military plans and intentions of the Soviet high command. As former CIA inspector general Frederick Hitz recalls the blow, "Aldrich Ames followed his sale of $150,000 worth of 'unimportant' spies to the Soviets in April 1985 with 'the big dump' in June of that year, in which he gave away every spy case the United States was running against the Soviets at the time, and every intelligence operation against the U.S.S.R. of which he was aware."[29] Ames was a thirty-year employee of the CIA and spied for the Soviets for nine years from 1985 to 1994 before being caught. His treason allowed the Soviets to catch and execute at least ten Soviets who were spying for the CIA. Ames was paid more than $4 million for his treason.[30] Ames also revealed American electronic eavesdropping operations to the Soviets.[31] Senior CIA officials have conceded, moreover, that "the best agents Ames killed were all 'walk-ins,' who had volunteered their services to the United States."[32]

How was it possible for Ames to have committed his treason for so long? A former DO officer gives probably the best and most straightforward answer, one that challenges the mystique of the DO: "spotting Ames psychologically, or by questioning his peers, would have been very difficult. In the CIA family there are many dysfunctional members," and "the truth is that Ames was not much different from many of his peers. He was disgruntled and he drank too much."[33]

Unfortunately, too many other Americans have suffered from vices like Ames and have volunteered their spying services to our adversaries. Robert Hanssen, an FBI officer, volunteered his services to Soviet intelligence and spied for them for fifteen years.[34] In 1968, a U.S. Navy chief warrant officer, John Walker, volunteered his espionage services to the Soviet Union and spied for the Soviets for nearly seventeen years.[35] Walker provided potentially war-winning intelligence to the Soviet Union had the Cold War ever turned into a hot war. As Robert Gates recalled, "Walker's information about U.S. encryption devices allowed the Soviets to decode nearly a million American military messages."[36] These are just a few of the American traitors who volunteered to share U.S. secrets with other countries.

The international security environment has changed substantially since the collapse of the Berlin Wall, but the CIA's business practices nurtured during the Cold War are still the same. A former DO officer who took the agency's case officer training class in 1999, for example, observes that the training she took for the CIA's program is still dominated by spotting, assessing, developing, and recruiting from the cocktail-party circuit.[37] But the trolling of cocktail parties is not going to bring CIA case officers in contact with terrorists from groups such as al-Qaeda, Hezbollah, Hamas, and Islamic Jihad who do not frequent these parties.

The CIA business practices place a heavy emphasis on targeting the diplomats of foreign countries, but these diplomats are not likely to have much access to their own country's strategic plans for and development of ballistic missiles and WMD. Judging from my own experience dealing with foreign diplomats from the Middle East and South Asia where ballistic missile and WMD proliferation are acute concerns, they are more often than not kept completely in the dark about their own country's national security plans, which are tightly held in the top leadership hierarchy, the military, and the intelligence services.

A more recent example of a significant diplomatic walk-in and subsequent defector to the United States in 1997 is the former North Korean ambassador posted in Egypt, Chang Sung Gil. Jeffrey Richelson reports: "It was believed that Chang could provide the CIA with a 'wealth of information about his country's sensitive dealings with Middle East nations.' Of particular interest would be North Korean sales of Scud-B missiles to Egypt and of other arms to Iran and Syria. Some of that information may have been provided prior to his defection; it was reported that Chang had been recruited by the CIA well before his defection. However, his defection would have allowed the CIA to debrief him at length about a variety of topics."[38] It is unclear, however, whether the North Korean ambassador was indeed privy to the scope and depth of information that U.S. officials apparently have leaked to the press.

Thinking Creatively about Future Human Intelligence Collection

Despite the DO's dismal performance over the years, it has escaped a sustained and rigorous examination of its operations and business practices. The DO bureaucracy is set in its ways and operates in a rut created during the Cold War, a rut that will be perpetuated under the DO's new guise as the NCS. The DO has no vested interest in instigating controversial reforms absent strong White House and congressionally imposed investigations to fathom the origins of DO systemic human intelligence collection failures or to chart a course of reforms that amount to anything more than window dressing to appease the House and Senate Intelligence Oversight Committees that approve the CIA's budget. The DO is even resistant to reform should the director of the CIA be so inclined and opts to wait out politically appointed directors and let any reform agendas whither on the vine after their departures from Agency headquarters. Although George Tenet had a longer tenure at the CIA than most of his predecessors, it is difficult to discern any revolutionarily changes he implemented in the DO.

The CIA's case officers need greater regional and country expertise to understand their operational environments. Today, they spend too little time in other countries. About one year is needed to learn the ropes in a new post, and by then, a case officer is already thinking about his or her next assignment. That is simply too little time to know the ins and outs of politics, society and culture, and language as well as the "who's who" in the power structure.

The CIA has traditionally refused to allow longer tours because of the fear that if case officers spent too long in one country, they would go "native" or suffer "clientitus" and associate and identify less with U.S. national interests and more with the interests of the posted country. Years ago, for example, a colleague of mine enjoyed back-to-back tours in Asia, but headquarters ordered him back to Langley just as his Chinese skills were hitting their stride. Rather than leave the thrill of operations in Asia and return to the doldrums of bureaucracy and paper pushing in Langley, my colleague chose to resign from the Agency. Too bad, he had a Ph.D.

from Harvard in history and was also fluent in Serbo-Croatian. Clientitus may indeed be a theoretical risk, but a far greater and more realistic risk is the consistent and systematic failure to have a deep bench of accomplished case officers with impressive hard language skills such as Chinese, Arabic, and Farsi. A sure means to redress the CIA's language-skills shortcomings is to allow case officers to extend their tours well beyond their traditional length.

The CIA needs to concentrate on vetting walk-ins who volunteer intelligence to CIA case officers overseas while encouraging and facilitating defections from the intelligence targets that matter most to U.S. interests. The most important intelligence the CIA acquired on the Soviet Union's biological warfare program, for example, came from two Russian defectors. The CIA had not identified the scope of the Soviet Union's massive biological warfare program until these two Soviet scientists who worked in the program defected. The defectors revealed that the Soviets continued their biological weapons program in violation of Russia's commitment to ban such weapons under the terms of the Biological Weapons Treaty signed in 1972.[39] In the cases of walk-ins from hard targets such as North Korea and Iran, the DO would be far better off trying to get them to defect for debriefings rather than trying to turn them around and go back into their countries to report in place. The CIA today, for example, should be sparing no expense or effort to encourage defections from Iran, whether from members of the Revolutionary Guard or technicians and scientists from the nation's suspected nuclear weapons program for intelligence as well as to disrupt Tehran's nuclear efforts.

Although defections offer a one-time snapshot of clandestine activities, one snapshot is better than none. If given a critical mass of reporting from dozens of defectors from Iran, the CIA's analysts would likely be better positioned to paste together an intelligence mosaic and a clearer picture of Iran's nuclear weapons program than the CIA has today. The CIA should be offering residence in the United States with a substantial cash bonus for those defectors who find their way to CIA case officers operating overseas and whose information proves to be significant.

Many commentators and observers take a "lesson learned" from the CIA's Iraq intelligence failure that defectors cannot be trusted. To be sure, defectors do have vested interests, but all human sources of information do. There is no one human source that could come to the CIA without personal biases. Even recruited agents spying in place have vested interests in telling the CIA what they think it wants to hear if only to keep their paycheck coming. These realities underscore the importance of encouraging wide swaths of defections to give CIA analysts, much like any competent national security investigative reporter working for a major newspaper, a strong empirical base on which to compare and contrast information to gauge ground truth. As the case in the Iraq WMD controversy clearly shows, basing strategic intelligence assessments on the reports of only one source, such as the Iraqi defector codenamed "Curveball," is not a wise business practice.

DO officers today receive little to no professional rewards for encouraging the defection and debriefing of high-level officials from "closed" or "denied area" nation-states. They may also lack the temperament and intellectual tools for systematically debriefing defectors and checking against information from other sources to establish source veracity, a process that is more analytic than operational. The CIA's analysts, on the other hand, are poorly organized to support broad and sustained defector debriefing programs. CIA analysts for the most part have introverted personalities not well suited to the assertive give-and-take of debriefings, are too chained to their headquarters desks and computer screens by micromanagers, and lack the linguistic skills that are invaluable for gaining the trust and confidence of defectors. In short, defector reporting falls between the two bureaucratic stools inside the CIA.

The DO's case officers have to become more passive receptors for vetting and debriefing walk-ins. The case officer's principal job in a new business model would be to solicit information from walk-ins who approach U.S. facilities overseas and to try to separate the minority of these individuals with access to unique sources of information of interest to U.S. policy makers from the majority of fabricators, some of whom are looking to make a quick buck and others who are controlled by foreign intelligence services that are trying to determine who works for the CIA and to provide misleading information to it. Until bona fide walk-ins with valuable information are identified, the identities of the CIA case officers could be protected with the use of one-way mirrored windows in debriefing rooms. Granted, this type of work is not as glamorous a self-image as the case officer of old who was charged with seducing agents, but separating the wheat from the chaff to get walk-ins to spy in place, or more likely to defect to the United States, would produce better intelligence than the DO's glorified recruitment method, just as the volunteer method produced better results during the Cold War even if the DO is unwilling to admit it.

The DO case officers in official cover capacities also need to interface with liaison services. Host-country liaison services are an invaluable means for the CIA to gain intelligence from on the ground. Host liaison services, for example, are much better able to gain access to terrorist cells in work that is more akin to police work than strategic intelligence collection. Yet terrorist cells in neighborhoods can be planning attacks of potential grave strategic consequence to U.S. national security. Liaison services also have unique perspectives and information on regional security issues that CIA analysts can take into account in their analyses.

The CIA in the post–9/11 world is using its larger budgets to build up liaison relationships. As reporter David Kaplan notes, "Millions of dollars in covert funding started flowing to friendly Muslim intelligence and security agencies. The top recipients: Egypt, Jordan, and Pakistan. Also on the list are Algeria, Morocco, and Yemen. Total payments have topped well over $20 million, intelligence sources say, an amount they consider a bargain."[40] Bob Woodward observes that the CIA moved quickly in the aftermath of the 9/11 attacks to get President Bush to authorize a quantum jump in funding for foreign liaison services. DCI George Tenet reasoned with Bush "that with hundreds of millions of dollars for new covert action, the CIA would 'buy' key intelligence services, providing training, new equipment, money for their agent networks, whatever they might need. Several intelligence services were listed: Egypt, Jordan, Algeria."[41]

The danger for the CIA is that it becomes overly dependent on liaison services and has no independent means to double-check liaison information. Just as walk-ins, defectors, and agents in place have biases, so, too, do liaison services. For all of the failings of the CIA and U.S. intelligence, it is still far superior in the objective collection and analysis of intelligence than most other foreign intelligence services. The CIA's personnel, for all of their weaknesses, are still on balance better trained and educated than their foreign intelligence counterparts. Foreign liaison services tend to be more vulnerable to shoddy analysis because of powerfully held worldviews than CIA analysts. The analysis of Arab intelligence services, for example, is all too easily influenced by worldviews colored by the Israeli-Palestinian conflict.

Nevertheless, foreign liaison service partnerships are invaluable for U.S. strategic intelligence. Under the auspices of the DO, I worked with more liaison services than the typical CIA analyst because of the Middle East topics on which I worked. I found these exchanges, especially with a few services that had substantial analytic expertise, to be invaluable opportunities to trade information and to assess intelligence judgments.

The rough-and-tumble, sometimes even hot and heated, liaison exchanges suited my extroverted personality, whereas my more typical, introverted colleagues dreaded liaison exchanges and likened them to "giving blood" to a blood bank. DO officers often depict their analysis counterparts as the "nerds" who do not perform well in the smoke-filled rooms of liaison exchanges or agent debriefings. To be fair, the DO officers were more right than not on this score. There's a joke that runs around the corridors at the CIA: "If one looks across the room and sees two DI [Directorate of Intelligence] analysts talking, how do you tell which one is the extrovert? He's the one talking to the other guy's shoes."

The CIA needs more robust techniques for intelligence collection outside the walls of official U.S. facilities overseas from human sources. The

Senate Select Committee on Intelligence found that human operations "against a closed society like Iraq prior to Operation Iraqi Freedom were hobbled by the Intelligence Community's dependence on having an official U.S. presence in-country to mount clandestine HUMINT collection efforts."[42] To be sure, case officers based undercover in these facilities will be critical to receiving and debriefing walk-ins and defectors. The United States, however, needs the means for more robust human intelligence collection against hard targets such as China, Iran, North Korea, Pakistan, Russia, Saudi Arabia, and Syria, where it has no official presence or where the counterintelligence environment is too tight for case officers under official cover to operate effectively.

The CIA needs to bolster substantially the use of nonofficial cover officers (NOCs) who have no connections to the U.S. infrastructure. Such officers can melt into areas rich in hard-target HUMINT collection opportunities such as the Muslim expatriate communities in Europe that are hotbeds for al-Qaeda recruitment, indoctrination, and logistics or in the Chinese expatriate communities in Asia. Unfortunately, the CIA's NOCs in the past have suffered from neglect at the hands of old-school DO managers who dominate the CIA's bureaucratic power structure. Former CIA case officer Melissa Boyle Mahle writes that "The NOC program, always small, has suffered from weak management and ossified vision. Although attempts to reform the program and increase its productivity and flexibility were made, the program remained troubled."[43]

The problems in revamping and energizing the NOC program probably stem, in no small measure, to resistance from the old-school DO senior officials who work to suppress the NOC program. As intelligence expert James Bamford has observed, NOCs are forced to operate under the authority of the DO's regional offices, which traditionally look down on their NOC counterparts.[44] One of the first orders of business for the DNI is to ensure that the CIA director gives NOC officers their own separate chain of command, which runs directly into his or her office. The infusion of competition between a rejuvenated and independent NOC program could be constructively managed by the CIA's director to light a fire under the backsides of the recalcitrant, risk-adverse, and old-school DO officers. As it stands today, the old-school DO is a monopoly that needs to be deregulated under the CIA director's authority.

The CIA's NOC program also has suffered in the past because of the salaries paid to its officers. NOCs might be earning six-figure salaries, for example, overseas and be required to surrender those earnings for substantially smaller government salaries. The Bush administration and Capitol Hill are moving in the right direction by passing legislation that appears to remove this problem.[45] The prospect of making heftier incomes might encourage more individuals to undertake a challenging NOC career as well as to help the NOC program recruit Americans with technical and scientific expertise needed to target WMD programs, skills that are not nurtured inside the CIA's bureaucratic walls. The CIA in the future would be wise to accept part-time services of American scientists and businesspeople who, in the course of their professional dealings, come across intelligence information that they could conveniently pass on to the CIA. The money that many business dealings entail, moreover, ensures access to real power and authorities in foreign governments and societies, access to which government-salaried Americans rarely even hear about.

Security Tail Wagging the Operational Dog

Onerous security procedures are formidable barriers to improving the CIA's human intelligence collection performance. The United States is blessed with an enormously diverse population, but the CIA and the intelligence community writ large have failed miserably at tapping this wealth of cultural and linguistic talent and harnessing it for intelligence collection and analysis. Security background investigations are loaded with ethnocentric biases that collectively border on xenophobia. Job candidates who are naturalized or second-generation U.S. citizens are assumed to be spies for hostile foreign powers until proved otherwise. Those job candidates with relatives or close friends overseas and extensive travel abroad have high chances of being precluded from intelligence service out of concern that they would be too vulnerable to foreign influences.[46] These are unacceptable cases of the security and counterintelligence tail wagging the operational and analytic dog. What U.S. citizen is going to be fluent in difficult languages such as Arabic or Chinese unless he or she has close friends and family abroad or has lived overseas for extended periods of time? Despite the CIA's security restrictions and expectations, one simply does not become fluent in difficult languages by living one's whole life inside the United States.

These overly burdensome security considerations prevent the intelligence community from making wise use of the government-sponsored National Security Education Program, which is designed to give scholarships to undergraduate and graduate students studying hard languages, frequently abroad. Recipients are required to pay off their scholarships with postgraduation service in the government, but I hear anecdotally and periodically from my graduate students that the security concerns often prevent scholarship recipients from serving in the CIA.

These security barriers are contributing substantially to chronic linguistic skill shortages in the CIA and increasing U.S. vulnerability to attack. As the congressional Joint Inquiry into the September 11 attacks and the intelligence community's performance determined, "the Intelligence Community was not prepared to handle the challenge it faces in translating the volumes of foreign language counterterrorism intelligence it collected. Agencies within the Intelligence Community experienced backlogs in material awaiting translation, a shortage of language specialists and language-qualified field officers, and a readiness level of only 30 percent in the most critical terrorism-related languages."[47]

The DO needs to have a workforce that is more ethnically diverse by tapping the ethnic diversity in the United States to fill its ranks. The CIA pays great lip service to the idea but has not delivered results commensurate with the claims coming from the CIA's Public Affairs Office. Former CIA case officer, Melissa Boyle Mahle, who had served in the CIA's Recruitment Center on 9/11, laments, "I can't tell you how many minority applicants – Arab Americans, Chinese Americans, Korean Americans, Indian Americans, and others – whom I lost to security or suitability, because the number is classified; however, it was not an insignificant number."[48]

All too frequently, Arab Americans, for example, are dissuaded from approaching the CIA and making their way through the CIA's security vetting procedures because they have relatives still living in the Middle East. The CIA's security officers too readily disqualify such individuals because they are potentially vulnerable to foreign pressure on their overseas relatives. But that consideration is more a problem in theory than in practice. The far greater problem is that the CIA still has too little cultural diversity and lacks an ethnically diverse workforce with a wide and deep range of fluency in Arabic dialects. People from such a workforce could more readily strike up a personal rapport with walk-ins and understand the cultural, tribal, and family ties that often lie at the heart of the politics in nation-states, insurgencies, and terrorists groups in the Middle East.

In the final analysis, the CIA needs to stop playing defense – which produces no strategic intelligence – and to play more offense, and it needs to take more risks to create a more ethnically diverse case officer corps. Robert Baer, a superb former DO case officer, suggests that one method to reduce the chances of compromising intelligence would be to institute tiered security clearances for case officers. "The CIA needs to establish a system with distinct clearance levels. Level One would cover typical CIA employees and would include a top-secret clearance, a polygraph every three years, a regular financial audit, and a thorough investigation of all foreign contacts... and a second class of CIA employees would be created: people who spend the majority of their lives outside the country. They attend foreign universities, marry foreign spouses, and have children who are not Americans: no access to intelligence from the National Security Agency, no access to advanced satellite-imaging systems, and no access to our nuclear secrets."[49] These are practical and readily doable solutions, although they undoubtedly are too innovative for the hidebound CIA to adopt absent outside pressure to do so, especially from the DNI.

The CIA also needs to work hand in hand with the FBI to cover the seam between international and domestic intelligence functions and responsibilities that al-Qaeda drove right through with the 9/11 attacks. The CIA and FBI need to cooperate to collect human intelligence from hard-target expatriate communities in the United States. The thought of such operations, of course, raises alarm bells over the potential to erode American civil liberties. But some balance must be struck between civil liberties and the fact that the United States offers a rich environment for running human intelligence agents. It is a safe bet that American universities are unwittingly training foreign scientific and engineering cadres that will in the near future staff the chemical, biological, and nuclear weapons and ballistic missile programs in India, Pakistan, China, and Egypt, to name only a few states. Further, terrorists from al-Qaeda, Hezbollah, Hamas, and Islamic Jihad still walk U.S. streets despite post–9/11 security measures.

The CIA's DO and the FBI still operate in the Cold War prism of a sharp dividing line between domestic and international operations, but in the era of globalization, no such line exists, and the world at large lives in the United States. U.S. human intelligence collection operators would be derelict in their responsibilities not to run human operations in foreign communities residing in the United States. Moreover, such operations would be inherently easier to run in the United States than abroad in the hard-target countries themselves.

The Way Ahead

One of the constant refrains one hears from defenders of the CIA's DO is that the Carter administration decimated the CIA's human intelligence operations. The reality, however, is that DO officials have been treading water on their own account and have no one to blame but themselves. They have perpetuated an empty and failed corporate culture that perpetuates a bureaucracy that consistently underperforms and is nearly incapable of delivering spies who report first-rate intelligence for the benefit of the commander in chief and his national security lieutenants. As intelligence expert Bruce Berkowitz rightly judges, "Four Presidents, twelve Congresses, and six directors of the CIA have come and gone. An intelligence officer could have served out his entire career in the CIA during that time. So if the United States has not been investing in HUMINT, we really need to stop blaming Stansfield Turner [director of central intelligence during the Carter administration]."[50] Admiral Turner may not have distinguished himself as DCI, but it is long past time to stop using him and the Carter administration as scapegoats for the DO's incompetence.

Another feeble defense of the DO's human intelligence performance is that it takes a long time to spot, assess, develop, and recruit spies. The DO conveniently and always needs more time to produce results. George Tenet long favored the DO and placed a high priority on revamping it during his tenure of seven years, which was the second longest tenure as DCI in the CIA's history.[51] Yet Tenet still made excuses in 2004 that the CIA needed five more years to revamp the DO's HUMINT operations, and Tenet's successor as head of CIA, Porter Goss, was even more pessimistic, telling Congress that five years was not enough time to get the DO performing.[52] Berkowitz makes another insightful observation on this score. "Despite the oft-repeated line that 'HUMINT sources take decades to rebuild,' that simply is not true. When William Casey was directing HUMINT operations in Europe for the Office of Strategic Services in World War II, he built a network of agents in just eighteen months. Casey was simply more aggressive and willing to take more chances than the CIA seems willing to accept today."[53]

The answer to the DO's woes certainly does not lie in fielding more officers to conduct the same business practices of human intelligence operations that have failed in the past. Former CIA Director Goss delivered to President Bush in February 2005 his plans for increasing by "50 percent" the number of case officers and analysts to get more people "in the field."[54] But a surge in hiring is hardly the answer to the CIA's woes.

The more telling and significant statistic will be how many of this deluge of new officers will stay longer in the CIA than the five to seven years needed at a minimum to develop competent case officers.

The CIA's human intelligence operations need to concentrate on the most critical issues facing U.S. national security decision makers. As a Council on Foreign Relations task force rightly argued, "collection priorities must not only be those subjects that are policy-relevant but also involve information that the intelligence community can best (or uniquely) ascertain."[55] Such targets would include a list of countries with power and interests that could potentially threaten the United States, especially because of nuclear weapons capabilities in China, Russia, North Korea, Pakistan, and potentially Iran and Saudi Arabia. U.S. policy makers can ill afford to have the CIA's human intelligence operations distracted by third- or fourth-tier collection issues, if only because the CIA finds information on these topics easier to collect than that on "hard targets." The commander in chief is desperate for human intelligence penetrations of hard-target countries to ascertain potentially hostile plans and intentions. It is long past due for the CIA to deliver, reliably and consistently.

6   Analysts Who Are Not Experts

THE CIA'S FAILURES IN STRATEGIC INTELLIGENCE DURING THE Cold War, post–Cold War, and 9/11 periods do not solely lay at the doorstep of poor human intelligence. Analysis, another core mission of the Agency, also bears a heavy burden for these intelligence failures. Just to tick off a few blunders, the CIA's analysts failed to warn of the intervention of Chinese forces in the Korean War, mistakenly judged that the Soviet Union would not be so "foolish" as to deploy nuclear-tipped ballistic missiles in Cuba, failed to predict that India would test a nuclear weapon in 1998, and completely misjudged the status of Iraq's weapons of mass destruction (WMD) programs in the run-up to the Iraq War.

The CIA has fallen a long way from where the father of strategic intelligence in the United States, Sherman Kent, wanted it to be. Kent envisioned an analytic corps in the CIA that would be akin to a major university's faculty with the research skills needed to exploit clandestine and public literature. Kent argued that strategic intelligence required "people to whom research and rigorous thought are the breath of life, and they must accordingly have tolerance for the queer bird and the eccentric with a unique talent. They must guarantee a sort of academic freedom of inquiry and must fight off those who derogate such freedom by pointing to its occasional crackpot finding. They must be built around a deference to the enormous difficulties which the search for truth often involves."[1] Kent lamented, however, that his expectations for a cadre of strategic intelligence analysts could not be met because of overly restrictive security vetting that ensured analysts would be "as alike as tiles of a bathroom floor – and about as capable of meaningful and original thought."[2] Kent's worse fears have unfortunately become the reality in spades in today's CIA.

What more beyond Kent's fears accounts for the CIA's analytic failures in strategic intelligence? Why have the CIA's analysts not been able to solve major strategic intelligence mysteries for U.S. policy makers? These failings are hard to square with the reputation outside the CIA that its analysts are experts. The reality inside the CIA is something different. In fact, the CIA has traditionally done a poor job of recruiting, nurturing, and maintaining nationally or internationally recognized experts in its analytic ranks. What follows is a critical examination of the analytic side of the CIA's strategic intelligence business. It examines why the Agency's analysis has been mediocre and has notably failed on key strategic issues. It also recommends changes in the Agency's business practices if it is to produce reliably first-rate strategic intelligence assessments for the commander in chief.

Lackluster Strategic Analysis

The analytic workhorse in foreign affairs analysis inside the U.S. government has been the Directorate for Intelligence (DI), the CIA's analytic corps. As former senior policy maker Robert Blackwill frames the DI's contribution, DI analysts "do 90 percent of the analysis by the USG [U.S. government] on foreign affairs. Policy officials, even those with academic backgrounds, are too busy with more pressing matters"[3] to do the analysis for themselves.

As has been noted in earlier chapters, the DI long considered the Presidential Daily Brief (PDB) as its flagship intelligence product for delivering strategic intelligence to the commander in chief and his key national security lieutenants. But high-level policy makers have found the PDB to be analytically wanting. The small group of PDB consumers told a presidential commission that they find the highly classified document of little value.[4] This sorry state of affairs has persisted for at least the past ten years. The Brown Commission in 1996 similarly assessed that "Often what they [policy makers] receive fails to meet their needs by being too late or too unfocused, or by adding little to what they already know."[5]

The CIA produced shoddy strategic intelligence before the cataclysmic events of 11 September 2001 and the run-up to the Iraq War. CIA analysis of the terrorist target was shallow, in no small measure, because "many analysts were inexperienced, unqualified, under-trained, and without access to critical information," according to the Joint House-Senate investigation.[6] The lack of analytic expertise in the CIA undoubtedly contributed to the series of intelligence failures surrounding the pre-war assessment of Iraq's WMD programs. The CIA was the most vocal in the intelligence community, arguing that Saddam's nuclear weapons program was robustly reconstituting. That argument stemmed from one lone CIA analyst in the Office of Weapons Intelligence, Proliferation, and Arms Control (WINPAC) who had questionable qualifications to make these judgments.[7] Another analyst in WINPAC was responsible for the assessment that the Iraqi defector, codenamed "Curveball," who was the prolific source – and subsequently proven fabricator – on Iraq's suspected mobile biological warfare program. The WINPAC analyst considered "Curveball" to be "fundamentally reliable" despite concerns from her Directorate of Operations (DO) counterparts.[8]

Perhaps more damning is that no manager in CIA's excessively heavy management layers had the expertise needed to question their analysts' critically flawed nuclear and biological assessments. WINPAC management even "rewarded judgments that fit the consensus view that Iraq had active WMD programs and discouraged those that did not."[9] And "analysts who raised concerns about the need for reassessments were not rewarded for having done so but were instead forced to leave WINPAC."[10]

Because of the CIA's shallow analytic expertise, for technical expertise, policy makers dealing with WMD proliferation know to turn to the National Laboratories run by the Department of Energy, not to the CIA. The dirty little secret in the intelligence community is that the National

Laboratories go out of their way to recruit and train highly qualified Ph.D.s in a variety of disciplines, whereas CIA management culturally discriminates against Ph.D.s. The CIA has even lost a few of its best analysts to the National Laboratories where the working environment is much better than that of Langley. As former Assistant Secretary of Defense and proliferation expert Ashton Carter has recommended, "the intelligence community needs to increase the size and technical training of its workforce. Because intelligence agencies have difficulty recruiting and training top talent with more lucrative prospects in private industry, they need to forge better links with the outside scientific community so that advice and insight are 'on call.'"[11]

The weaknesses of CIA intelligence analyses on Iraq are easier to see when juxtaposed to British intelligence assessments. Loch Johnson characterizes the American–British partnership thusly: "perhaps the most exhaustively researched foreign intelligence relationship, is a special case with an extensive, intertwined history between two enduring democracies that share a common language and culture."[12] British intelligence in 1995 accurately judged, "We assess that [Iraq] may also have hidden some specialized equipment and stocks of precursor chemicals but it is unlikely they have a covert stockpile of weapons or agent in any significant quantity; Hussein Kamil claims there are no remaining stockpiles of agents."[13] More generally, British intelligence in 1998 assessed that "UNSCOM [United Nations Special Commission] and the IAEA [International Atomic Energy Agency] have succeeded in destroying or controlling the vast majority of Saddam's 1991 weapons of mass destruction (WMD) capability."[14] British intelligence, to be sure, suffered from inadequate assessments of Iraq's programs, but its judgments were closer to the mark than the CIA's assessments contained in the October 2002 National Intelligence Estimate (NIE).

What, then, accounts for the discrepancies between British and American estimates on Iraq that were presumably based on shared raw intelligence? The answer must lie in the superior quality of British intelligence analysis. The United States would be well advised to seek some pointers from its British comrades in arms on how to recruit, train, and retain first-rate analysts for working the demanding strategic intelligence problems such as WMD.

Obstacles to Strategic Analysis at the Grassroots

People outside the intelligence community often mistakenly believe that the DI is the CIA's equivalent of a "think tank" or major research university and is loaded with Ph.D.s. Nothing could be farther from the truth. As David Ignatius, who has keen judgment regarding the intelligence world, assesses, "The DI analysts work hard, but their product is too often mediocre.... America's intelligence analysts should be a match for the best college faculty in the world. They're far from that now, and life outside the CIA cocoon might do them some good."[15]

The DI claims publicly to have expertise, but few if any analysts are nationally, much less internationally, recognized experts in their fields. DI management will claim they cannot be publicly known because of the classified nature of their work, but that argument holds little merit. Many analysts at major research centers such as the RAND Corporation have security clearances and are nationally and internationally recognized experts. Why couldn't the CIA do likewise? The reality is that any analyst who aspires to be a serious scholar cannot develop the necessary expertise inside the CIA and must leave to do so.

The DI does not have a large number of Ph.D.s in its ranks, but that does not stop it from pretending it does. Although the CIA does not publicly release figures, I would guess that about 10 percent of the DI analysts have doctorates and a substantially larger percentage have master's degrees. The DI has analysts and managers who came up the ranks following economic issues and refer to themselves as "economists." But these analysts and managers simply do not have the professional backgrounds to be considered actual economists in the outside world. I have a bachelor's degree in economics but would not for a moment pretend to be an economist. As my undergraduate advisor long ago told me, one must have a Ph.D. to be considered an economist; even a master's does not grant that stature because it is just a way station en route to a doctorate. Yet few of my DI colleagues who analyzed economies of other countries had Ph.D.s. I even worked alongside a DI "economist" who worked on Middle Eastern economies and was well regarded by CIA management who had a bachelor's degree in history.

The DI's economic talent pool is a far cry from academe in the United States or in the banking and financial world where doctorates are requisites for economists. A more direct and comparable institutional and functional comparison to the CIA would be the World Bank and the International Monetary Fund (IMF). The vast majority of World Bank and IMF economists actually have Ph.D.s, whereas the vast majority of the CIA's "economists" do not. To be sure, the government and the CIA cannot afford to pay economists the salaries that they can command at those organizations or on Wall Street. Nevertheless, the CIA's analysis would be qualitatively better if CIA management leveraged its personnel budgets for hiring and retaining fewer experts at higher salaries than for hiring quantities of inexperienced and inexpert analysts.

The DI management has an almost palpable disdain for Ph.D.s. The common wisdom is that individuals with doctorates are "too scholarly" and are unable to make the transition from the perceived "staid" life in academe to the fast-paced, rough-and-tumble world of intelligence analysis. Management also thinks that scholars are prone and trained to write jargon for other scholars and are incapable of writing short, snappy, and concise prose in short memos for harried policy makers. To be fair, there is some merit to these charges. But if given time, attention, and good management, many Ph.D.s who have an intellectual bent toward policy-relevant intelligence problems could make the transition to the benefit of CIA analysis.

The DI's concentration on current intelligence production places a premium on analysts who are generalists and can write well and quickly meet tight deadlines. In evaluating analysts for promotion, managers tend to reward those analysts who work on issues that command daily current intelligence headlines and write more than those analysts who would prefer to specialize and work on "slower" and less high-profile issues for longer periods of time. Crises often are unanticipated and force DI managers to "surge" analysts or bodies against the crisis of the day, and in promotion panels they consequently tend to favor generalists who are more versatile and willing to bounce from hot topic to hot topic than individuals who would prefer to stay put and work on "slower" accounts for longer periods of time and to develop a specialty. The excessive DI concentration on current intelligence has, however, over time had a corrosive and deleterious impact on the building of knowledge and expertise that is the intellectual fruit of longer-term and scholarly research. It also denies analysts practice and expertise in critical analysis, weighing of evidence, and evaluation of alternatives.[16]

The DI's management holds firmly to these negative stereotypes of scholars even though a small minority of their analysts have Ph.D.s and have proven that they can be scholarly and at the same time valuable and productive intelligence analysts. I know a handful of the DI's well-seasoned analysts who have Ph.D.s under their belt, but they do not acknowledge their doctorates out of a fear that they will be dismissed by management. The DI's bureaucratic culture is such that no one ever uses the title "Dr.," and one senior DI analyst once even confessed to me in a hallway chat that he preferred to "hide" his Ph.D.

An intellectual inferiority complex explains part of the DI management's general hostility toward scholars in their ranks. The vast majority of the DI's management team do not have doctorates, and they resent people who do. In fact, many do not even have academic degrees relevant to the study of international affairs. One former senior manager in the CIA's Counterterrorism Center (CTC) who rose up the DI ranks only had a master's degree in English. Another former senior-most official in the CTC had only a bachelor's degree in forestry.

I had the privilege in the mid-1990s to work with a colleague who had a doctorate in Middle Eastern history from a major U.S. university and spoke Hebrew and Arabic. As he came on duty at the CIA, the division chief in charge of the analysis of the Persian Gulf called him into his office for the customary "welcome aboard" chat. Instead of an exchange of pleasantries and small talk, the division chief barked at him, "There's been all this fanfare about getting you with your doctorate and language capabilities on board, but I want you to know that in my book you're just a GS-9 [a junior level analyst]." My colleague left the division chief's office scratching his head thinking, "Now what did I ever do to him?" The irony – or tragedy would be a better word – was that my colleague was an intellectual but also a very able analyst who demonstrated a quick ability to transition from academe to the business of intelligence. He eventually grew in less than a couple of years to feel undervalued and left the DI to pursue a career as a case officer in the DO. To add insult to injury, the division chief who could barely contain his disdain for scholars was promoted up the ranks to become the deputy director for intelligence (DDI), the CIA's top analyst and head of the analytic corps.

Few of the DI's managers have ever written a book or even devote significant attention to reading them. One high-level DI official once claimed that analysts could become "experts" – presumably just like he had, at least in his own mind – by writing a steady stream of short memos. Only inside the CIA would such a standard be acceptable to establish intellectual legitimacy and expertise. In academe and the think-tank world, the research, writing, and publication of substantive analysis in books is rightly seen as the means to nurture and develop expertise. The DI managers generally do not even keep abreast of scholarly literature in their fields of responsibility. I remember sharing the news with my Middle East division chief that distinguished Harvard professor and political scientist Joseph Nye was named the chairman of the National Intelligence Council. My division chief looked at me curiously and asked, "Who is Joseph Nye?" To which I had to reply, "Oh, he's just one of the most highly regarded political scientists of his generation."

If the DI's managers have no regard for the writing, and even the reading, of books, they obviously are not going to allow their subordinates to do so either. I remember once sitting at my CIA cubicle reading a scholarly book on the Middle East when a manager passed by my desk, took a double-take at my book, and told me to get back to "work," meaning to get back to monitoring classified cable traffic – reports coming from overseas on my computer. DI managers foolishly believe that all they have to do is sit analysts down at computers and get them to read cable traffic for at least a week, and – presto – they've got an expert!

What is remarkable is that DI management gives no time, resources, or attention to having analysts read or study the publicly available scholarship on the countries or topics they are responsible for before assuming their analytic responsibilities on an account. Management, for example, might take a newly hired CIA analyst without an academic or professional background on, say, South Asia, sit the staffer at a computer, and call him or her an expert on South Asia. If a studious and conscientious analyst wants to read a boatload of books, journal articles, magazines, and monographs on their countries or topics, management wants them to do it on their "own time," not during the workday. The cultural bias of the CIA's managers in the analytic corps in the end produces cable readers and summary writers, not experts.

CIA managers are poorly suited intellectually to oversee strategic analysis, the intersection of the realms of politics and military affairs. They most often come up the analytic ranks as political and economic analysts who are unfamiliar with even a basic knowledge of military affairs. Only a small percentage of Agency managers have backgrounds in military affairs, a longstanding fact at the CIA. As scholar Richard Shultz has observed regarding this neglect of the study of force in international relations, "Unfortunately, the intelligence community, particularly the CIA – both during the Cold War and in its aftermath – has thought about and dealt with armed groups in an *episodic*, *transitory*, and *ad hoc* manner."[17] I vividly recall being counseled by veteran agency military analysts who got their analytic spurs in the heated disputes with military intelligence and policy makers over the course of the Vietnam War. They advised me in the late 1980s that specializing in military analysis was a career dead end and no place to stay for any analyst who aspired to advance to senior ranks.

What was true in the late 1980s and through the 1990s about the CIA's neglect of strategic and military analysis is true today. The military expertise honed in the Cold War against the Soviet Union and by the Warsaw Pact withered of neglect and retirements after the Berlin Wall collapsed. Agency managers saw no need to replenish its ranks because they labored under a mistaken and philosophically liberal "End of History" worldview that military affairs would not be relevant to the post–Cold War world. During the 1990s, a small cadre of military analysts was a beleaguered band of misfits analyzing conflicts in the Balkans and the Persian Gulf. Agency management judged that conducting military analysis was a tertiary function and put substantially more investment into political and economic analysis, even while policy makers most often judged the quality of these analyses to be mixed at best.

All the while, Agency managers increasingly allowed military analyst workloads to be driven by tasking from the military services and Pentagon, while forcing military analysts to devote less attention to more significant customers of strategic analysis in the White House. By the end of the 1990s, most CIA military analysts judged that their collective manpower was so limited by answering the daily deluge of questions – especially from the tactical and operationally oriented military – they were unable to look over the horizon to examine longer-range warning challenges for civilian policy makers. These civilian policy makers are not always well served by intelligence analysis coming from operationally oriented military services, as the American experiences at Pearl Harbor and in Vietnam, Iraq, and Kosovo have shown. The CIA's dismissive mindset against military and strategic analysis permeates managerial ranks.

The DI managers as a whole are a timid bunch and rarely live up to the "speak truth to power" standard within the CIA's halls. They are careerists and are always worried about the prospect of offending their next boss or someone who will sit on the board considering their next promotion. They will bend over backward to avoid a heated debate or argument with other managers or superiors even if they are substantively right on an intelligence issue.

This anti-intellectual mindset is reinforced by management's view that analyses are "corporate" products and not the result of the individual intellectual capital of the working-level analysts. The Agency clearly articulated this managerial viewpoint in a report written for Director of Central Intelligence (DCI) Robert Gates: "We do produce a corporate product. If the policymaker wants the opinion of a single individual, he can (and frequently does) consult any one of a dozen outside experts on any given issue. Your work, on the other hand, counts because it represents the well-considered view of an entire directorate and, in the case of National Estimates, the entire intelligence community. Analysts … must discard the academic mindset that says their work is their own."[18] The obvious implicit subtext of this statement is that if analysts want to be experts, "don't let the CIA door hit you on the backside on your way out." The statement, however, utterly fails to appreciate that insightful strategic intelligence is not written by gaggles of government bureaucrats but is more likely the product of fruitful and insightful minds, as Sherman Kent knew well. The CIA's corporate culture needs to be reminded that the profoundly incorrect assessments of Iraq's nuclear, biological, and chemical weapons were "corporate products" extensively reviewed by layers of CIA managers who all failed to prevent the Iraq intelligence debacle.

The CIA's analysis managers do not have foreign-language skills or other expertise comparable to their State Department and National Security Council staff counterparts. I have come to this conclusion in my many dealings with Foreign Service officers – our diplomats – over the years. To its credit and despite its meager resources compared with the CIA, the State Department, for example, has done a superb job of ensuring that its Middle East officers received full-time Arabic language training. In comparison to the State Department, CIA analysts and managers have little to no Arabic training. The last head of the CIA's Middle East office to be an Arabic speaker was twenty years ago with Robert Ames, who came up in the Agency as a DO case officer. He was a highly regarded Arabist and a close adviser to Secretary of State George Shultz. Sadly, Ames was killed in the 1983 bombing of the U.S. Embassy in Beirut. But

Ames was an extraordinary individual in CIA history in that he was a brilliant case officer, analyst, and expert Arabist. The CIA just does not produce Arabists like Ames.

Because CIA managers working on the Middle East do not have Arabic, they really have no appreciation for the intense and prolonged study required to achieve a rudimentary understanding of the language, and they do not give their subordinates the time or the money to gain intensive training. An analyst interested in studying Arabic should not be surprised in light of the CIA management's ignorance to get a response such as, "Study your Arabic on weekends." When the House-Senate inquiry investigated the causes of the 9/11 intelligence failure, the finding that the intelligence community's and the CIA's Arabic capabilities were abysmal should not surprise taxpayers.[19] The CIA's management has to be held accountable for this inexcusable lapse, especially because the State Department has done much better in producing Arabists with a budget that is miniscule compared with that of the CIA.

Although the CIA's management is a dim bulb, the country was blessed with the wisdom of former Senator David Boren, chair of the Senate Select Committee on Intelligence, who moved to increase the intelligence community's hard-language capabilities in Arabic, Chinese, Farsi, Japanese, and Korean, to name just a few. He provided funding for the National Security Education Program that provides scholarships to undergraduate and graduate students to study hard languages. In exchange for these scholarships, which in many cases entail study abroad for total language emersion, the recipients must agree to work for the federal government for some time, depending on the amount of funding they received, after receiving their degree.

The Boren fellowships make eminent and practical sense, but the CIA has failed to tap the expertise created by these government fellowships as intended by Senator Boren. As with all things, the workings of the CIA are seldom straightforward or logical. I routinely recommend the Boren fellowships to my graduate students only to hear later about the difficulty the National Security Education Program recipients have landing postgraduation jobs in the intelligence community, especially at the CIA, to fulfill their fellowship obligations. Because many receive language training overseas in Asia or the Middle East, they naturally come into contact with a wide array of foreigners. Those contacts – precisely the ones that allow dedicated American students to develop language capabilities and regional expertise that would be invaluable to the CIA – cause these students to be weeded out in the security checks that are a central component of the CIA's employment application process.

The CIA's Office of Security puts too many red flags on applicants with extensive foreign travel. But people cannot be fluent in hard languages unless they have extensive travel and living experience with extensive contacts overseas. For the CIA's analytic ranks, the Office of Security prefers to approve individuals who have little to no foreign travel experience or contacts and no family living abroad. Further, the DI's management does have the collective courage needed to wag the Office of Security tail, instead of allowing the tail to wag the rest of the CIA.

The same narrow mindset that works against U.S. interests plays against first-generation Arab American citizens who are fluent in Arabic. The CIA says publicly that it is now recruiting first- and second-generation Americans with Arabic skills, but my anecdotal evidence suggests otherwise. A first-generation Egyptian Arab American intern who performed excellent research assistance for me on a project that examined al-Qaeda and militant Islamic insurgency was eager to join the CIA to contribute to the U.S. war effort. He approached three middle-aged, white male CIA recruiters at a job fair in 2005, who told him not to bother even applying to the CIA because he still had relatives in the Middle East. The three CIA recruiters also told two of his friends, who were Lebanese Americans interning for the Department of State, that they, too, need not apply to the CIA because they had relatives in the Arab world.

The CIA's recruitment practices are simply too defensive and inexcusably fail to tap the enormous wealth of multicultural talent here in the United States. The CIA today is so busy playing defense in worrying about notional counterintelligence vulnerabilities that it is not playing offense to gain access, contacts, human intelligence, and cultural and linguistic expertise from the Arab world. These ridiculous practices are setting the United States up for more intelligence failures, the likes of which we suffered on 9/11.

Bureaucratic Process over Analytic Substance

The DI made a failed effort in 1996 to flatten the bureaucratic hierarchy. The well-intentioned effort to cut managerial levels to free up resources to devote to analytic talent was predictably suffocated by entrenched bureaucratic interests. Today, a working-level analyst is separated from the director of the CIA by about eight bureaucratic rungs. This is a far cry from the flat and flexible organization charts of companies that thrive in the information technology era. Further, the CIA's bureaucracy artificially divides world affairs into units or fiefdoms, which frustrates the formulation of broader strategic analysis. As Robert Jervis aptly captures the problem, "The specialization, division of labor, and caution that characterize a large intelligence organization like CIA is more conducive to studying trees than the forest."[20]

Analysis moves painstakingly slowly through the bureaucratic structure, and iconoclastic views that challenge conventional wisdom are likely to have their edges substantially smoothed in the laborious review process. Analysts suffer considerable frustration. Their charge is to write analyses for the senior levels of the national security policy-making community. Even uncontroversial analysis suffers from pronounced dumbing-down effects as it passes up and through the chain of command. More often than not, policy makers are substantially more conversant with international issues than the CIA managers, who in the review act more as overpaid editors – without the technical expertise of professional editors – to make analysis more understandable for themselves rather than the far more expert consumers in the policy community.

The production of intelligence analysis takes the form of an inverted pyramid. One or a few junior analysts, for example, might draft a piece of intelligence analysis. It then passes through a chain of command loaded with senior managers, who typically impose more stylistic than substantive changes. The piece of analysis then passes to a current intelligence staff stuffed with senior individuals, who further massage the analysis into stale and boring prose before publication in the PDB or the more widely disseminated Senior Executive Intelligence Brief.

The CIA briefers returned from policy community runs to Langley each morning with tasking in hand. Unfortunately for analysts, that tasking slowly and laboriously flows down the chain of command, reaching them only late in the day. In many instances, analysts might be able to write a piece of analysis in relatively short order, only to be confronted with the time-consuming and cumbersome internal bureaucratic review process to get the answers for policy makers back up the CIA's chain of command. In my career as an analyst, the wisest and most seasoned analysts would opt to wait for managers to go home for the evening before moving a draft forward to avoid several rungs of review by Agency managers.

The Agency today still operates on a top-down organizational model rather than utilizing the bottom-up model that succeeds in the private information-technology sector. The CIA's analytic managers frequently push down orders for intelligence analyses. Such orders often force analysts to produce analyses whether or not there is a critical mass of intelligence that fills the knowledge gaps in publicly available information and assessments for policy makers. The top-down cultural ethos has grown stronger in recent years. As the working-level analytic workforce becomes younger and more inexperienced, the aging ranks of Agency managers are increasingly insecure about the quality, timeliness, and policy relevance of analysis. They compensate by micromanaging the intelligence production cycle. Micromanagement, in turn, discourages analysts and stifles intellectual innovation among inexperienced and veteran analysts alike.

Nothing could better illustrate the clash of cultures between the Cold War mentality of the Agency's senior managerial ranks and the young recruits who represent the Agency's future than the security restrictions at the front door of the George Bush Center for Intelligence, the CIA's headquarters in Langley, Virginia. Agency personnel and visitors are prohibited from bringing in laptop computers, cell phones, Palm pilots, Blackberries, and the like out of an unrealistic fear that these items could be used for espionage. These security prohibitions would hardly deter a traitor from committing espionage. Agency rules have always prohibited employees from taking classified information home with them, for example, but that restriction did not stop Aldrich Ames's years of betrayal by walking out the CIA's front door with classified information stuffed in his pants. These pieces of technology are the lifeblood of private and professional lives today in the information-technology era. The security prohibitions undoubtedly are more effective in deterring a younger generation of analysts, who want to hone and keep current on the professional skills needed to stay competitive in the information-technological revolution, from pursuing long-term CIA careers. The young and new analysts at the CIA are likely to look at the antiquated security boards and conclude that this is no place to spend more than a couple of years lest their skills atrophy to the point where they are no longer on a par with their cohort on the outside of the CIA's suffocating security walls.

The CIA's Office of Security often adopts policies and procedures that defy common sense. I recall while working European security issues in the mid-1990s, for example, that our office had a competent summer intern working with us. My colleagues and I wanted to tap her talent to help our analytic efforts. We decided to have her peruse the Internet looking for a variety of topics and Web sites that we did not have time to monitor. For some reason – I suspect it was an act of bureaucratic cowardice – my team chief decided to consult the Office of Security to see if it had any objections. Sure enough and true to form, the Office of Security objected to tasking the intern to monitoring the Internet because she "wasn't cleared for it." When our team chief announced – without a hint of embarrassment – the Office of Security's wisdom, I was aghast, furious, and at the same time laughing so hard I could barely breathe.

The CIA's security concerns also collectively act as concrete barriers to the nourishing of CIA analytic contacts with outside experts. As the

Brown Commission rightly judged, "The failure to make greater use of outside expertise at the CIA appears to result in part from a lack of financial resources and in part from onerous security requirement – particularly the polygraph examination and the requirement to submit subsequent publications for review – that discourages some outside experts from participating in intelligence work."[21] The CIA's analysts might have occasion to chat with a foreign scholar over substantive issues at an academic or professional conference in the United States, but the wrath of security officers would fall on an analyst's head if he or she had a one-on-one discussion with the same expert abroad. The CIA still has not caught up to the consequences of globalization for the intelligence business. As Berkowitz and Goodman perceptively assess, "Secrecy runs counter to the essence of the Information Revolution, where the free flow of information drives productivity and creativity. The procedures and technologies of the Information Revolution – open architectures, public data bases, and the ability to form networks with almost anyone, anywhere – are all defeated by secrecy."[22]

One of the most damning criticisms of the Agency is that it fails miserably at recruiting, nurturing, and retaining experts of its own, whereas it excels at producing bureaucrats. The Brown Commission found that "While there are some analysts in the Intelligence Community who are nationally known experts in their respective fields, they are the exception rather than the rule."[23] To underscore this point, few of this book's readers, off the top of their heads, would be able to name a handful of Agency analysts who are widely respected experts. Are the CIA's "team leaders" or "issue managers" who are responsible for the multidisciplinary teams that produce analysis on North Korea, China, Iraq, Iran, the Persian Gulf, Russia, Pakistan, India, or weapons proliferation and terrorism nationally or internationally recognized experts? The answer by and large is that no CIA analyst on any of these topics is a top expert. In marked contrast, many readers would likely be able to identify numerous foreign affairs experts from the halls of academe or think tanks such as the Council on Foreign Relations, the Brookings Institution, and the RAND Corporation.

This sorry state of affairs is such that although the CIA has few experts of national or international standing, guessing from the bureaucratic wire diagram of the analytic corps posted on the Agency's Web site, the DI alone has managers numbering in triple digits. The U.S. policy-making community and the general public have the right to ask, What is the Agency's contribution to national security, expert analysts who make sense of the world for our decision makers or bureaucrats who push paper?

With much fanfare, the DI launched in the mid-1990s a new career path in the analytic ranks, the senior analytic service (SAS), designed to counter criticisms of its analytic prowess – or lack thereof. In theory, the career path was intended to offer greater financial compensation for analysts who choose to remain analysts and hone their expertise rather than leave the analytic ranks for the more remunerative management ranks. But, in actuality, for all intents and purposes, the CIA broadly conferred the status of SAS on its senior analysts, a move that accomplished little in addressing the Brown Commission's criticisms. Over time, the SAS, as in the case of the failed effort to flatten the DI's management hierarchy, will likely suffer slow asphyxiation to make more funds available for the managerial ranks that control the Agency and DI purse strings.

The DI today is too tactically driven by day-to-day and current intelligence reporting at the expense of deep analytic research and study.[24] The pressure of daily intelligence demands has only increased since 11 September and the wars in Afghanistan and Iraq. The CIA, for example, "pulled about 160 analysts from their jobs watching global political, economic, and military trends and turned them into counterterrorism specialists."[25] Although the CIA keeps its workforce numbers classified – in many instances to its detriment, because the public perception is that the CIA is a large agency despite the reality that it is relatively small compared with other government departments and agencies – 160 people is a sizable chunk of its analytic ranks. Stripping the analytic ranks for the counter-terrorism war may meet the crisis du jour, but it risks denying the

United States the analytic capabilities needed to forecast the next battles, crises, and wars. Rather than being forward-leaning in analysis, the CIA is constantly playing catch-up. Indeed, one of the most critical functions of the CIA is strategic warning, a mission that it is increasingly incapable of doing. Without the benefits of strategic analytic warning, civilian policy makers will again be unable to take measures that might avert the deaths of American citizens.

To be even-handed, however, it is important to note that policy makers crave current intelligence and have little interest or time for longer-term strategic intelligence analysis. Further, because CIA analysts are now closer to policy makers than they had been in the formative days of the Agency, they naturally gravitate toward current intelligence analysis that brings laurels and attention from policy makers. As Harold Ford, a former senior intelligence official, captured the dilemma, "Estimates often do not rank high on the list of the types of intelligence digested by senior consumers. Time and time again, polls taken among decisionmakers over the years have yielded similar results: policymakers invariably value current intelligence reports the most, Estimates less so."[26]

The demand for current intelligence saps research needed to develop expertise, which is of practical importance because the Agency's long-standing failings in this area have come back to roost with devastating consequences to U.S. security. The Joint House–Senate Inquiry faulted the lack of analytic expertise in large measure for the intelligence failure of 11 September. It found that the intelligence community's understanding of al-Qaeda was "hampered by insufficient analytic focus and quality, particularly in terms of strategic analysis.... The quality of counterterrorism analysis was inconsistent, and many analysts were inexperienced, unqualified, under-trained, and without access to critical information. As a result, there was a dearth of creative, aggressive analysis targeting Bin Ladin and a persistent inability to comprehend the collective significance of individual pieces of intelligence. These analytic deficiencies seriously undercut the ability of U.S. policymakers to understand the full nature of the threat, and to make fully informed decisions."[27]

The CIA needs experts who master the vast wealth of information that is constantly growing in the information-technology age. The critical importance of publicly available information to strategic intelligence analysis is underscored by former Secretary of State James Baker, who wrote of the PDB and other highly classified intelligence papers for senior policy makers that "much of the analysis and information would revolve around public statements by foreign officials and assessments of the extent to which these public statements accurately reflected the confidential plans of the government involved."[28]

A great many of the "mysteries" of international politics can be fathomed by the mining of publicly available literature in libraries. George Kennan, the diplomat-scholar and author of the Cold War policy of containment against the Soviet Union, commented on the overemphasis on classified sources of information to the detriment of the public. Kennan assessed that "the need by our government for secret intelligence about affairs elsewhere in the world has been vastly overrated. I would say that something upward of 95 percent of what we need to know could be very well obtained by the careful and competent study of perfectly legitimate sources of information open and available to us in the rich library and archival holdings of this country."[29] That observation is true today even against al-Qaeda, which is an adversary far different from the former Soviet Union because the terrorist group uses the Internet heavily for recruitment and indoctrination of its membership.

Although publicly available information is the lion's share of the grist needed for the CIA's analysis, intelligence work is still required to synthesize analyses directly relevant to the needs of U.S. national security, which often are not produced in academe or even in the increasingly partisan think-tank world. As Bruce Berkowitz and Allan Goodman rightly assess, "Most information U.S. officials use is, and always will be, from open sources. The reason for an intelligence apparatus is to find and interpret information concerning national security that the government needs, but cannot obtain from the media or from other commercial sources."[30]

The Allure of the "Devil's Advocate Fix"

The string of the CIA's intelligence failures has naturally led to a slew of commissions and investigations over the past ten years to ferret out the causes of poor to abysmal intelligence analysis. Invariably and like clockwork, they recommend the use of alternate analysis, red teaming, and devil's advocacy as analytic methods to test common assumptions and analytic judgments. The Jeremiah Panel that investigated the 1998 India nuclear tests, for example, recommended the use of devil's advocacy. Then-DDI John McLaughlin placed a senior analyst in the post of devil's advocate for the analytic corps as a means to test and challenge analytic assumptions. These steps seem eminently reasonable, but as with all things in the CIA, rarely is anything straightforward and logical. As Roger George points out, the DI today is still struggling with employing devil's advocacy as well as other alternative analysis tools.[31]

The idea behind devil's advocacy, Michael Handel explains, "is to encourage an individual to freely express unpopular, dissenting opinions, which allows decision-makers to consider alternative views while protecting those who present them."[32] Robert Jervis elaborates that "To make it more likely that they [policy makers and intelligence analysts] will consider alternative explanations of specific bits of data and think more carefully about the beliefs and images that underlie their policies, they should employ devil's – or rather devils' – advocates...those who listen to the arguments are in a good position to learn what perspectives they are rejecting, what evidence they should examine more closely, and what assumptions need further thought. As a result, fewer important questions will be overlooked because everyone agrees on the answer."[33]

The culture inside the Agency's analytic corps today is simply too intellectually rigid to do devil's advocate analysis. Under DCI George Bush, the CIA resisted the team A and team B exercise that examined competing analyses of Soviet strategic forces and plans. The common folklore inside the Agency is that the exercise threatened the autonomy of the

CIA's analysis and should never be repeated. That mindset undoubtedly would have stopped any notion of doing competitive devil's advocate analysis on India's nuclear strategy before the 1998 intelligence failure to warn of New Delhi's impending nuclear weapons test. Robert Gates, during his tenure as DDI, was lambasted by the CIA's recalcitrant analytic ranks who opposed his support for a devil's advocate analysis that put together the best case for the Soviet Union's support of the 1981 assassination attempt against Pope John Paul II. The evidence for a case was thin, but it was a potentially useful analytic device for testing the strengths and weaknesses of the conventional wisdom that the Soviets did not back the assassination attempt.[34]

The CIA's bureaucratic culture that prevents intellectual curiosity and unconventional wisdom critical to effective devil's advocacy analysis was evident in spades in the Iraq WMD debacle. The Presidential Commission on WMD found that over the twelve years after the 1991 Gulf War, "not a single analytic product that examined the possibility that Saddam Hussein's desire to escape sanctions, fear of being 'caught' decisively, or anything else would cause him to destroy his WMD."[35] The National Intelligence Officer for the Near East and South Asia noted that "such an hypothesis was so far removed from analysts' understanding of Iraq that it would have been very difficult to get such an idea published even as a 'red-team' exercise."[36] The Presidential Commission determined that "An intellectual culture or atmosphere in which certain ideas were simply too 'unrespectable' and out of synch with prevailing policy and analytic perspectives pervaded the Intelligence Community."[37]

I learned from personal experience that CIA analysts and managers would not recognize the need, utility, or desirability of devil's advocacy analysis even if it hit them on their foreheads. On my own time and initiative, I was teaching a security studies graduate course at George Washington University. In delivering lectures on Asian security, I was struck by the amount of conventional wisdom that held that China lacked the military wherewithal and political incentive to invade Taiwan. I decided to write a devil's advocate analysis to expose the weaknesses of the common wisdom. I made good use of the university's library because the CIA's library was simply not up to the standards of a major university. I also exploited the desktop computer in the basement of our townhouse to write an article arguing that China could invade Taiwan and laid out the political calculus and military means for doing so as well as the implications for the United States. I submitted the scholarly and entirely unclassified analysis to the CIA Publication Review Board to ensure that nothing was classified. The board approved the piece.

I subsequently received a call from the DI's devil's advocate who had read the piece as a member of the review board. This thoughtful and well-experienced senior analyst was intrigued by my paper and asked if I would be willing to debate the issue with the DI's political and military analysts on China. I said I would be delighted, but the DI's devil's advocate later told me that the China shop had read my analysis only to comment, "The Chinese aren't going to like this if it is published." As if I cared what the Chinese government thought of my analysis! I was writing as a private citizen on my own time and with my own resources to warn U.S. policy makers and military commanders of the gaps in the common wisdom regarding China's capabilities against Taiwan. I had also thought that this was what the CIA was supposed to do. In the end, the China shop wanted no part in a debate despite the DI's devil advocate's wisest of intentions. I eventually managed to publish the article as "What if . . . 'China Attacks Taiwan!'" in the Army War College's journal *Parameters*, which was subsequently written about in two *Washington Post* articles.[38] Notwithstanding serious public attention paid to the article, it failed to generate a whimper of intellectual curiosity in the halls of the CIA.

That lack of intellectual courage or inquisitiveness was not unique to the Asia hands at the CIA. The Middle East and weapons proliferation analysts and managers too were not the least bit interested in provocative analysis that challenged conventional wisdom, as shown by the CIA's failure to warn policy makers of India's detonation of a nuclear weapon and to gauge Iraq's dilapidated WMD programs. Again, on my own time, initiative, and resources, I wrote another provocative analysis in the 2001 arguing that although the United States and American intelligence are preoccupied with nuclear programs among the usual list of suspects such as North Korea and Iraq – the CIA would later be surprised by the scope and sophistication of Libya's and Iran's suspected nuclear weapons programs after 9/11 – it risked overlooking a potentially grave proliferation threat in Saudi Arabia. I argued in the paper that Saudi Arabia had plenty of strategic reasons as well as the means by working with its Pakistani and Chinese partners to develop nuclear weapons capability. I published the article in the British journal *Survival* under the title "A Saudi Nuclear Option?"[39]

The argument did not raise an eyebrow among the CIA's top managers. I gave the *Survival* article to the director of the Office of Near East and South Asian Analysis in the DI, and he never responded to it. I also gave it to the deputy of the Office of Weapons Intelligence, Proliferation, and Arms Control. He at least got back to me and said, "It's an interesting argument, but there's no evidence for it." My counter-argument was that just because no CIA agents are saying that Saudi Arabia wants nuclear weapons does not mean that the Saudi Kingdom is not pursuing the option. That would be akin to arguing that if a tree falls in the forest but doesn't hit a CIA agent on the head, the tree did not fall. My argument was intended as a hypothesis that could be used to generate an intelligence collection strategy to try to confirm or disprove the hypothesis.

But that line of inquiry, as routine and second nature as it is in the social and natural sciences, is lost on bureaucrats at the CIA. Senior CIA officials are bureaucrats who by and large have advanced their careers by looking at the intelligence process as the product rather than as a means to produce substantive intelligence for policy makers. A colleague and I used to joke that the CIA's management motto is not "speak truth to power" but "process is our product." In the DI, there are simply too many layers of management, and the only way for midlevel management to get recognition and promotion is to distinguish themselves to their superiors by creating more process. No one in the CIA except the lowly analyst pays anything other than passing interest in the intellectual substance of intelligence.

An influential review of intelligence by the Council on Foreign Relations in 1996 called for the establishment of a reserve corps to bolster expertise,[40] but the implementation has been problematic. Just days before my resignation in July 2001, I felt a pang of guilt about the imminent end of my nearly two decades as a political-military analyst at the CIA. I phoned the National Intelligence Council staff, which had been tasked to form an outside group of analysts called the Reserve Officer Corps, available for consultations with CIA analysts during crises. I explained to the man at the other end of the secure "green line" that was routinely used by intelligence community staffers for classified conversations that I was an experienced analyst who had worked on security issues in the Middle East and Europe, including wars between nation-states, civil wars, insurgencies, militant Islamic governments, and the proliferation of weapons of mass destruction. I further explained that I was resigning from the CIA to accept a professorship at the National Defense University where I would be teaching senior diplomats and military officers from the Middle East and South Asia.

The man at the other end of the phone listened politely and said, "Thank you, Mr. Russell. But the Agency already is well stocked with analysts with your expertise. What we really are looking for is expertise in sub-Sahara Africa. Do you have any expertise there?" I said "no." And he declined to take my forwarding contact information. Two months later, al-Qaeda attacked, in October we were waging war in Afghanistan, and in early 2002 events in Iraq were heating up, and by spring 2003, U.S. forces were fighting in Baghdad. It seems these days that one cannot open a major newspaper or magazine without seeing a CIA advertisement for military analysts with expertise in the Middle East. As is the case more often than not, however, the CIA's management seems to always shut the barn door after the horses have all fled.

Are CIA's Days in Strategic Intelligence Numbered?

President Bush's order to the CIA to increase by 50 percent the number of operations officers and analysts – paying special attention to terrorism and WMD proliferation – represents a surge in hiring and a veiled acknowledgment of the CIA's analytic failings.[41] But now is in many respects too late. U.S. policy makers need expert analysis today in the heat of battle, not five to seven years from now when new recruits begin to emerge as competent analysts. As a stopgap measure, Agency managers are press-ganging analysts to work on Afghanistan, Iraq, and al-Qaeda. That management philosophy is akin to lemmings jumping from a cliff. Siphoning analysts from other issues will further erode the CIA's already poor ability to conduct strategic warning for policy makers of armed conflicts that have yet to break out.

Merely throwing a quantity of analysts at a problem will not yield qualitatively better intelligence. The net result of the CIA's current hiring binge will be an analytic corps with young and inexperienced analysts to stuff ranks that are already filled with the same. As Mark Lowenthal, a former senior CIA official and intelligence expert observes, "The net result is an analytic corps that is younger and less experienced than before. Former CIA Deputy Director of Intelligence Jami Miscik captured this fact when she noted that 40 percent of analysts in the directorate of intelligence had worked for only one DCI, George Tenet, who resigned after exactly seven years. The analytic work force can mature only if retention is kept high."[42]

The CIA does a poor job of keeping the highest caliber analysts on board, however. Bureaucratic and security idiocies are prompting younger CIA analysts, as well as case officers, to resign, although the CIA's management hides the attrition rate under the cloak of classifying personnel numbers. The CIA's Public Affairs Office might tout a low attrition figure of less than 5 percent, but that figure masks what must be a higher figure for younger employees, who have the equivalent of a 401(k) retirement fund and can roll over their CIA retirement contributions into private accounts after they resign. On the other hand, in the past CIA employees had to stay on a full career of twenty or more years to be fully vested in the retirement plan; this applies to employees who started with the Agency before the early 1980s. The CIA's retirement plans encouraged the old CIA dinosaurs to hang on in the management ranks for as long as possible, while the younger blood took off even before the five to seven years needed at a minimum to nurture a competent analyst or case officer. The most telling statistic on CIA retention would be for the employees hired in the last five years, but I suspect that the CIA would pronounce those embarrassing statistics "classified."

The CIA needs a strong bureaucratic culture of education and learning that does not exist today. As William Nolte wryly and perceptively observes, "We also need leadership that understands the need for career development paths and that investment in career development takes time. An average military officer can easily spend, in the course of a full career, two to four years in full-time professional education and training. His or her civilian counterpart can often put a supervisor into fibrillation by suggesting enrollment in a two-week course."[43]

Sherman Kent's frustrations over the homogenization and dumbing-down of intellectual talent due to security vetting was spawned in the early 1950s. But the problem remains ever present today in the CIA's DI where there is little intellectual, professional, cultural, and ethnic diversity notwithstanding the pronouncements coming from the CIA's Office of Public Affairs. The CIA's founding in 2000 of the Sherman Kent School for Intelligence Analysis to train its intelligence analysts was probably one of the wisest and most innovative measures that the Agency undertook in the post–Cold War period.[44] Today its classrooms are filled with an onslaught of new Agency hires, but the bulk of these students are young, inexperienced – both in intellectual accomplishments as well as "street smarts" – and a culturally homogeneous lot. In short, the Kent School is probably well short of fulfilling the vision set out by its namesake half a century ago.

What is clear is that CIA managers have to foster an environment in which analysts are encouraged to have fresh ideas that challenge the conventional wisdom. Analysts also need to be freed from oppressive security requirements to have a broad and diverse array of professional contacts at home and abroad. These contacts are essential in the globalized world to gather information to compensate for huge gaps in human intelligence and to shed light on how foreign decision makers view their interests, position, power, and policy options.

Information gathered from these professional channels and relationships would help hedge against the persistent problem of mirror imaging that often lies at or near the root causes of intelligence failures. Another safeguard against the dangers of mirror imaging and of not rigorously challenging conventional wisdom is to ensure that CIA managers and analysts study the regrettably long and persistent history of CIA strategic intelligence failures, their root causes, and how former senior U.S. policy makers have assessed the CIA's contributions to national security. Intense study of such a curriculum should, at a minimum, induce a fair dose of humility to the CIA, where intellectual arrogance, especially in the managerial ranks, runs rampant.

As it stands today, analysts are ill-equipped and unempowered by CIA managers to undertake the critical task of expertly monitoring WMD proliferation. Managers force-feed a data stream from classified sources to analysts, an intellectual feeding tube that deprives them from opportunities to exploit fully the explosion in publicly available literature relevant to WMD proliferation. Analysts would do much better in monitoring WMD if they had the charge, responsibilities, and freedom to track down open-source leads and have discussions inside American and foreign scientific and WMD-related communities, much as an investigative reporter does when working for a major news organization. If CIA analysts were given freedom from oppressive management chains and excessive security concerns, they could collect an enormous amount of information via their own contacts, conversations, travels, and debriefings.

The bureaucratic reality of day-to-day life as an analyst inside the CIA, as I know all too well, is that managers insist their analysts sit in their cubicles all day long to monitor the steady stream of classified information that comes from abroad via the DO, intercepted communications, diplomatic reports, defense attaché reports, satellite imagery, and, to a lesser extent, a slice of the massive amount of media reporting. But in the information-technology age, most of the information – a less-than-scientific guess off the top of my head would be about 95 percent – is available in open and public sources, unlike during the Cold War when the CIA and the intelligence community had a near monopoly on access to information.

Today analysts are almost looking at international reality through a "soda straw" comprising the classified data stream, thus missing the lion's share of reality that is available through the explosion of open-source information. What CIA analysts need to be able to do today to be first-rate experts is to work in a manner more akin to the business practices of investigative journalists, not as minions subordinate to the Cold War–minded, isolated, and obsolete DO, where counterintelligence concerns constantly blow back on DI analysts who need greater freedom to practice their trade. Alas, the security bubble in which analysts work is simply too restrictive, if not oppressive, for such business practices. If the United States is to improve its intelligence performance against WMD, it needs to lessen substantially the defensive counterintelligence and security crouch in which it has dwelt for too long.

The CIA's managers complain that they cannot hire Ph.D.s because they have not been a good fit with the Agency's needs in the past. To be sure, many Ph.D.s in the political science field produced by major university departments would find life inside the CIA's analytic ranks difficult because their educations have trained them to be more comfortable with theory than practice. Nevertheless, if the CIA's management were to be more enlightened and to give the time and attention to newly minted Ph.D.s than it has done in the past, the Agency might be able to retain more of them and nurture them into productive intelligence analysts for the benefit of policy makers.

Maintaining a strong cadre of nationally and internationally recognized experts would not eliminate intelligence failures given the complexity of human affairs. One of the United States' most distinguished political scientists, Professor Robert Jervis, points out, for example, that the senior CIA analyst who failed to predict the Iranian revolution in 1979 "had an excellent command of the country's language, religion, culture, and politics."[45] Nevertheless, getting, nurturing, and keeping experts certainly would increase the quality of analysis and reduce, but not eliminate, the chances and frequency of analytic failings. To use a baseball analogy, more experts in the CIA's analytic ranks would bump up the Agency's batting average toward the .400 Ted Williams range but probably not beyond that, given the complexity of human and international affairs that bedevils even the wisest of scholars.

Many of the recommendations made here are not new. Robert Jervis, for example, conducted a review for the CIA on its intelligence failure in the Iranian revolution. Jervis recommended constant training of analysts, development of specialization and expertise, alternative and competing analyses, greater contact with outside experts, and an intellectual environment in which analysts could discuss and criticize each other's views, rewarding them for being first-rate analysts rather than forcing them to become second-rate managers to make career advances.[46] But since the mid-1980s, the Agency has ignored Jervis's sage calls to action and gone about doing business as usual. The CIA appears to be doing the same today in the wake of the 9/11 and Iraq WMD debacles.

In light of this track record, it might be comparatively easier for the Director of National Intelligence (DNI) to gradually dismantle the DI by shifting resources away from the CIA and moving them to new analytic organizations directly under the DNI's wing. With the right leadership, new DNI analytic units could start fresh with modern business practices to fit the challenges of this century, not the last, the period in which the DI appears to retain its focus.

7 Facing Future Strategic Intelligence Challenges

THE DEATHS OF 3,000 PEOPLE ON AMERICAN SOIL AT THE hands of a ruthless adversary along with the CIA's profound misreading of Iraq's weapons of mass destruction (WMD) capabilities are only the latest and greatest and in a long string of U.S. intelligence failures. The American public should no longer be duped by the mystique surrounding the CIA and the greater intelligence community that is propagated by Hollywood, spy novels, and the glorified memoirs of retired CIA case officers. The CIA for too long has been given a pass in the court of public opinion by whitewashing past intelligence failures with the retort that "We have more successes that cannot be shared publicly." The American public needs to ask direct, tough questions of the intelligence community and demand that the CIA's "business as bureaucracy" attitude will no longer be tolerated. This book is aimed at providing scholarly ammunition for that much-needed and much-belated debate and challenge.

United States government officials and the public in the aftermath of 9/11 have concentrated on bureaucratic, or top-down, approaches to fix intelligence in general and the CIA in particular with the creation of the director of national intelligence (DNI). Post–9/11 investigations including the Joint House–Senate Investigation, the Senate Select Committee's investigation, the 9/11 Commission, and, most recently, the Presidential Commission on Intelligence Capabilities against WMD all found profound shortcomings in human intelligence collection and the quality of

intelligence analysis. The 9/11 Commission's report in particular, however, shied away from a menu of deep, thoughtful recommendations on
how best to improve these performances from the grassroots up at the
CIA. It instead defaulted to the easier task of making superficial recommendations for changing bureaucratic wiring diagrams.

The DNI post by itself will do nothing to fix the root causes of intelligence failures that lie in the bowels of the CIA with its poor human
intelligence collection operations and shoddy intelligence analysis. These
core failings will need to be addressed not by rewiring bureaucratic diagrams but by changing the institutional culture and business practices at
the grassroots at the CIA. Would-be reformers need to retrain their sights
from extremities such as the DNI to the vital organs of human intelligence
collection and analysis.

The DNI post does not fix our strategic intelligence woes, but it is here
to stay and portends the demise of the CIA's traditional access and influence in presidential decision making. To use a baseball analogy, the establishment of the DNI essentially has pushed the CIA from the majors down
to the minor leagues. To be sure, the CIA's demotion is justified because
of its systematic and sustained human intelligence collection and analytic
failings. Nevertheless, these functions and skill sets will have to be retooled
and nurtured somewhere under the DNI's authority if the president is to
receive reliable and insightful strategic intelligence on U.S. adversaries.

The DNI and the CIA are likely in coming years to add even more
intelligence failures to this extensive list of blunders unless dramatic
efforts to fix the United States' human intelligence collection and analysis
capabilities are undertaken. As it stands today, the intelligence agencies
are bureaucratically modeled after the management layers and hierar-
chies of the blue-chip companies of old such as IBM, which failed in the
1980s, and General Motors, which is failing today. Whereas the market
weeds out noncompetitive companies that are too inflexible and sluggish
to be successful in the private sector, noncompetitive organizations are
perpetuated by inertia in the public sector.

The DNI will need to impose himself or herself on the CIA to mold it into a modern institution that is capable of efficiently operating in the globalized information-technology era. Intelligence, in its boiled-down essence, is information, and information is critical to the power of competitive businesses as well as to the power of terrorists and nation-states. The intelligence community, however, has profoundly lost its once-competitive advantage over the private sector for the collection and analysis of publicly available information.

The intelligence community's antiquated capabilities are devoted to the exploitation of clandestinely acquired information that collectively sheds only a narrow light on the broad array of national security threats. To gain greater access to the secrets that transnational organizations and nation-states seek to deny the United States as well as to exploit the explosion in public information, the community must sharpen its collection and analytic tools. The near-term outlook for the DNI and the CIA is one of uncertainty and chaos, but this unsettled situation just might open opportunities for initiative, creativity, and aggressiveness that too often has alluded the Agency. As Richard Betts insightfully notes, "The current crisis presents the opportunity to override entrenched and outdated interests, to crack heads and force the sorts of consolidation and cooperation that have been inhibited by bureaucratic constipation."[1]

The Illusion of Bureaucratic Fixes for Strategic Intelligence Problems

Well-meaning intelligence reform advocates, including members of Congress and families of 9/11 victims, mistakenly fixed their sights on measures recommended by the 9/11 Commission, most notably the creation of the DNI. The establishment of the DNI, however, unconstructively adds to the already bureaucratically bloated intelligence community. Analysts and human intelligence operators at the CIA had roughly eight layers of bureaucracy separating them from their boss, the CIA director. The DNI adds at least another couple of layers between the CIA director and the president to further separate intelligence officers and their products from their most important customer.

The DNI office, which now oversees some sixteen intelligence agencies in the intelligence community, runs the risk of evolving into another bloated component of the intelligence community. Congress had mistakenly expected the DNI office to be a lean management organization, but its staff in 2006 numbers about 1,539 people and its budget is about $1 billion per year, a steep increase from the $200 million spent annually by the Intelligence Community Management Staff, which the DNI office replaced.[2] This additional bureaucratic layering at the top in the DNI's office will likely make the CIA's strategic intelligence even more sluggish in serving the commander in chief because the intelligence community is moving even farther away from the flatter organizations in the significantly more nimble information-technology firms in the private sector.

The bureaucratic rot at the CIA alone is a long-standing problem that reaches back decades but has only more recently come to public attention with the intelligence failures of 9/11 and Iraq's lack of WMD. As far back as 1981, Robert Gates, as a senior CIA official, wrote in a memorandum to his boss, Director of Central Intelligence (DCI) William Casey, an insightful and remarkably candid assessment that is worthy of quoting at length:

> As a result of the lack of innovative and creative personnel management, I believe this Agency is chock full of people simply awaiting retirement: some are only a year or two away and some are twenty-five years away, but there are far too many playing it safe, proceeding cautiously, not antagonizing management, and certainly not broadening their horizons, especially as long as their own senior management makes it clear that it is not career enhancing. How is the health of CIA? I would say that at the present time it has a case of advanced bureaucratic arteriosclerosis: the arteries are clogging up with careerist bureaucrats who have lost the spark. It is my opinion that it is this steadily increasing proportion of intelligence *bureaucrats* that has led to the decline in the quality

of our intelligence collection and analysis over the past fifteen years – more so than our declining resources ... or Congressional investigations or legal restrictions. CIA is slowly turning into the Department of Agriculture.[3]

By Gates's assessment, the bureaucratic sclerosis began setting in at the CIA in the mid-1960s. To take Gates's medical analogy further, by the time of my resignation in 2001, the CIA patient was bedridden and on life support.

The government's proposed solution for our strategic intelligence woes was to add yet even more bureaucracy – ostensibly to "connect the dots" more effectively – among members of the intelligence community. The DNI post and his staff added several more vertical layers to the intelligence community bureaucracy, which does nothing to promote the working-level lateral sharing or pooling of intelligence. These additions to the wiring diagram are essentially irrelevant in getting the FBI to share intelligence generated by field investigations with the CIA. It would have been a much easier fix to the all-source fusion problem to have had the president simply order his attorney general and the FBI director to share intelligence on al-Qaeda and ordered the CIA director to monitor the FBI's intelligence sharing to ensure compliance of the president's order. In other words, all that was needed was a robust exercise in executive and managerial power, not more flabby and lethargic bureaucracy to dilute intelligence community accountability still further.

The government also created the National Counterterrorism Center (NCTC) under direct authority of the DNI. The NCTC combines the former Terrorist Threat Integration Center with counterterrorism elements from the CIA, FBI, and the Departments of Defense and Homeland Security.[4] Unfortunately, the NCTC undoubtedly will siphon away from the CIA's Counterterrorism Center (CTC) personnel before they have had time to season in expertise, diluting its capability to conduct terrorism analysis. The Joint House–Senate Investigation of the 9/11 attacks assessed that the CIA's CTC was staffed by too many young and inexperienced analysts to be able to do sophisticated strategic analysis of the al-Qaeda and terrorism threat.[5]

Even more damaging to all-source fusion is that the NCTC will not have direct access to the CIA's case officers. The divide will break the important synergizing effects of colocating operations officers with analysts that the CIA's CTC had nurtured for some twenty years. That divorce over the longer run will give the CIA's operational officers too much flexibility to drift off and collect human intelligence that is easiest to collect and of little consequence to U.S. national security. Analysts looking over operational officers' shoulders had a tendency in CTC to pressure CIA operational officers to go for harder human targets whose potential information would be of more interest to U.S. policy makers.

In 2005, the director of the CIA, Porter Goss, announced the establishment of the National Clandestine Service (NCS) at the CIA, taking over what has been the called the DO for most of the Agency's history. The NCS will coordinate but not direct the increasing spying and covert activities conducted by the Pentagon and FBI.[6] A critical observer, however, looks at this move as little more than a change of the DO's nameplate in the hallway of CIA headquarters. The odds are strong that notwithstanding the name change, the CIA will simply go about doing human intelligence collection as usual just as it had done in the wake of past reform efforts.

The DNI announced the Open Source Center (OSC), which is intended to "gather and analyze information from the Web, broadcasts, newspapers and other unclassified sources around the world."[7] Much as in the case of the creation of the NCS, however, creation of the OSC may be less than meets the eye. It probably reflects a name change for the former Foreign Broadcast Information Service (FBIS), not a revolution in past CIA business practices. The FBIS throughout the Cold War and post–Cold War periods was the unsung hero of U.S. intelligence. It performed yeoman's service in translating countless articles from the foreign media for the intelligence community and made much of its unclassified translations available to scholars. The former head of the CIA's bin Laden unit, Michael Scheuer, paid appropriate tribute to the FBIS by writing that

"Though intelligence-community leaders have little regard for unclassified information – it cannot be important if it is not secret, after all – the FBIS should take comfort in knowing that it provided as much warning about bin Laden's lethal intentions as any other community component."[8]

The CIA's institutional bias, however, had always been tilted toward espionage and analysis, which always pulled resources away from FBIS and the exploitation of publicly available information. FBIS operations were expensive undertakings that fell between the bureaucratic cracks and never benefited from the personal and budgetary support its mission deserved, especially not in the era of globalization in which the floodgates of information have opened. The DNI will have to keep a watchful eye to protect the new OSC from the budgetary poaching of the CIA's human intelligence operations and analysis, as well as from competing and expensive technical and clandestine collection programs such as satellites.

The DNI has yet to demonstrate real power and authority as a "unified commander" of the intelligence community. One potentially bold and constructive move to exert real DNI control and to facilitate all-source fusion would be to order a cut roughly by half the number of hierarchical bureaucratic layers inside intelligence community agencies. Major eliminations of bureaucratic rungs would make flatter and more nimble organizations across the intelligence community. Working-level analysts responsible for connecting the dots and fusing intelligence would be able to spend more time sharing and exchanging information laterally between flatter and less bureaucratically top-heavy organizations. As it stands today, these overworked and underpaid analysts spend too much of their time pushing intelligence ponderously up excessive layers of bureaucrats who rarely add anything of qualitative substance to intelligence. These layers of bureaucrats routinely retard the timely all-source fusion of intelligence, something that the intelligence community can ill afford with the quickened pace of international security and policy making in the globalized and wired world. The DNI would do well to review the manager-analyst ratios in the intelligence community, especially at the CIA, and compare them with private-sector information-technology firms to identify where support staff and managerial layers could be eliminated and compressed so that resources could be devoted to the grassroots level where most of the lion's share of intelligence collection and analysis needs to be conducted.

The globalized world puts an even greater premium on scholarship and expertise in strategic intelligence than was the case during the Cold War. During the American–Soviet rivalry, the intelligence community had a virtual monopoly on information – primarily clandestinely collected – against the principal intelligence target, the Soviet Union.[9] Since the 1990s, globalization, the information-technology revolution, and the Internet have transformed the information environment and substantially diminished the CIA's comparative advantage. The CIA no longer has a monopoly on information; today, it is one of numerous competing entities, including universities, think tanks, consulting firms, and media, shopping information wares and competing for the very limited time available for the commander in chief and his senior national security lieutenants to read and absorb.

The narrow sliver of clandestinely acquired information – whether from diplomatic, military attaché, or human intelligence sources, satellite imagery, or intercepted communications – in its raw intelligence form is now directly and readily available to policy makers on their desktop computers, who, unlike during the Cold War, can try to process, synthesize, and analyze the material for themselves.[10] Of course, they are more readily able than intelligence analysts to discern what raw intelligence reporting is most directly relevant to their policy interests and responsibilities. These factors have eroded the CIA's once-dominant advantage in intelligence. The CIA has yet to develop and tap sophisticated expertise that can be leveraged against strategic intelligence problems that policy makers still do not have the time and expertise to tackle and to provide unique services to the policy world.

A significant omission in the DNI's reforms is the creation of an intelligence community strategic studies center. The presidential commission on weapons proliferation smartly recommended the creation of "at least one not-for-profit 'sponsored research institute' to serve as a critical window into outside expertise for the Intelligence Community" and that its "primary purpose would be to focus on strategic issues."[11] Such a center would be separated from the taxing burden of current intelligence production, have more expertise, and be better positioned than the CIA's rank-and-file to fuse the information flows from public and clandestine sources to form strategic intelligence assessments.

American statecraft needs first-rate analysts and scholars to make sense of the contemporary deluge of publicly available information. Measures have to be taken under the DNI's direction to ensure that analysts will be rewarded for the time and study required to be nationally or internationally recognized experts. The CIA's management needs to protect its experts from the often trivial and parochial concerns that are obstacles to their recruitment and retention. The Agency should be compelled to have a freer flow of experts to and from academe and the think-tank world to keep Directorate of Intelligence (DI) analysis fresh and competitive. As a task force of the Council on Foreign Relations years ago recommended, to no avail, "A greater flow of talented people into the agency from academia and business is essential. Greater provision ought to be made for lateral and mid-career entry as well as for short-term entry."[12]

Mid- and senior-level hires of experts could bolster the DI's analysis and immediately infuse the organization with a respect, appreciation, and dedication to the demands of research and analysis. Middle East terrorism expert and former CIA analyst Daniel Byman has quipped that he could join the CIA at the bottom as a junior analyst or at the very top as the head of the analysis directorate, but nowhere in between, a true characterization that shows how poorly the CIA taps the intellectual capital that lies in the United States.[13] Such an infusion of intellectual talent would move the DI away from the bulk of its shallow current intelligence work toward a professional atmosphere that rewards analysts for creating cutting-edge research and strategic warning for policy makers.

The DNI would be wise to nurture a stable of experts under his or her own authority divorced from the CIA. The National Intelligence Council

(NIC) – which has been pulled out from underneath the director of CIA and put under the DNI's wing – would be a natural fit for this recommendation. The presidential commission on WMD came to the same conclusion: "Analysts cannot maintain their expertise if they cannot conduct long-term and strategic analysis. Because this malady is so pervasive and has proven so resistant to conventional solutions, we recommend establishing an organization to perform only long-term and strategic analysis under the National Intelligence Council, the Community's existing focal point for interagency long-term analytic efforts."[14]

A revamped NIC could be a pool of expertise drawn from inside and outside government with its principal mission of crafting long-term strategic assessments for senior policy makers. As a distinguished group of scholar-practitioners wisely recommended years ago, "the NIC could better enable its insiders to share ideas and learn from the best minds outside government – in academia, think tanks, business, and importantly in today's world, non-governmental organizations."[15] A reenergized NIC could build on its past legacy of drawing first-rate minds from academe, starting with the founder Sherman Kent from Yale and more recently Joseph Nye and Gregory Treverton from Harvard and Robert Hutchings from Princeton.

Under the DNI's tutelage, the NIC would be able to perform the strategic intelligence fusion function, but its manpower and resources would have to be significantly expanded. The NIC has long been too sparsely manned and funded to perform more than a modest role of serving as a focal point for coordinating intelligence community assessments, the National Intelligence Estimates (NIEs). The NIC traditionally lacked the analytic bench strength to write its own NIEs or write strategic intelligence analyses to challenge critically the analyses bubbling up from the separate intelligence agencies, the most active of which are the CIA, the Defense Intelligence Agency, and the State Department's Bureau of Intelligence and Research. As seasoned intelligence officers have commented, "NIEs rarely represent new analysis or bring to bear more expertise than already exists in analytic offices; indeed, drafters of

NIEs are usually the same analysts from whose work the NIE is drawn. Little independent knowledge or informed outside opinion is incorporated in estimative products."[16]

The NIC also would have to shun its now-increased role in writing and delivering the Presidential Daily Brief (PDB), which undoubtedly forces the NIC to be focused on current intelligence to the detriment of strategic, long-term intelligence analysis. The DNI has taken over the PDB responsibility from the CIA because the Agency squandered its privileged access to the president and his key national security lieutenants through the massive intelligence failures discussed in previous chapters. The CIA is no longer the sole contributor to writing the PDB.[17] The head of the NIC argues that he has established a "Long Range Analysis" unit as recommended by the WMD Commission that is "walled off from current intelligence demand."[18] Those walls, however, are probably paper thin. Even though the DNI's office is growing, it still probably does not have intellectual resources to spare from the huge demands of current intelligence, especially as the DNI works to establish his influence with the president and in the intelligence community.

The bolstering of the NIC's staff could improve its sometimes-lackluster strategic assessments. As former director of the National Security Agency and former senior official on the National Security Council Lieutenant General William Odom rightly judged of NIEs, "The utility of such products for policymaking is not great, and they have become the focus of a lot of criticism and dispute, especially within congressional oversight committees."[19] This observation is all the more relevant in light of the justified controversy surrounding the 2002 NIE on Iraq's WMD program. Despite the shortcomings and questionable relevancy to policy makers of many NIEs, Odom wisely points out that "The estimate process has the healthy effect of making analysts communicate and share evidence. If the NIEs performed no other service, they would still be entirely worth the effort."[20]

A rejuvenated and more muscular NIC would also be better placed and more competent to carry out devil's advocate analysis on critically

important strategic intelligence problems than personnel inside the bowels of the CIA, where contrarian analysis would likely be strangled to
death. Richard Betts wisely recommends the ad hoc use of "real devils"
that have real substantive objections to "common wisdom" analysis on
critical strategic intelligence problems. He advises, "This selective or
biased form of multiple advocacy may be achieved by periodically giving a platform within the intelligence process to minority views that
can be argued more persuasively by prestigious analysts outside the
bureaucracy."[21]

A bolstered and intellectually heavyweight NIC would give the intelligence community the expertise that it has not had for far too long. The idea
that a bolstered NIC would have the intellectual horsepower to produce
strategic intelligence for the commander in chief appears to be behind
former senior national security official Richard Clarke's criticisms of the
quality of CIA analysis: "The list of important analytical failures by the
CIA is now too long for us to conclude that the current system is acceptable. It is time now to do what so many veteran observers of the intelligence community have recommended: remove the intelligence analysis
function from CIA and establish a small independent bureau with a staff
of career professionals and outside experts."[22] The idea of getting the
CIA out of the analysis business all together is probably a bridge too far,
however. The CIA will still be needed to produce the gush of daily intelligence reporting. The idea of a new and revamped NIC with substantially
more clout and a federally funded research center are good ideas that
have been bantered about for sometime,[23] however, and the 9/11 and
Iraq WMD fiascos should give enough political impetus to make these
wise proposals a reality.

The strengthening of the NIC and the addition of a real, independent strategic intelligence shop would go a long way to redress the running subtext of the CIA's poor strategic intelligence due to the problem
of "mirror imaging." Richards Heuer defines mirror imaging as "filling
gaps in the analyst's own knowledge by assuming that the other side is
likely to act in a certain way because that is how the US would act under

similar circumstances.... But mirror-imaging leads to dangerous assumptions, because people in other cultures *do not* think the way we do."[24] Michael Handel elaborates on the mirror-imaging problem by explaining that "perceptual errors are the result of either projecting one's own culture, ideological beliefs, military doctrine, and expectations on the adversary" or of "wishful thinking, that is, molding the facts to conform to one's hopes."[25]

The problem of mirror imaging comes up time and time again in the history of U.S. strategic intelligence failures. Many attribute the blame for the failure on analysis. Equally culpable, however, are the failures in intelligence collection, especially from human sources. As I have discussed in this book, analysts are often forced to resort to mirror imaging – usually implicitly rather than explicitly – because the CIA's Directorate of Operations had failed in its core mission to steal the secrets needed to illuminate the thinking and policy deliberations of U.S. adversaries.

Balancing Civil-Military Relations in Strategic Intelligence

An important reason for establishing the DNI was to infuse a greater degree of civilian influence into the intelligence community. As it stands today, the majority of agencies and organizations are funded and operationally controlled by the military. The DNI should be leveraged as an important institutional tool for ensuring that civilian policy makers maintain control over the military, which has slipped with the loss of civilian influence in strategic intelligence assessments. John Deutch's tour as DCI led to the erosion of the CIA as an independent civilian intelligence agency. As Loch Johnson observed, "'Support for Military Operations!' and 'Tactical Intelligence for the Warfighter!' became the battle cries of the new Deutch team."[26] The trend was set in motion for "the demise of the CIA's traditional responsibility: providing the president with global intelligence on military, political, and economic matters that could prevent the outbreak of war."[27] As Gregory Treverton astutely comments, "If, on the civilian side of intelligence, irrelevance is more of a problem than politicization, on the military side a form of politicization seems more of a problem."[28]

The military gained a huge edge over civilians in strategic intelligence assessments in particular with its monopoly on satellite imagery collection and analysis. The 1996 creation of the National Imagery and Mapping Agency, specifically assigned the responsibilities of a "combat support agency" – subsequently renamed the National Geospatial Intelligence Agency – essentially ripped out from underneath the CIA an autonomous and expert imagery-analysis shop manned by civilians. As Jeffrey Richelson rightly recommends, "Action should be taken to restore an independent imagery interpretation capability to the CIA, by the establishment either of the National Photographic Interpretation Center or the Office of Imagery Analysis that had existed within the Directorate of Intelligence. Although it does not automatically follow that the failure to provide tactical warning of the Indian nuclear detonations of May 1998 resulted from the elimination of an independent CIA capability – it does highlight the importance of *national* intelligence as well as the need for a key element in the production of that intelligence to be placed in an agency outside of the Department of Defense, in an agency for whom support to military operations is not the key mission."[29]

But the commander in chief's loss of independent civilian analytic checks on military intelligence analysis began even earlier. The CIA's loss of responsibility for conducting battle damage assessments as a result of disputes with the military during the 1990–1 Gulf War stripped the opportunity for civilian policy makers to have another set of eyes, divorced from the military's vested interests in operational success, to analyze satellite imagery. Although the muzzling of the CIA's independent voice on this score may have reduced the potential areas of analytic dispute in the intelligence community, the move has not led to a sharpening of the military's ability to conduct objective intelligence analysis, as is evident from the military's wildly inaccurate battle damage assessments during the 1999 Kosovo War.

The long history of differing analytic assessments between the CIA and the military intelligence services over strategic assessments

underscores the validity and continuing relevance of one critical rationale for the CIA's inception. The DNI needs to continue to strengthen
this role of providing independent and objective assessments, particularly on political-military strategic issues, to national-level policy makers,
the most important of whom are the president and his closest national
security advisers. The DNI's bureaucratic autonomy from the Pentagon
increases – but by no means guarantees – the prospects for the president
to receive intelligence assessments that are removed from vested military
service and operational interests. The military, notwithstanding the best
of intentions, will likely remain influenced by operational concerns that
will taint its intelligence analysis.

More steps to bolster the civilian influence of the intelligence community are in order to "keep the military honest." The staff of the DNI
needs to be dominated by civilian personnel and not filled to the gills
with military officers serving in rotations as is too often the case in a wide
array of positions in the entire national security bureaucracy. Strategic
intelligence that is collected and analyzed by civilians for the commander in chief would best insulate assessments from military operational
prerogatives and help the commander in chief exercise civilian direction
over military operations to achieve political national interests. Allowing
CIA Director Michael Hayden to remain an active-duty U.S. Air Force
four-star general was a move in the wrong direction on this score. Civilians will not always be right in analyzing strategic intelligence problems,
as the past performances in the Cold War, post–Cold War, and 9/11 histo-
ries show, but at least they will stand a better chance of crafting strategic
intelligence that does not unduly reflect the operational prerogatives of
the military as happened during the Vietnam War, the 1990–1 Gulf War,
and the 1999 Kosovo War, which went largely unnoticed by the American
public.

A Symbiotic Relationship: Intelligence Officers and Policy Makers

The fusing of information in the intelligence community is the process
by which finished intelligence is produced. But the production of finished

intelligence analysis is not an end in and of itself. That analysis has to be shared with U.S. policy makers. The relations between all-source intelligence analysts – especially those at the CIA – and U.S. policy makers are complicated. How these relationships govern both the provision of intelligence to policy makers and the role that policy makers play in setting intelligence agency collection and analysis agendas has been a perpetually running debate among intelligence professionals since the inception of the modern American intelligence community in 1947.

A large and unsettled question is whether the DNI will have the stature and strength needed to deliver bad news to the White House. Some observers argue that the DNI will be too close to the White House and too beholden to the president to "speak truth to power" as a voice independent from policy considerations, as a long line of directors of central intelligence by and large had been. The concern cuts directly into the problem of intelligence officers delivering intelligence that conforms to policy expectations, or politicization for short.

How to avoid the pitfalls of politicization is a bone of contention between two competing schools of intelligence on what constitutes the healthiest intelligence-policy relationship. As Richard Betts explains the "Kent" and "Gates" schools of thought, "Kent warned against the danger of letting intelligence personnel get too close to policymaking circles, least their objectivity and integrity be compromised by involvement."[30] Kent wanted intelligence analysts to keep an arm's length from policy makers lest their analyses become tainted by policy interests. In contrast, the Gates model "arose from critiques of ineffective intelligence contributions to policymaking, and the view that utility is the *sine qua non*. To be useful, intelligence analysis must engage policymakers' concerns. Policymakers who utilize analysis need studies that relate to the objectives they are trying to achieve. Thus analysis must be sensitive to the policy context, and the range of options available, to be of any use in making policy."[31] Gates judged that such an awareness of policy was essential for producing timely and relevant intelligence analyses to inform policy decisions.

The debate on the nature of the relationship between intelligence officials and policy makers in the post–9/11 environment has taken on a new intensity. Some observers charge that policy officials unduly influenced intelligence assessments to reflect policy, especially on Iraq's WMD programs and alleged links to al-Qaeda in the run-up to the Iraq War. Others counter that policy makers did not tell intelligence communities what their assessments were to be as much as they completely ignored intelligence assessments in making the decision to wage war against Iraq. Most notably, Paul Pillar, former national intelligence officer for the Middle East, assesses, "What is most remarkable about prewar U.S. intelligence on Iraq is not that it got things wrong and thereby misled policymakers; it is that it played so small a role in one of the most important U.S. policy decisions in recent decades."[32]

The largest downside of the Kent school philosophy is irrelevance, which may well be a greater pitfall than the risks of political subservience run by the Gates school advocates. At the risk of stating the obvious, the intelligence community does not exist as an end in itself but as a collection of institutions purposefully designed to serve national interests as articulated by policy makers supported by the American public. A strict adherence to the Kent school runs too great a risk of perpetuating an intelligence community and a CIA that sees its own internal processes as justifying its existence rather than intelligence products that are relevant to the interests of policy makers trying to advance national political interests. On balance, the ideal intelligence-policy relationship is a pendulum swing toward the Gates school and away from the Kent school. But, at the end of the day, the ability of the DNI to give the president bad news ultimately will depend on the personal integrity and courage of the individual that occupies the DNI's chair, not the bureaucratic wiring diagram.

Scanning the Horizon for Future Threats

The intelligence community needs to be on the lookout for strategic surprises that lie over the horizon. The strong and natural tendency to throw resources almost exclusively at the terrorism and al-Qaeda challenge will have to be resisted. Al-Qaeda is indeed a serious threat, but it is not the only threat that the United States will likely face in the next generation. Wars and crises involving armed forces, more often than not, come as a surprise, and the intelligence community must do a better job of warning policy makers of their coming.

In many respects, the intelligence community runs the risk of fighting in the rearview mirror by devoting too many resources against al-Qaeda to the potential detriment of guarding against other potential sources of strategic surprise. The presidential commission on WMD, for example, prudently warned that "The loose nukes problem is in many ways indicative of problems facing the Intelligence Community as a whole. Analysts and collectors are too consumed with daily intelligence requirements to formulate or implement new approaches. The war on terrorism and ongoing military operations has distracted the Community from longer-term threats of critical importance to national security. The perception is that there is no 'crisis' until a weapon or fissile material is stolen."[33]

Other sources of strategic surprise are likely to stem from nation-states, especially Russia, China, Pakistan, Iran, and Saudi Arabia. In each of these countries, which are either armed with nuclear weapons now or might soon be, the CIA and intelligence community – much like the case in the run-up to the Iranian revolution – is overly dependent on liaison service relationships and too risk adverse in going after unilateral human intelligence and defectors from these countries. As the President's Commission on WMD rightly warns, "Across the board, the Intelligence Community knows disturbingly little about the nuclear programs of many of the world's most dangerous actors. In some cases, it knows less now than it did five or ten years ago."[34] Human intelligence collection and analytic assets need to be focused on areas prone for geopolitical convulsions that would threaten vital and major U.S. strategic interests.

The critical importance of intelligence to U.S. statecraft has come to the fore as the nation grapples with its new, uncertain, and risky security environment. An American consensus has emerged over the concern that nation-states and transnational terrorist groups could use WMD – chemical, biological, radiological, and nuclear weapons – to strike U.S. territory, citizens, and interests. More controversially, President George W. Bush has ardently argued that given the potential death and destruction that WMD attacks could wreak on the United States, the commander in chief can no longer afford the risk of waiting and absorbing the first blow from a WMD-armed adversary. Accordingly, President Bush articulated in his National Security Strategy a policy of preemptive and preventive strikes to protect U.S. national interests.[35]

The articulation of a policy of preemptive and preventive strikes generates considerable partisan debate in Washington. Democratic critics charge that Bush's policy threatens to destabilize the international system by giving international legitimacy as well as incentive to all nation-states for waging preemptive and preventive war. What these critics forget or conveniently overlook, though, is that Democratic President Bill Clinton launched cruise missile strikes against al-Qaeda–related targets in Afghanistan and Sudan in 1998 in part to preempt al-Qaeda's suspected planning for chemical weapons attacks against the United States.[36] The Clinton administration, moreover, contemplated preventive strikes against North Korea's nuclear weapons program, but lacked specific intelligence needed for military targeting of Pyongyang's nuclear weapons infrastructure.[37] Partisan politics aside, the stubborn reality is that future U.S. presidents, whether Republican or Democrat, are likely to need viable policy options for militarily striking adversaries preemptively or preventively even if they are armed with WMD.

Intelligence will be a load-bearing pillar of U.S. policy against WMD-armed adversaries. Without high-quality and timely intelligence reports and analysis, the policy of preemptive or preventive military action will simply not be feasible. Much ink has been spilt on the pros and cons of preemptive and preventive military action in the counter-proliferation campaign, but without timely and accurate intelligence, the debate becomes academic. If the United States does not have sufficient intelligence to know the "what, when, where, and how" to attack an adversary's WMD capabilities – including WMD weapon stocks, production facilities, and delivery systems – U.S. precision munitions will stand idle because neither preemptive nor preventive military options will be viable for the commander in chief to order. Although much debate, research, and thought has gone into the transformation of the U.S. military to meet the challenges posed by new security threats, no comparable effort has been made to examine how intelligence collection and analysis needs to keep pace with threats to enable military options for the president in the information-technology era.

U.S. national security today has a narrower margin for error because of the technological advances that allow nation-states as well as nonstate actors such a terrorist groups to project force farther and WMD that allow them to strike with more devastating effects. In this environment, the United States needs to rectify the substantial shortcomings in human intelligence collection operations if it is to deal successfully with issues of war and peace in the future. The CIA or some other entity under the DNI must make qualitative improvements in its human intelligence operations to increase the odds that U.S. policy makers and military commanders will have access to the thoughts and intentions of our adversaries. Even if the intentions of U.S. adversaries prove elusive and remain hidden, a critical task for human intelligence is to illuminate the policy pressures at play on foreign leaders and to help analysts narrow the range of ambiguity for U.S. policy makers.

A Solid Footing to Face Future Challenges

Defenders of the CIA's performance argue that no matter how diligent, intelligent, and creative the CIA may be, intelligence failures are inevitable. There is a grain of truth in this defense in that, as is the case in all human affairs, complexity rules supreme, and human beings are incapable of perfect and routine clairvoyance. Nevertheless, the argument too easily becomes a way to escape responsibility of the CIA's dismal strategic intelligence performances and too readily provides cover for dodging tough decisions needed to undertake major, not cosmetic, reforms. The Senate Select Committee on Intelligence rightly diagnosed the root cause of the CIA's failure on Iraq as "a broken corporate culture and poor management," which "will not be solved by additional funding and personnel."[38] John McLaughlin, then the acting DCI, asked at a press conference defending the Agency's performance, "How do you measure, how do you balance a hundred successes against one failure?" McLaughlin's defense is hardly a credible one in light of the CIA's failures in 9/11 and Iraq, arguably the gravest intelligence debacles in the Agency's sixty-year history, coming in a short span of about two years. These intelligence failures show the American public that the CIA is broken, no matter how deep into denial the Agency's senior management sinks. Reforms cannot be postponed until after the United States destroys al-Qaeda and stabilizes the security environments in Afghanistan and Iraq.

The chalice has been thrown down, and the DNI and the CIA director will have to move boldly to redress profound intelligence collection and analysis shortcomings if they are to give the commander in chief the high-quality intelligence he needs to inform policy in an international security environment littered with nation-states armed with WMD and Islamic extremists seeking to lay their hands on them. The last thing the United States needs is for the series of post–9/11 investigations and the creation of the DNI to, as Shakespeare might have put it, be "full of sound and fury, signifying nothing." The DNI and CIA director will have to move decisively against the bureaucracies that have produced a dismal showing against WMD threats for the past couple of decades. Unless the DNI is willing to take on the vested status quo interests, especially in the CIA, the intelligence community will add yet another victory to what the president's WMD commission aptly called its *almost perfect record of resisting external recommendations.*[39]

Notes

1. STRATEGIC INTELLIGENCE AND AMERICAN STATECRAFT

1. The intelligence community's budget is classified, but a senior official in the director of national intelligence's office publicly disclosed the $44 billion figure. See Scott Shane, "Official Reveals Budget for U.S. Intelligence," *New York Times*, 8 November 2005.
2. Scott Shane, "Official Reveals Budget for U.S. Intelligence."
3. Mark Mazzetti, "Spymaster Tells Secret of Size of Spy Force," *New York Times*, 21 April 2006.
4. Bob Woodward, *Plan of Attack* (New York: Simon & Schuster, 2004), 68.
5. National Commission on Terrorist Attacks upon the United States, *The 9/11 Commission Report* (Washington, DC: Government Printing Office, July 2004), 411. Available at http://www.9–11commission.gov/report/index.htm.
6. Richard A. Posner, *Preventing Surprise Attacks: Intelligence Reform in the Wake of 9/11* (New York: Rowman & Littlefield, 2005), 6.
7. Daniel Yankelovich, "Poll Positions: What Americans Really Think about U.S. Foreign Policy," *Foreign Affairs* 84, no. 5 (September/October 2005), 13.
8. One notable exception is Robert M. Gates, "An Opportunity Unfulfilled: The Use and Perceptions of Intelligence at the White House," *Washington Quarterly* 12, no. 1 (winter 1989).
9. John Keegan, *Intelligence in War: Knowledge of the Enemy from Napoleon to Al-Qaeda* (New York: Alfred A. Knopf, 2003), 7.
10. *The New American Bible*, Saint Joseph Edition (New York: Catholic Book, 1992), 169 and 213.
11. Sherman Kent, *Strategic Intelligence for American World Policy* (Princeton, NJ: Princeton University Press, 1951), vii.
12. Adda B. Bozeman, *Strategic Intelligence & Statecraft: Selected Essays* (Washington, DC: Brassey's, 1992), 2.

13. Michael Herman, *Intelligence Power in Peace and War* (Cambridge: Cambridge University Press, 1996), 3.

14. Loch K. Johnson and James J. Wirtz (eds.), *Strategic Intelligence: Windows into a Secret World* (Los Angeles, CA: Roxbury, 2004), 2.

15. Bruce D. Berkowitz and Allan E. Goodman, *Strategic Intelligence for American National Security* (Princeton, NJ: Princeton University Press, 1989), 4.

16. This definition of strategic intelligence owes an intellectual debt to a traditional conceptualization of security studies as the study of "the threat, use, and management of military force, and closely related topics." The author is grateful on this score to Richard Shultz, Roy Godson, and Ted Greenwood (eds.), *Security Studies for the 1990s* (New York: Brassey's, 1993), 2–3.

17. Loch K. Johnson, *Secret Intelligence Agencies: U.S. Intelligence in a Hostile World* (New Haven: Yale University Press, 1996), 2.

18. Gregory Treverton and Joseph Nye have probably been the most prominent scholar-practitioners to make the distinction between *secrets* and *mysteries*. See Treverton, *Reshaping National Intelligence for an Age of Information* (Cambridge: Cambridge University Press, 2003), 11, and Joseph S. Nye, Jr., "Peering into the Future," *Foreign Affairs* 77, no. 4 (July/August 1994).

19. Berkowitz and Goodman, *Strategic Intelligence for American National Security*, 88.

20. Berkowitz and Goodman, *Strategic Intelligence for American National Security*, 103.

21. Carnes Lord, *The Modern Prince: What Leaders Need to Know Now* (New Haven: Yale University Press, 2003), 23.

22. Lord, *The Modern Prince*, 24.

23. Richard K. Betts, "Should Strategic Studies Survive?," *World Politics* 50, no. 1 (October 1997), 7–8.

24. Maurice R. Greenberg and Richard N. Haass (eds.), *Making Intelligence Smarter: The Future of U.S. Intelligence*, Report of an Independent Task Force (New York: Council on Foreign Relations, 1996), 13.

25. For drawing the distinction between covert action and special activities, I am indebted to William J. Daugherty, *Executive Secrets: Covert Action and the Presidency* (Lexington: University Press of Kentucky, 2004), 12–16. For a broader discussion of covert action, see Roy Godson, *Dirty Tricks or Trump Cards: U.S. Covert Action and Counterintelligence* (Washington, DC: Brassey's, 1995). For an examination of the history of covert actions reaching back to the American Founding Fathers, see Stephen F. Knott, *Secret and Sanctioned: Covert Operations and the American Presidency* (New York: Oxford University Press, 1996). And for an insightful treatment of the CIA's role in paramilitary operations during the Vietnam War, see Richard H. Shultz, Jr., *The Secret War against*

Hanoi: Kennedy's and Johnson's Use of Spies, Saboteurs, and Covert Warriors in North Vietnam (New York: HarperCollins, 1999).

26. Dana Priest, "Covert CIA Program Withstands New Furor," *Washington Post*, 30 December 2005.

27. For examinations of the CIA's important role in the 2001 Afghanistan War, see Bob Woodward, *Bush at War* (New York: Simon & Schuster, 2002); Steve Coll, *Ghost Wars: The Secret History of the CIA, Afghanistan, and bin Laden, from the Soviet Invasion to September 10, 2001* (New York: Penguin Press, 2004); George Crile, *Charlie Wilson's War: The Extraordinary Story of How the Wildest Man in Congress and a Rogue CIA Agent Changed the History of Our Times* (New York: Grove Press, 2003); Gary C. Schroen, *First In: An Insider's Account of How the CIA Spearheaded the War on Terror in Afghanistan* (New York: Presidio Press, 2005); and Gary Berntsen and Ralph Pezzullo, *Jawbreaker, The Attack on bin Laden and al-Qaeda: A Personal Account by the CIA's Key Field Commander* (New York: Crown, 2005).

28. Ray S. Cline, *Secrets, Spies, and Scholars: Blueprint of the Essential CIA* (Washington, DC: Acropolis Books, 1976), 226.

29. For an account of the Iran covert action program, see Rhodri Jeffreys-Jones, *The CIA and American Democracy* (New Haven: Yale University Press, 1989), 89–90.

30. John Lewis Gaddis, *The Cold War: A New History* (New York: The Penguin Press, 2005), 166.

31. See Coll, *Ghost Wars*.

32. Efraim Halevy, *Man in the Shadows: Inside the Middle East Crisis with a Man Who Led the Mossad* (New York: St. Martin's Press, 2006), 210.

33. For a concise history of congressional oversight of the CIA and covert action, see Loch K. Johnson, "Presidents, Lawmakers, and Spies: Intelligence Accountability in the United States," *Presidential Studies Quarterly* 34, no. 4 (December 2004), 828–37.

34. Shaun Waterman, "Goss Says CIA Ban Excludes Terrorists," *Washington Times*, 25 March 2005, A5.

35. Josh Meyer, "CIA Expands Use of Drones in Terror War," *Los Angeles Times*, 29 January 2006, A1.

36. *The 9/11 Commission Report*, 113.

37. Stephen Grey and Don Van Natta, "In Italy, Anger at U.S. Tactics Colors Spy Case," *New York Times*, 26 June 2005, A1.

38. For informative treatments of the CIA's covert activity and ethical dilemmas with maintaining prison facilities for rendition individuals, see Dana Priest, "CIA Holds Terror Suspects in Secret Prisons," *Washington Post*, 2 November 2005, and Dana Priest, "Covert CIA Program Withstands New Furor," *Washington Post*, 30 December 2005.

39. James Risen, *State of War: The Secret History of the CIA and the Bush Administration* (New York: Free Press, 2006), 32–3.
40. Risen, *State of War*, 33.
41. Douglas Jehl, "Qaeda-Iraq Link U.S. Cited Is Tied to Coercion Claim," *New York Times*, 9 December 2005, A1.
42. Robert M. Gates, "The CIA and Foreign Policy," *Foreign Affairs* 66, no. 2 (winter 1987/88), 216.
43. For the landmark study of the Pearl Harbor intelligence failure, see Roberta Wohlstetter, *Pearl Harbor: Warning and Decision* (Stanford, CA: Stanford University Press, 1962). Also see David Kahn, "The Intelligence Failure of Pearl Harbor," *Foreign Affairs* 70, no. 5 (winter 1991/92).
44. Gates, "The CIA and Foreign Policy," 225.
45. L. Britt Snider, *Sharing Secrets with Lawmakers: Congress as a User of Intelligence* (Washington, DC: Center for the Study of Intelligence, Central Intelligence Agency, February 1997), 24–5.
46. Treverton, *Reshaping National Intelligence for an Age of Information*, 2.
47. Herman, *Intelligence Power in Peace and War*, 143.
48. Herman, *Intelligence Power in Peace and War*, 144.
49. George Bush and Brent Scowcroft, *A World Transformed* (New York: Vintage Books, 1998), 30.
50. Robert M. Gates, *From the Shadows: The Ultimate Insider's Story of Five Presidents and How They Won the Cold War* (New York: Touchstone, 1997), 30.
51. John L. Helgerson, *Getting to Know the President: CIA Briefings of Presidential Candidates, 1952–1992* (Washington, DC: Center for the Study of Intelligence, Central Intelligence Agency, n.d.), 1.
52. James Bamford, *A Pretext for War: 9/11, Iraq, and the Abuse of America's Intelligence Agencies* (New York: Doubleday, 2004), 118.
53. See Richard K. Betts, "Analysis, War, and Decision: Why Intelligence Failures Are Inevitable," *World Politics* 31, no. 1 (October 1978).
54. Eliot A. Cohen and John Gooch, *Military Misfortunes: The Anatomy of Failure in War* (New York: Vintage Books, 1991), 26–7.
55. Bamford, *A Pretext for War: 9/11, Iraq, and the Abuse of America's Intelligence Agencies*, 117.
56. Treverton, *Reshaping National Intelligence for an Age of Information*, xiii–xiv.
57. John Diamond and Judy Keen, "Bush's Daily Intel Briefing Revamped," *USA Today*, 25 August 2005, A1.
58. Gates, "An Opportunity Unfulfilled," 35.
59. See Senate Select Committee on Intelligence, *Report on the U.S. Intelligence Community's Prewar Intelligence Assessments on Iraq* (Washington, DC:

NOTES TO PAGES 22–35

175

Government Printing Office, 7 July 2004). Available at http://www.gpoaccess.gov/ serialset/creports/iraq.html.

60. See Commission on the Intelligence Capabilities of the United States Regarding Weapons of Mass Destruction, *Report to the President* (Washington, DC: United States Government, 31 March 2005). Available at http://www.wmd.gov/report.

2. DEBUNKING COLD WAR MYTHS

1. Ernest R. May, "The Twenty-First Century Challenge for U.S. Intelligence," in Jennifer E. Sims and Burton Gerber (eds.), *Transforming U.S. Intelligence* (Washington, DC: Georgetown University Press, 2005), chap. 1, p. 3.

2. John Ranelagh, *The Agency: The Rise and Decline of the CIA* (New York: Simon and Schuster, 1986), 186.

3. Eliot Cohen, "'Only Half the Battle': American Intelligence and the Chinese Intervention in Korea, 1950," *Intelligence and National Security* 5, no. 1 (January 1990), 138. Cohen cites a CIA memorandum, "Threat of Full Chinese Communist Intervention in Korea," 12 October 1950 in U.S. Department of State, *Foreign Relations of the United States, 1950*, vol. 8 (Washington, DC: Government Printing Office, 1976), 933–4.

4. Harold P. Ford, *Estimative Intelligence: The Purposes and Problems of National Intelligence Estimating*, rev. ed. (Lanham, MD: University Press of America, 1993), 68.

5. National Intelligence Estimate, *Iraq's Continuing Programs for Weapons of Mass Destruction* (Washington, DC: National Intelligence Council, October 2002). Available at http://www.fas.org/irp/cia/product/iraq-wmd.html.

6. James G. Blight and David A. Welch, "What Can Intelligence Tell Us about the Cuban Missile Crisis, and What Can the Cuban Missile Crisis Tell Us about Intelligence?" *Intelligence and National Security* 13, no. 3 (autumn 1998), 5.

7. Klaus Knorr, "Failures in National Intelligence Estimates: The Case of the Cuban Missile Crisis," *World Politics* 16, 3 (fall 1964), 461.

8. Richard Helms with William Hood, *A Look over My Shoulder: A Life in the Central Intelligence Agency* (New York: Random House, 2003), 217.

9. John Lewis Gaddis, *We Now Know: Rethinking Cold War History* (New York: Oxford University Press, 1997), 276.

10. See Harold P. Ford, *CIA and Vietnam Policy Makers: Three Episodes, 1962–1968* (Washington, DC: Center for the Study of Intelligence, 1998).

11. Quoted in Ranelagh, *The Agency*, 420.

12. James J. Wirtz, "Intelligence to Please? The Order of Battle Controversy during the Vietnam War," in Loch K. Johnson and James J. Wirtz (eds.), *Strategic Intelligence: Windows into a Secret World* (Los Angeles, CA: Roxbury, 2004), chap. 15, 186.

13. James J. Wirtz, *The Tet Offensive: Intelligence Failure in War* (Ithaca: Cornell University Press, 1991), 3.

14. Wirtz, "Intelligence to Please?," 189.

15. Ibid.," 186.

16. For insightful treatments of the CIA's role in supporting strategic forces negotiations with the Soviets during the Cold War, see Strobe Talbott, *Endgame: The Inside Story of SALT II* (New York: Harper & Row, 1980); and William C. Potter (ed.), *Verification and SALT: The Challenge of Strategic Deception* (Boulder, CO: Westview Press, 1980).

17. Raymond L. Garthoff, "Estimating Soviet Military Intentions and Capabilities," in Gerald K. Haines and Robert E. Leggett (eds.), *Watching the Bear: Essays on CIA's Analysis of the Soviet Union* (Washington, DC: Center for the Study of Intelligence, 2003), chap. V, 33. Available at www.odci.gov/csi/books/watching thebear/article05.html.

18. Ranelagh, *The Agency*, 173.

19. Ibid., 322–3.

20. Rhodri Jeffreys-Jones, *The CIA and American Democracy* (New Haven: Yale University Press, 1989), 114.

21. For discussions of the Cold War controversies on estimates of Soviet bombers and ballistic missiles, see John Prados, *The Soviet Estimate: U.S. Intelligence Analysis and Soviet Strategic Forces* (Princeton: Princeton University Press, 1986), 43–50 and 114–20.

22. Lawrence Freedman, "The CIA and the Soviet Threat: The Politicization of Estimates, 1966–1977," *Intelligence and National Security* 12, no. 1 (January 1997), 138.

23. Judith Miller, Stephen Engelberg, and William Broad, *Germs: Biological Weapons and America's Secret War* (New York: Touchstone, 2002), 94–6 and 136–7.

24. Ibid., 167–8.

25. James Bamford, *Body of Secrets: Anatomy of the Ultra-Secret National Security Agency* (New York: Doubleday, 2001), 40–1.

26. David S. Robarge, "Getting It Right: CIA Analysis of the 1967 Arab-Israeli War," *Studies in Intelligence* 49, no. 1 (2005), 1.

27. Henry Kissinger, *Years of Upheaval* (Boston: Little, Brown, 1982), 464–5.

28. Robert M. Gates, *From the Shadows: The Ultimate Insider's Story of Five Presidents and How They Won the Cold War* (New York: Touchstone, 1997), 40–1.

29. Douglas J. MacEachin, *Predicting the Soviet Invasion of Afghanistan: The Intelligence Community's Record* (Washington, DC: Center for the Study of Intelligence, Central Intelligence Agency, April 2002), 44.

30. MacEachin, *Predicting the Soviet Invasion of Afghanistan*, 45.

31. George P. Shultz, *Turmoil and Triumph: My Years as Secretary of State* (New York: Charles Scribner's Sons, 1993), 1086.

32. Shultz, *Turmoil and Triumph*, 1087–8.
33. Ibid., 1093–4.
34. Douglas MacEachin, "Analysis and Estimates: Professional Practices in Intelligence Production," in Jennifer E. Sims and Burton Gerber (eds.), *Transforming U.S. Intelligence* (Washington, DC: Georgetown University Press, 2005), chap. 7, 121.
35. MacEachin, "Analysis and Estimates," 121.
36. Ibid., 123.
37. Douglas J. MacEachin, *U.S. Intelligence and the Confrontation in Poland, 1980–1981* (University Park: Pennsylvania State University Press, 2002), 231.
38. Earnest R. May, "Capabilities and Proclivities," in Earnest R. May (ed.), *Knowing One's Enemies: Intelligence Assessment before the Two World Wars* (Princeton: Princeton University Press, 1984), 537.
39. Quoted in Gary Sick, *All Fall Down: America's Tragic Encounter with Iran* (New York: Random House, 1985), 92.
40. Barry Rubin, *Paved with Good Intentions: The American Experience and Iran* (New York: Penguin Books, 1981), 180.
41. Sick, *All Fall Down*, 90.
42. Ibid., 90.
43. Zbigniew Brzezinski, *Power and Principle: Memoirs of the National Security Advisor, 1977–1981* (New York: Farrar, Straus, & Giroux, 1983), 367.
44. William J. Daugherty, "Behind the Intelligence Failure in Iran," *International Journal of Intelligence and CounterIntelligence* 14, no. 4 (winter 2001), 450.
45. Brzezinski, *Power and Principle: Memoirs of the National Security Advisor, 1977–1981*, 367.
46. Rubin, *Paved with Good Intentions*, 202.
47. Michael Ledeen and William Lewis, *Debacle: The American Failure in Iran* (New York: Alfred A. Knopf, 1981), 132.
48. Gates, *From the Shadows*, 238. For a detailed examination of how Kuklinski's reporting influenced CIA intelligence assessments, see MacEachin, *U.S. Intelligence and the Confrontation in Poland, 1980–1981*.
49. Gates, *From the Shadows*, 239.
50. For an interesting account of East Germany's ties with Palestinian terrorists, see Markus Wolf with Anne McElvoy, *Man without a Face: The Autobiography of Communism's Greatest Spymaster* (New York: Random House, 1997), 269–81.
51. Christopher Andrew and Oleg Gordievsky, *KGB: The Inside Story of its Foreign Operations from Lenin to Gorbachev* (New York: HarperCollins Publishers, 1990), 639–40.
52. George Weigel, *Witness to Hope: The Biography of Pope John Paul II, 1920–2005* (New York: HarperPerennial, 2001), 397–8.

53. For fascinating accounts of Operation RYAN, see Ben B. Fischer, *A Cold War Conundrum: The 1983 Soviet War Scare* (Washington, DC: Center for the Study of Intelligence, Central Intelligence Agency, September 1997); and Andrew and Gordievsky, *KGB: The Inside Story of Its Foreign Operations from Lenin to Gorbachev*, 583–605.

54. Don Oberdorfer, *From the Cold War to a New Era: The United States and the Soviet Union, 1983–1991* (Baltimore: Johns Hopkins University Press, 1998), 65–8.

55. Christopher Andrew and Oleg Gordievsky, *KGB*, 605.

56. Daniel P. Moynihan, "Do We Still Need the CIA?" *New York Times*, 19 May 1991, E17.

57. Bruce D. Berkowitz and Jeffrey T. Richelson, "The CIA Vindicated," *The National Interest* 41 (fall 1995), 37.

58. Gates, *From the Shadows*, 343–5.

59. Ibid., 525.

60. Ibid., 526.

61. Berkowitz and Richelson, "The CIA Vindicated," 45. For another defense of the CIA's analytic performance, written by the CIA's former director of Soviet analysis, see Douglas J. MacEachin, *CIA Assessments of the Soviet Union: The Record Versus the Charges* (Washington, DC: Center for the Study of Intelligence, Central Intelligence Agency, May 1996).

62. Gates, *From the Shadows*, 560.

3. STUMBLING AFTER THE COLD WAR

1. Milt Bearden and James Risen, *The Main Enemy: The Inside Story of the CIA's Final Showdown with the KGB* (New York: Random House, 2003), 470.

2. See Francis Fukuyama, *The End of History to the Last Man*, reprinted edition (New York: Free Press, 2006), which popularized this liberal philosophy, one that easily caught the imagination and worldview of the CIA's management.

3. For a more in-depth analysis of strategic intelligence during the 1990–1 war, see Richard L. Russell, "CIA's Strategic Intelligence in Iraq," *Political Science Quarterly* 117, no. 2 (summer 2002), 191–207.

4. H. Norman Schwarzkopf and Peter Petre, *It Doesn't Take a Hero* (New York: Bantam Books, 1992), 319.

5. James A. Baker III with Thomas M. DeFrank, *The Politics of Diplomacy: Revolution, War and Peace, 1989–1992* (New York: G. P. Putnam's Sons, 1995), 7.

6. Baker and DeFrank, *The Politics of Diplomacy*, 268.

7. Thomas A. Keaney and Eliot A. Cohen, *Revolution in Warfare? Airpower in the Persian Gulf War* (Annapolis, MD: Naval Institute Press, 1995), 53.

8. Rick Atkinson, *Crusade: The Untold Story of the Persian Gulf War* (Boston: Houghton Mifflin, 1993), 266.

9. Ibid., 347.

10. House Armed Services Committee, Subcommittee on Oversight and Investigations, *Intelligence Successes and Failures in Operations Desert Shield/ Storm* (Washington, DC: Government Printing Office, August 1993), 4 and 31.

11. Atkinson, *Crusade*, 347.

12. For an account of the al Firdos bunker bombing during the 1991 Gulf War, see Michael R. Gordon and Bernard E. Trainor, *The General's War: The Inside Story of the Conflict in the Gulf* (New York: Little, Brown, 1995), 324–6.

13. For a discussion of the creation of the chain of command inside CIA by DCI John Deutch to support the military and to vet military targets proposed by the CIA, a legacy of the Gulf War, see Richard L. Russell, "Tug of War: The CIA's Uneasy Relationship with the Military," *SAIS Review* XXII, no. 2 (summer-fall 2002), 9–12.

14. Timothy V. McCarthy and Jonathan B. Tucker, "Saddam's Toxic Arsenal: Chemical and Biological Weapons in the Gulf Wars," in Peter R. Lavoy, Scott Sagan, and James Wirtz (eds.), *Planning the Unthinkable: How New Powers Will Use Nuclear, Biological, and Chemical Weapons* (Ithaca: Cornell University Press, 2000), chap. 2, 72.

15. For a more thorough analysis, see Richard L. Russell, "Iraq's Chemical Weapons Legacy: What Others Might Learn from Saddam," *Middle East Journal* 59, no. 2 (spring 2005), 187–208.

16. Keaney and Cohen, *Revolution in Warfare?*, 67.

17. Gregory F. Treverton, *Reshaping National Intelligence for an Age of Information* (Cambridge: Cambridge University Press, 2003), 177.

18. National Intelligence Estimate, *Yugoslavia Transformed* (Washington, DC: National Intelligence Council, 18 October 1990), v. Available at http://www.foia.cia.gov/nic_collection.asp.

19. Ibid.

20. Quoted in Thomas W. Shreeve, "The Intelligence Community Case Method Program: A National Intelligence Estimate on Yugoslavia," Chapter 26, in Roger Z. George and Robert D. Kline (eds.), *Intelligence and the National Security Strategist: Enduring Issues and Challenges* (Washington, DC: National Defense University Press, 2004), 338.

21. John Barry and Evan Thomas, "The Kosovo Cover-Up," *Newsweek*, 15 May 2000, 23.

22. Steven Lee Myers, "Chinese Embassy Bombing: A Wide Net of Blame," *New York Times*, 17 April 2000, A1 and A10.

23. Richard L. Russell, "The Fog of War: NATO's Bombing of the Chinese Embassy in Belgrade," Pew Case Study, no. 253 (Washington, DC: Institute for the Study of Diplomacy, Georgetown University, 2002), 5–6.

24. Ibid., 5–6.

25. Ibid., 3–4.

26. Melissa Boyle Mahle, *Denial and Deception: An Insider's View of the CIA from Iran-Contra to 9/11* (New York: Nation Books, 2004), 273.

27. Richard L. Russell, "American Military Retaliation for Terrorism: Judging the Merits of the 1998 Cruise Missile Strikes in Afghanistan and Sudan," Pew Case Study, no. 238 (Washington, DC: Institute for the Study of Diplomacy, Georgetown University, 2000), 2, 5, and 7.

28. James Risen, "To Bomb Sudan Plant, or Not: A Year Later, Debate Rankle," *New York Times*, 27 October 1999, A12.

29. Russell, "American Military Retaliation for Terrorism: Judging the Merits of the 1998 Cruise Missile Strikes in Afghanistan and Sudan," 7–9.

30. See Richard H. Shultz, Jr., "Showstoppers: Nine Reasons Why We Never Sent Our Special Operations Forces after al Qaeda before 9/11," *The Weekly Standard*, 26 January 2004, 32.

31. Quoted in Shultz, "Showstoppers: Nine Reasons Why We Never Sent Our Special Operations Forces after al Qaeda before 9/11," 32.

32. Richard A. Clarke, *Against All Enemies: Inside America's War on Terror* (New York: Free Press, 2004), 204.

33. Risen, "To Bomb Sudan Plant, or Not," A12.

34. Daniel Benjamin and Steven Simon, *The Age of Sacred Terror: Radical Islam's War against America* (New York: Random House, 2003), 256–62, 354–6, and 368–70.

35. For background on the formation of NIMA, see A Series Roundtable, "Creating the National Imagery and Mapping Agency," *Studies in Intelligence* 42, no. 1 (1998).

4. BLUNDERING IN THE "WAR ON TERRORISM"

1. Bob Woodward, *Bush at War* (New York: Simon & Schuster, 2002), 43, 51, and 53.

2. See National Commission on Terrorist Attacks upon the United States, *The 9/11 Commission Report* (Washington, DC: Government Printing Office, July 2004), hereafter referred to as the *9/11 Commission Report*. Available at http://www.9–11commission.gov/report/index.htm; House Permanent Select Committee on Intelligence and Senate Select Committee on Intelligence, *Joint Inquiry into Intelligence Community Activities before and after the Terrorist Attacks of September 11, 2001* (Washington, DC: United States Government Printing Office,

December 2002), hereafter referred to as House–Senate Joint Inquiry. Available at http://www.gpoaccess.gov/serialset/creports/911.html. Senate Select Committee on Intelligence, *Report on the U.S. Intelligence Community's Prewar Intelligence Assessments on Iraq* (Washington, DC: Government Printing Office, 7 July 2004). Available at http://www.gpoaccess.gov/serialset/creports/iraq.html. Commission on the Intelligence Capabilities of the United States Regarding Weapons of Mass Destruction, *Report to the President* (Washington, DC: United States Government, 31 March 2005), hereafter referred to as WMD Commission Report. Available at http://www.wmd.gov/report.

3. Richard Miniter, *Losing Bin Laden: How Bill Clinton's Failures Unleashed Global Terror* (Washington, DC: Regnery, 2003), 34.
4. Daniel Benjamin and Steven Simon, *The Age of Sacred Terror: Radical Islam's War against America* (New York: Random House, 2003), 304.
5. House–Senate Joint Inquiry, xiii.
6. Scott Shane and Neil A. Lewis, "At Sept. 11 Trial, Tale of Missteps and Management," *New York Times*, 31 March 2006, A1.
7. Richard A. Posner, *Preventing Surprise Attacks: Intelligence Reform in the Wake of 9/11* (New York: Rowman & Littlefield, 2005), 31–2.
8. Richard A. Posner, *Uncertain Shield: The U.S. Intelligence System in the Throes of Reform* (New York: Rowman & Littlefield, 2006), 105.
9. Daniel Benjamin and Steven Simon, *The Age of Sacred Terror*, 341.
10. Steve Coll, *Ghost Wars: The Secret History of the CIA, Afghanistan, and Bin Laden, From the Soviet Invasion to September 10, 2001* (New York: Penguin Press, 2004), 561.
11. *The 9/11 Commission Report*, 261.
12. Coll, *Ghost Wars*, 561.
13. Richard K. Betts, *Surprise Attack: Lessons for Defense Planning* (Washington, DC: Brookings Institution Press, 1982), 18.
14. Betts, *Surprise Attack*, 18.
15. *The 9/11 Commission Report*, 118.
16. Daniel Byman, "Strategic Surprise and the September 11 Attacks," *Annual Review of Political Science* 8, no. 1 (2005), 157.
17. National Intelligence Estimate, *Iraq's Continuing Programs for Weapons of Mass Destruction* (Washington, DC: National Intelligence Council, October 2002). Available at http://www.fas.org/irp/cia/product/iraq-wmd.html.
18. Bob Woodward, *Plan of Attack* (New York: Simon & Schuster, 2004), 249.
19. Colin Powell, "Iraq's Failure to Disarm," remarks to the United Nations Security Council (Washington, DC: Bureau of Public Affairs, Department of State, 5 February 2003). Available at http://www.state.gov/p/nea/disarm/.
20. Woodward, *Plan of Attack*, 299–300.

21. For an excellent examination of the turning point from hiding, preserving, and rebuilding WMD capabilities to weathering economic hardships until UN sanctions would be lifted, see Barton Gellman, "Iraq's Arsenal of Ambitions," *Washington Post*, 7 January 2004.

22. Special advisor to the director of central intelligence on Iraq's WMD, "Delivery Systems: Key Findings," *Comprehensive Report*, Volume I (Washington, DC: Central Intelligence Agency, 30 September 2004). Hereafter, referred to as the Duelfer Report. Available at http://www.cia.gov/cia/reports/iraq_wmd_2004/.

23. Duelfer Report, "Chemical: Key Findings."

24. Duelfer Report, "Biological: Key Findings."

25. Ibid.

26. Duelfer Report, "Nuclear: Key Findings."

27. WMD Commission Report, 84.

28. Bob Drogin, "Spy Work in Iraq Riddled by Failures," *Los Angeles Times*, 17 June 2004, A1.

29. Senate Select Committee on Intelligence, "Conclusions," *Report on the U.S. Intelligence Community's Prewar Intelligence Assessments on Iraq*, 14.

30. WMD Commission Report, 14.

31. See Richard L. Russell, "CIA's Strategic Intelligence in Iraq," *Political Science Quarterly* 117, no. 2 (summer 2002), 201.

32. WMD Commission Report, 117.

33. Ibid., 122.

34. Central Intelligence Agency Report, "Further Comments on Iraqi Weapons of Mass Destruction," August 1995, Gulf Link Declassified Document. Available at http://www.gulflink.osd.mil/declassdocs/cia/19960705.

35. Steve Rodan, "All in the Family," *Jerusalem Post*, 13 June 1997.

36. WMD Commission Report, 162.

37. Ibid., 162.

38. Robert Jervis, "Reports, Politics, and Intelligence Failures: The Case of Iraq," *Journal of Strategic Studies*, 29, no. 1 (February 2006), 25.

39. Scott Shane, "Iraqi Official, Paid by CIA, Gave Account of Weapons," *New York Times*, 22 March 2006.

40. James Risen, *State of War: The Secret History of the CIA and the Bush Administration* (New York: Free Press, 2006), 106.

41. Senate Select Committee on Intelligence, *Report on the U.S. Intelligence Community's Prewar Intelligence Assessments on Iraq*, 273.

42. WMD Commission Report, 11.

43. Senate Select Committee on Intelligence, *Postwar Findings about Iraq's WMD Programs and Links to Terrorism and How They Compare with Prewar Assessments*, 110.

44. Jervis, "Reports, Politics, and Intelligence Failures: The Case of Iraq," *Journal of Strategic Studies*, 35.

45. Bob Woodward, *Plan of Attack*, 196–7.

46. WMD Commission Report, 408.

47. Walter Pincus, "Spy Agencies Faulted for Missing Indian Tests," *Washington Post*, 3 June 1998, A18. For an analysis of the role of intelligence against WMD threats, see Jason D. Ellis and Geoffrey D. Kiefer, *Combating Proliferation: Strategic Intelligence and Security Policy* (Baltimore, MD: The Johns Hopkins University Press, 2004).

48. Ronald Kessler, *The CIA at War: Inside the Secret Campaign against Terror* (New York: St. Martin's Press, 2003), 212.

49. David Albright and Corey Hinderstein, "Unraveling the A. Q. Khan and Future Proliferation Networks," *The Washington Quarterly* 28, no. 2 (spring 2005), 111. Also see Douglas Frantz, "A High-Risk Nuclear Stakeout," *Los Angeles Times*, 27 February 2005.

50. David E. Sanger and William J. Broad, "Pakistan's Nuclear Earnings," *New York Times*, 16 March 2004.

51. William J. Broad and David E. Sanger, "The Bomb Merchant," *New York Times*, 26 December 2004, A1.

52. Douglas Franz and William C. Rempel, "New Find in a Nuclear World," *Los Angeles Times*, 28 November 2004, A1.

53. For an examination of the strategic rationale for nuclear weapons in Saudi Arabia, see Richard L. Russell, "Saudi Nukes: A Looming Intelligence Failure," *Washington Times*, 5 January 2004, A17.

54. David E. Sanger and William J. Broad, "From Rogue Nuclear Programs, Web of Trails Leads to Pakistan," *New York Times*, 4 January 2004, A1.

55. Douglas Frantz, "Iran Moving Methodically toward Nuclear Capability," *Los Angeles Times*, 21 October 2004, A1. For more discussion of the massive scope and sophistication of Iran's uranium-enrichment program, see Joby Warrick and Glenn Kessler, "Iran's Nuclear Program Speeds Ahead," *Washington Post*, 10 March 2003, A1. For a discussion of Iran's strategic rationale for nuclear weapons, see Richard L. Russell, "Iran in Iraq's Shadow: Dealing with Tehran's Nuclear Weapons Bid," *Parameters* XXXIV, no. 3 (autumn 2004), 32–4.

56. David E. Sanger, "Pakistan Found to Aid Iran Nuclear Efforts," *New York Times*, 2 September 2004.

57. David E. Sanger and William J. Broad, "From Rogue Nuclear Programs, Web of Trails Leads to Pakistan," *New York Times*, 4 January 2004, A1.

58. Jonathan D. Pollack, "The United States, North Korea, and the End of the Agreed Framework," *Naval War College Review* LVI, no. 3 (summer 2003), 13.

59. Douglas Jehl, "Bush's Arms Intelligence Panel Works in Secret," *New York Times*, 6 December 2004.

60. Quoted in Barbara Demick, "North Korea's Ace in the Hole," *Los Angeles Times*, 14 November 2003.

61. Phillip van Niekerk, "South Africa Had Six A-Bombs," *Washington Post*, 25 March 1993. For analyses of South Africa's nuclear weapons program and its decision to abandon it, see Peter Liberman, "The Rise and Fall of the South African Bomb," *International Security* 26, no. 2 (fall 2001), 45–86; and J. W. de Villiers, Roger Jardine, and Mitchell Reiss, "Why South Africa Gave Up the Bomb," *Foreign Affairs* 72, no. 5 (November/December 1993), 98–109.

62. National Intelligence Estimate, *Trends in South Africa's Nuclear Security Policies and Programs* (Washington, DC: National Intelligence Council, 5 October 1984), 1. Available at http://www.foia.cia.gov/nic_collection.asp. Parenthetically, the NIE also noted that "There is still considerable disagreement as to whether the flash in the South Atlantic detected by a US satellite in September 1979 was a nuclear test, and if so, by South Africa." The debate today remains unsettled. For a detailed discussion of the issue, see Jeffrey T. Richelson, *Spying on the Bomb: American Nuclear Intelligence from Nazi Germany to Iran and North Korea* (New York: W. W. Norton, 2006), 283–316.

63. Jim Mann, "Threat to Mideast Military Balance: US Caught Napping by Sino-Saudi Missile Deal," *Los Angeles Times*, 4 May 1988, A1.

64. For an analysis of Saudi interest in a nuclear deterrent, see Richard L. Russell, *Weapons Proliferation and War in the Greater Middle East* (New York and London: Routledge, 2005), 108–19.

65. Quoted in Jeffrey Goldberg, "The Unknown," *The New Yorker* 78, no. 46 (10 February 2003).

66. Mitchell Reiss, *Bridled Ambition: Why Countries Constrain Their Nuclear Capabilities* (Baltimore, MD: The Johns Hopkins University Press, 1995), 14–15 and 30–1.

67. House-Senate Joint Inquiry, 40.

68. Ibid., 59.

69. Ibid., 59–60.

70. Lawrence Freedman, "War in Iraq: Selling the Threat," *Survival* 46, no. 2 (summer 2004), 7.

71. Richard K. Betts, "Intelligence Warning: Old Problems, New Agendas," *Parameters* (spring 1998), 30.

5. SPIES WHO DO NOT DELIVER

1. Richard Helms with William Hood, *A Look over My Shoulder: A Life in the Central Intelligence Agency* (New York: Random House, 2003), 318.

2. Edward G. Shirley [a pen name for Reuel Marc Gerecht], "Can't Anybody Here Play This Game?" *Atlantic Monthly* 281, no. 2 (February 1998), 53.

3. Robert M. Gates, *From the Shadows: The Ultimate Insider's Story of Five Presidents and How They Won the Cold War* (New York: Touchstone, 1997), 560.

4. Markus Wolf with Anne McElvoy, *Man without a Face: The Autobiography of Communism's Greatest Spymaster* (New York: Random House, 1997), 284.

5. Ibid., 285.

6. James Risen, *State of War: The Secret History of the CIA and the Bush Administration* (New York: Free Press, 2006), 193–4.

7. John Walcott and Brian Duffy, "The CIA's Darkest Secrets," *U.S. News & World Report*, 4 July 1994, 34.

8. Greg Miller, "CIA Operation in Iran Failed When Spies Were Exposed," *Los Angeles Times*, 12 February 2005.

9. House Permanent Select Committee on Intelligence and Senate Select Committee on Intelligence, *Joint Inquiry into Intelligence Community Activities before and after the Terrorist Attacks of September 11, 2001* (Washington, DC: U.S. Government Printing Office, December 2002), 90. Hereafter referred to as House–Senate Joint Inquiry. Available at http://www.gpoaccess.gov/serialset/creports/911.html.

10. Quoted in John Diamond, "CIA's Spy Network Thin," *USA Today*, 22 September 2004, 13A.

11. Senate Select Committee on Intelligence, "Conclusions," *Report on the U.S. Intelligence Community's Prewar Intelligence Assessments on Iraq* (Washington, DC: U.S. Government Printing Office, 7 July 2004), 24–25. Available at http://www.gpoaccess.gov/serialset/creports/iraq.html.

12. Ibid., 24. For more in-depth examinations of the CIA's human collection and analytic shortcomings, see Richard L. Russell, "Spies Like Them," *National Interest* 77 (fall 2004), 59–62; and Richard L. Russell, "Intelligence Failures: The Wrong Model for the War on Terror," *Policy Review* 123 (February & March 2004), 61–72.

13. Senate Select Committee on Intelligence, 25.

14. Reuel Marc Gerecht, "A New Clandestine Service: The Case for Creative Destruction," in Peter Berkowitz (ed.), *The Future of American Intelligence* (Stanford, CA: Hoover Institution Press, 2005), chap. 4, 105.

15. House Permanent Select Committee on Intelligence, *Intelligence Authorization Act for Fiscal Year 2005* (Washington, DC: U.S. Government Printing Office, 21 June 2004), 24. Available at http://intelligence.house.gov/Reports.aspx?Section=56).

16. Reuel Marc Gerecht, "I Spy with My Little Eye . . . ," *Wall Street Journal*, 9 November 2005.

17. Lindsay Moran, *Blowing My Cover: My Life as a CIA Spy* (New York: G. P. Putnam's Sons, 2005), 274.

18. Shirley, "Can't Anybody Here Play This Game?," 50.

19. Helms with Hood, *A Look over My Shoulder*, 145.

20. Christopher Andrew, *For the President's Eyes Only: Secret Intelligence and the American Presidency from Washington to Bush* (New York: HarperPerennial, 1996), 213–14. For a fascinating account of the Popov case, see William Hood, *Mole* (New York: W. W. Norton, 1982).

21. Andrew, *For the President's Eyes Only*, 267.

22. See Arkady N. Shevchenko, *Breaking with Moscow* (New York: Alfred A. Knopf, 1985).

23. Robert Baer, *See No Evil: The True Story of a Ground Soldier in the CIA's War on Terrorism* (New York: Three Rivers Press, 2002), 143.

24. Reuel Marc Gerecht, "The Sorry State of the CIA," *The Weekly Standard*, 19 July 2004.

25. Baer, *See No Evil*, 118–19.

26. Duane R. Clarridge with Digby Diehl, *A Spy for All Seasons: My Life in the CIA* (New York: Scribner, 1997), 76.

27. Clarridge with Diehl, *A Spy for All Seasons*, 124.

28. James Lilley with Jeffrey Lilley, *China Hands: Nine Decades of Adventure, Espionage, and Diplomacy in Asia* (New York: Public Affairs, 2004), 86.

29. Frederick P. Hitz, *The Great Game: The Myth and Reality of Espionage* (New York: Alfred A. Knopf, 2004), 29.

30. Hitz, *The Great Game*, 58–9.

31. David Wise, *Nightmover: How Aldrich Ames Sold the CIA to the KGB for $4.6 Million* (New York: HarperCollins Publishers, 1995), 315 and 326.

32. Shirley, "Can't Anybody Here Play This Game?," 48.

33. Ibid., 47–8.

34. Hitz, *The Great Game*, 69.

35. Gates, *From the Shadows*, 22.

36. Ibid., 22–3.

37. See L. Moran, *Blowing My Cover*.

38. Jeffrey T. Richelson, *The U.S. Intelligence Community*, 4th ed. (Boulder, CO: Westview Press, 1999), 267.

39. Judith Miller, Stephen Engelberg, and William Broad, *Germs: Biological Weapons and America's Secret War* (New York: Touchstone, 2002), 166–8.

40. David E. Kaplan, "Playing Offense: The Inside Story of How U.S. Terrorist Hunters Are Going after al Qaeda," *U.S. News & World Report*, 2 June 2003.

41. Bob Woodward, *Bush at War* (New York: Simon & Schuster, 2002), 76–7.

42. Senate Select Committee on Intelligence, 25.

43. Melissa Boyle Mahle, *Denial and Deception: An Insider's View of the CIA from Iran-Contra to 9/11* (New York: Nation Books, 2004), 149.
44. James Bamford, *A Pretext for War: 9/11, Iraq, and the Abuse of America's Intelligence Agencies* (New York: Doubleday, 2004), 200.
45. Walter Pincus, "Intelligence Efforts Get Boost: Undercover Officers to Keep Salaries from Civilian Jobs Abroad," *Washington Post*, 10 December 2004, A6.
46. For a mild rebuke of the intelligence community's security bias against Arab Americans, see Bob Graham with Jeff Nussbaum, *Intelligence Matters: The CIA, the FBI, Saudi Arabia, and the Failure of America's War on Terror* (New York: Random House, 2004), 247–8.
47. House-Senate Joint Inquiry, 70.
48. Melissa Boyle Mahle, *Denial and Deception*, 311.
49. Robert Baer, "Wanted: Spies Unlike Us," *Foreign Policy* (March/April 2005).
50. Bruce Berkowitz, *The New Face of War: How War Will Be Fought in the 21st Century* (New York: The Free Press, 2003), 201.
51. David S. Robarge, "A Look Back: Directors of Central Intelligence, 1946–2005," *Studies in Intelligence* 49, no. 3 (2005), 4. According to Robarge, who is the CIA's chief historian, the longest serving DCI was Allen Dulles with almost nine years' tenure, whereas the average tenure for DCIs is about three years.
52. Diamond, "CIA's Spy Network Thin," 13A.
53. Berkowitz, *The New Face of War*, 201–2.
54. Walter Pincus, "Goss Plan to Strengthen CIA Is Ready," *Washington Post*, 16 February 2005, A2.
55. Maurice R. Greenberg and Richard N. Haass (eds.), *Making Intelligence Smarter: The Future of U.S. Intelligence*, Report of an Independent Task Force (New York: Council on Foreign Relations, 1996), 14.

6. ANALYSTS WHO ARE NOT EXPERTS

1. Sherman Kent, *Strategic Intelligence for American World Policy* (Princeton: Princeton University Press, 1951), 74.
2. Kent, *Strategic Intelligence for American World Policy*, 74, fn. 2.
3. Robert D. Blackwill and Jack Davis, "A Policymaker's Perspective on Intelligence Analysis," in Loch K. Johnson and James J. Wirtz (eds.), *Strategic Intelligence: Windows into a Secret World* (Los Angeles, CA: Roxbury, 2004), chap. 10, 121.
4. Scott Shane and David E. Sanger, "Daily Intelligence Briefings Are Vague, Officials Say," *New York Times*, 3 April 2005.
5. Commission on the Roles and Capabilities of the United States Intelligence Community, *Preparing for the 21st Century: An Appraisal of U.S. Intelligence* (Washington, DC: U.S. Government Printing Office, 1 March 1996), 83. Hereafter

referred to as Brown Commission Report. Available at http://www.access.gpo. gov/su_docs/dpos/epubs/int/pdf/report.html.

6. House Permanent Select Committee on Intelligence and Senate Select Committee on Intelligence, *Joint Inquiry into Intelligence Community Activities before and after the Terrorist Attacks of September 11, 2001* (Washington, DC: U.S. Government Printing Office, December 2002), 59. Hereafter referred to as the House–Senate Joint Inquiry. Available at http://www.gpoaccess.gov/serialset/creports/911.html.

7. For an examination of how one analyst of questionable authority in the CIA dominated the analytic assessment that Iraq was actively reconstituting its nuclear weapons program, see David Barstow, "Who the White House Embraced Disputed Arms Intelligence," *New York Times*, 3 October 2004.

8. WMD Commission Report, 97.

9. Ibid., 191.

10. Ibid., 193.

11. Ashton B. Carter, "How to Counter WMD," *Foreign Affairs* 83, no. 5 (September/October 2004), 85.

12. Loch K. Johnson, *Bombs, Bugs, Drugs, and Thugs: Intelligence and America's Quest for Security* (New York: New York University Press, 2000), 151.

13. Report of a Committee of Privy Counsellors, *Review of Intelligence on Weapons of Mass Destruction* (Norwich, UK: Her Majesty's Stationery Office, 14 July 2004), 47.

14. Report of a Committee of Privy Counsellors, 49.

15. David Ignatius, "Spying: Time to Think outside the Box," *Washington Post*, 29 August 2004, B7.

16. I am indebted to Robert Jervis for this point. Correspondence with the author, 13 June 2006.

17. Richard H. Shultz, Jr., "The Era of Armed Groups," in Peter Berkowitz (ed.), *The Future of American Intelligence* (Stanford, CA: Hoover Institution Press, 2005), chap. 1, 2.

18. Quoted in Richard K. Betts, "Politicization of Intelligence: Costs and Benefits," in Richard K. Betts and Thomas G. Mahnken (eds.), *Paradoxes of Strategic Intelligence* (Portland, OR: Frank Cass, 2003), 64.

19. House–Senate Joint Inquiry, 70–2.

20. Robert Jervis, "Reports, Politics, and Intelligence Failures: The Case of Iraq," *Journal of Strategic Studies* 29, no. 1 (February 2006), 41.

21. Brown Commission Report, 88.

22. Bruce D. Berkowitz and Allan E. Goodman, *Best Truth: Intelligence in the Information Age* (New Haven: Yale University Press, 2000), 151.

23. Brown Commission Report, 86.

24. For anecdotal comments from interviews and focus groups that flash the frustrations of CIA analysts due to time constraints and the pressure of current intelligence publication that prevents long-term strategic research, see Rob Johnston, *Analytic Culture in the U.S. Intelligence Community: An Ethnographic Study* (Washington, DC: Center for the Study of Intelligence, Central Intelligence Agency, 2005), 9–29.

25. Dana Priest, "CIA Feels Strain of Iraq and Al Qaeda," *Washington Post*, 17 November 2002, A26.

26. Harold P. Ford, *Estimative Intelligence: The Purposes and Problems of National Intelligence Estimating*, rev. ed. (Lanham, MD: University Press of America, 1993), 176.

27. House-Senate Joint Inquiry, 59.

28. James A. Baker III with Thomas M. DeFrank, *The Politics of Diplomacy: Revolution, War and Peace, 1989–1992* (New York: G. P. Putnam's Sons, 1995), 154.

29. George F. Kennan, "Spy and Counterspy," *New York Times*, 18 May 1997, A17.

30. Berkowitz and Goodman, *Best Truth*, 40.

31. George details these challenges in his "Fixing the Problem of Analytic Mindsets," in Roger Z. George and Robert D. Kline (eds.), *Intelligence and the National Security Strategist: Enduring Issues and Challenges* (Washington, DC: National Defense University Press, 2004), chap. 25, 311–26.

32. Michael I. Handel, "Intelligence and the Problem of Strategic Surprise," *Journal of Strategic Studies* 7, no. 3 (September 1984), 269.

33. Robert Jervis, *Perception and Misperception in International Politics* (Princeton, NJ: Princeton University Press, 1976), 416.

34. Robert M. Gates, *From the Shadows: The Ultimate Insider's Story of Five Presidents and How They Won the Cold War* (New York: Touchstone, 1997), 355–6. For an insightful analysis of this controversy and its central role in Gates's 1991 confirmation hearings to become DCI, see Gregory F. Treverton, *Reshaping National Intelligence for an Age of Information* (Cambridge: Cambridge University Press, 2003), 198–9.

35. WMD Commission Report, 155–6.

36. Ibid., 156.

37. Ibid., 156.

38. See Richard L. Russell, "What if . . . 'China Attacks Taiwan!' " *Parameters* XXXI, no. 3 (autumn 2001); Thomas Ricks, "War College Details New Taiwan Attack Scenario," *Washington Post*, 31 August 2001, A21; and George F. Will, "Another Unthinkable Scenario," *Washington Post*, 7 October 2001, B8.

39. See Richard L. Russell, "A Saudi Nuclear Option?" *Survival* 43, no. 2 (summer 2001).

40. Maurice R. Greenberg and Richard N. Haass (eds.), *Making Intelligence Smarter: The Future of U.S. Intelligence*, Report of an Independent Task Force (New York: Council on Foreign Relations, 1996), 5.

41. Walter Pincus, "Bush Orders the CIA to Hire More Spies," *Washington Post*, 24 November 2004, A4.

42. Mark M. Lowenthal, "Intelligence Analysis: Management and Transformation Issues," in Jennifer E. Sims and Burton Gerber (eds.), *Transforming U.S. Intelligence* (Washington, DC: Georgetown University Press, 2005), chap. 13, 231.

43. William M. Nolte, "Rethinking War and Intelligence," in Anthony D. McIvor, *Rethinking Principles of War* (Annapolis, MD: Naval Institute Press, 2005), chap. 23, 435.

44. For background on the Kent School, see Stephen Marrin, "CIA's Kent School: Improving Training for New Analysts," *International Journal of Intelligence and Counterintelligence* 16, no. 4 (winter 2003).

45. Robert Jervis, "What's Wrong with the Intelligence Process?," *International Journal of Intelligence and Counterintelligence* 1, no. 1 (spring 1986), 32.

46. Ibid., 31–7.

7. FACING FUTURE STRATEGIC INTELLIGENCE CHALLENGES

1. Richard K. Betts, "Fixing Intelligence," *Foreign Affairs* 81, no. 1 (January/February 2002), 52.

2. Walter Pincus, "Intelligence Director's Budget May Near $1 Billion, Report Finds," *Washington Post*, 20 April 2006, A11.

3. Robert M. Gates, *From the Shadows: The Ultimate Insider's Story of Five Presidents and How They Won the Cold War* (New York: Touchstone, 1997), 223–4.

4. Walter Pincus, "Bush's Intelligence Panel Gains Stature," *Washington Post*, 7 February 2005, A19.

5. House Permanent Select Committee on Intelligence and Senate Select Committee on Intelligence, *Joint Inquiry into Intelligence Community Activities before and after the Terrorist Attacks of September 11, 2001* (Washington, DC: U.S. Government Printing Office, December 2002), 59. Hereafter referred to as House–Senate Joint Inquiry. Available at http://www.gpoaccess.gov/serialset/creports/911.html.

6. Walter Pincus, "CIA Spies Get a New Home Base," *Washington Post*, 14 October 2005, A6.

7. Scott Shane, "Intelligence Center is Created for Unclassified Information," *New York Times*, 9 November 2005.

8. Anonymous [Michael Scheuer], *Imperial Hubris: Why the West Is Losing the War on Terror* (Washington, DC: Brassey's, 2004), xiii.

9. Central Intelligence Agency, *Intelligence and Policy: The Evolving Relationship* (Washington, DC: Center for the Study of Intelligence, June 2004), 7. Available at http://www.cia.gov/csi/books/Roundtable_june2004/IntelandPolicyRelationship_ Internet.pdf.

10. James E. Steiner, *Challenging the Red Line between Intelligence and Policy* (Washington, DC: Institute for the Study of Diplomacy, Georgetown University, n.d.), 1.

11. Commission on the Intelligence Capabilities of the United States Regarding Weapons of Mass Destruction, *Report to the President* (Washington, DC: U.S. Government, 31 March 2005), 399. Hereafter referred to as WMD Commission Report. Available at http://www.wmd.gov/report.

12. Maurice R. Greenberg and Richard N. Haass (eds.), *Making Intelligence Smarter: The Future of U.S. Intelligence* (New York: Council on Foreign Relations, 1996).

13. Correspondence with the author, 22 June 2006.

14. WMD Commission Report, 25.

15. Allan E. Goodman, Gregory F. Treverton, and Philip Zelikow, *In from the Cold: Report of the Twentieth Century Fund Task Force on the Future of U.S. Intelligence* (Twentieth Century Fund Press, 1996), 8.

16. Richard Kerr, Thomas Wolfe, Rebecca Donegan, and Aris Pappas, "Issues for the US Intelligence Community," *Studies in Intelligence* 49, no. 3 (2005), 7. Available at https://www.cia.gov/csi/studies/vol49no3/html_files/index.html.

17. Walter Pincus, "CIA Morale on Hayden's Menu," *Washington Post*, 18 May 2006.

18. Thomas Fingar, "Questionable Intelligence," Correspondence, *The New Republic*, 10 July 2006. Fingar was attempting to refute criticisms made of the NIC's preoccupation with current intelligence chronicled in Spencer Ackerman, "Under Analysis," *The New Republic*, 29 May 2006.

19. William E. Odom, *Fixing Intelligence for a More Secure America*, 2d ed. (New Haven: Yale University Press, 2004), 80.

20. Ibid., 81.

21. Richard K. Betts, "Analysis, War, and Decision: Why Intelligence Failures Are Inevitable," *World Politics* 31, no. 1 (October 1978), 80.

22. Richard A. Clarke, *Against All Enemies: Inside America's War on Terror* (New York: Free Press, 2004), 252.

23. A. Goodman, G. Treverton, and P. Zelikow, *In from the Cold, Report of the Twentieth Century Fund Task Force on the Future of U.S. Intelligence*, 9.

24. Richards J. Heuer, Jr., *Psychology of Intelligence Analysis* (Washington, DC: Center for the Study of Intelligence, Central Intelligence Agency, 1999), 70.

25. Michael I. Handel, "Intelligence and the Problem of Strategic Surprise," *Journal of Strategic Studies* 7, no. 3 (September 1984), 250.

26. Loch K. Johnson, *Secret Intelligence Agencies: U.S. Intelligence in a Hostile World* (New Haven: Yale University Press, 1996), 51.

27. Ibid., 51.

28. Gregory F. Treverton, *Reshaping National Intelligence for an Age of Information* (Cambridge: Cambridge University Press, 2003), 202.

29. Jeffrey T. Richelson, *The U.S. Intelligence Community*, 4th ed. (Boulder, CO: Westview Press, 1999), 456.

30. Richard K. Betts, "Politicization of Intelligence: Costs and Benefits," in Richard K. Betts and Thomas G. Mahnken (eds.), *Paradoxes of Strategic Intelligence* (Portland, OR: Frank Cass, 2003), 60–1.

31. Ibid., 61.

32. Paul R. Pillar, "Intelligence, Policy, and the War in Iraq," *Foreign Affairs* 85, no. 2 (March/April 2006), 16.

33. WMD Commission Report, 518.

34. WMD Commission Report, 4.

35. President George W. Bush, *The National Security Strategy of the United States of America* (Washington, DC: The White House, September 2002), 15. Available at http://www.whitehouse.gov/nsc/nss.pdf. In strategic discourse, a preemptive strike traditionally has referred to attacking an adversary in anticipation of an impending, imminent war while preventive strikes generally refer to destroying a potential adversary's nascent capabilities to stop them from growing into a significant threat over time. In the contemporary debate, preemptive and preventive strikes are commonly used interchangeably.

36. See Richard L. Russell, "Military Retaliation for Terrorism: The 1998 Cruise Missile Strikes against al-Qaeda in Afghanistan and Sudan," Pew Case Study (Washington, DC: Institute for the Study of Diplomacy, 2002).

37. Jason D. Ellis and Geoffrey D. Kiefer, *Combating Proliferation: Strategic Intelligence and Security Policy* (Baltimore: Johns Hopkins University Press, 2004), 62.

38. Senate Select Committee on Intelligence, *Report on the U.S. Intelligence Community's Prewar Intelligence Assessments on Iraq* (Washington, DC: U.S. Government Printing Office, 7 July 2004), 24. Available at http://www.gpoaccess.gov/serialset/creports/iraq.html.

39. WMD Commission Report, 6. Italics are from original text.

Selected Bibliography

BOOKS AND MONOGRAPHS

Anonymous [Michael Scheuer], *Imperial Hubris: Why the West Is Losing the War on Terror* (Washington, DC: Brassey's, 2004).

Christopher Andrew, *For the President's Eyes Only: Secret Intelligence and the American Presidency from Washington to Bush* (New York: Harper-Perennial, 1996).

Christopher Andrew and Oleg Gordievsky, *KGB: The Inside Story of Its Foreign Operations from Lenin to Gorbachev* (New York: Harper Collins Publishers, 1990).

Rick Atkinson, *Crusade: The Untold Story of the Persian Gulf War* (Boston: Houghton Mifflin, 1993).

Robert Baer, *See No Evil: The True Story of a Ground Soldier in the CIA's War on Terrorism* (New York: Three Rivers Press, 2002).

James A. Baker III, with Thomas M. DeFrank, *The Politics of Diplomacy: Revolution, War and Peace, 1989–1992* (New York: G. P. Putnam's Sons, 1995).

James Bamford, *A Pretext for War: 9/11, Iraq, and the Abuse of America's Intelligence Agencies* (New York: Doubleday, 2004).

James Bamford, *Body of Secrets: Anatomy of the Ultra-Secret National Security Agency* (New York: Doubleday, 2001).

Milt Bearden and James Risen, *The Main Enemy: The Inside Story of the CIA's Final Showdown with the KGB* (New York: Random House, 2003).

Daniel Benjamin and Steven Simon, *The Age of Sacred Terror: Radical Islam's War Against America* (New York: Random House, 2003).

Bruce Berkowitz, *The New Face of War: How War Will Be Fought in the 21st Century* (New York: The Free Press, 2003).

Bruce D. Berkowitz and Allan E. Goodman, *Best Truth: Intelligence in the Information Age* (New Haven: Yale University Press, 2000).

Bruce D. Berkowitz and Allan E. Goodman, *Strategic Intelligence for American National Security* (Princeton: Princeton University Press, 1989).

Peter Berkowitz (ed.), *The Future of American Intelligence* (Stanford, CA: Hoover Institution Press, 2005).

Richard K. Betts, *Surprise Attack: Lessons for Defense Planning* (Washington, DC: Brookings Institution Press, 1982).

Richard K. Betts and Thomas G. Mahnken (eds.), *Paradoxes of Strategic Intelligence* (Portland, OR: Frank Cass, 2003).

Adda B. Bozeman, *Strategic Intelligence & Statecraft: Selected Essays* (Washington, DC: Brassey's, 1992).

Zbigniew Brzezinski, *Power and Principle: Memoirs of the National Security Adviser, 1977–1981* (New York: Farrar, Straus, & Giroux, 1983).

George Bush and Brent Scowcroft, *A World Transformed* (New York: Vintage Books, 1998).

Richard A. Clarke, *Against All Enemies: Inside America's War on Terror* (New York: Free Press, 2004).

Duane R. Clarridge with Digby Diehl, *A Spy for All Seasons: My Life in the CIA* (New York: Scribner, 1997).

Ray S. Cline, *Secrets, Spies, and Scholars: Blueprint of the Essential CIA* (Washington, DC: Acropolis Books, 1976).

Eliot A. Cohen and John Gooch, *Military Misfortunes: The Anatomy of Failure in War* (New York: Vintage Books, 1991).

Steve Coll, *Ghost Wars: The Secret History of the CIA, Afghanistan, and Bin Laden, From the Soviet Invasion to September 10, 2001* (New York: Penguin Press, 2004).

William J. Daugherty, *Executive Secrets: Covert Action and the Presidency* (Lexington: University Press of Kentucky, 2004).

Jason D. Ellis and Geoffrey D. Kiefer, *Combating Proliferation: Strategic Intelligence and Security Policy* (Baltimore: Johns Hopkins University Press, 2004).

Ben B. Fischer, *A Cold War Conundrum: The 1983 Soviet War Scare* (Washington, DC: Center for the Study of Intelligence, Central Intelligence Agency, September 1997).

Harold P. Ford, *Estimative Intelligence: The Purposes and Problems of National Intelligence Estimating*, rev. ed. (Lanham, MD: University Press of America, 1993).

John Lewis Gaddis, *The Cold War: A New History* (New York: The Penguin Press, 2005).

John Lewis Gaddis, *We Now Know: Rethinking Cold War History* (New York: Oxford University Press, 1997).

Robert M. Gates, *From the Shadows: The Ultimate Insider's Story of Five Presidents and How They Won the Cold War* (New York: Touchstone, 1997).

Roger Z. George and Robert D. Kline (eds.), *Intelligence and the National Security Strategist: Enduring Issues and Challenges* (Washington, DC: National Defense University Press, 2004).

Allan E. Goodman, Gregory F. Treverton, and Philip Zelikow, *In from the Cold: Report of the Twentieth Century Fund Task Force on the Future of U.S. Intelligence* (New York: Twentieth Century Fund Press, 1996).

Michael R. Gordon and Bernard E. Trainor, *The General's War: The Inside Story of the Conflict in the Gulf* (New York: Little, Brown, 1995).

Bob Graham with Jeff Nussbaum, *Intelligence Matters: The CIA, the FBI, Saudi Arabia, and the Failure of America's War on Terror* (New York: Random House, 2004).

Maurice R. Greenberg and Richard N. Haass (eds.), *Making Intelligence Smarter: The Future of U.S. Intelligence*, Report of an Independent Task Force (New York: Council on Foreign Relations, 1996).

Gerald K. Haines and Robert E. Leggett (eds.), *Watching the Bear: Essays on CIA's Analysis of the Soviet Union* (Washington, DC: Center for the Study of Intelligence, Central Intelligence Agency 2003), 33.

Efraim Halevy, *Man in the Shadows: Inside the Middle East Crisis with a Man Who Led the Mossad* (New York: St. Martin's Press, 2006).

John L. Helgerson, *Getting to Know the President: CIA Briefings of Presidential Candidates, 1952–1992* (Washington, DC: Center for the Study of Intelligence, Central Intelligence Agency, n.d.).

Richard Helms with William Hood, *A Look over My Shoulder: A Life in the Central Intelligence Agency* (New York: Random House, 2003).

Michael Herman, *Intelligence Power in Peace and War* (Cambridge: Cambridge University Press, 1996).

Richards J. Heuer, Jr., *Psychology of Intelligence Analysis* (Washington, DC: Center for the Study of Intelligence, Central Intelligence Agency, 1999).

Frederick P. Hitz, *The Great Game: The Myth and Reality of Espionage* (New York: Alfred A. Knopf, 2004).

Rhodri Jeffreys-Jones, *The CIA and American Democracy* (New Haven: Yale University Press, 1989).

Robert Jervis, *Perception and Misperception in International Politics* (Princeton: Princeton University Press, 1976).

Loch K. Johnson, *Bombs, Bugs, Drugs, and Thugs: Intelligence and America's Quest for Security* (New York: New York University Press, 2000).

Loch K. Johnson, *Secret Intelligence Agencies: U.S. Intelligence in a Hostile World* (New Haven: Yale University Press, 1996).

Loch K. Johnson and James J. Wirtz (eds.), *Strategic Intelligence: Windows into a Secret World* (Los Angeles, CA: Roxbury, 2004).

Thomas A. Keaney and Eliot A. Cohen, *Revolution in Warfare? Airpower in the Persian Gulf War* (Annapolis, MD: Naval Institute Press, 1995).

John Keegan, *Intelligence in War: Knowledge of the Enemy from Napoleon to Al-Qaeda* (New York: Alfred A. Knopf, 2003).

Sherman Kent, *Strategic Intelligence for American World Policy* (Princeton: Princeton University Press, 1951).

Ronald Kessler, *The CIA at War: Inside the Secret Campaign against Terror* (New York: St. Martin's Press, 2003).

Henry Kissinger, *Years of Upheaval* (Boston: Little, Brown, 1982).

Peter R. Lavoy, Scott Sagan, and James Wirtz (eds.), *Planning the Unthinkable: How New Powers Will Use Nuclear, Biological, and Chemical Weapons* (Ithaca: Cornell University Press, 2000).

Michael Ledeen and William Lewis, *Debacle: The American Failure in Iran* (New York: Alfred A. Knopf, 1981).

James Lilley with Jeffrey Lilley, *China Hands: Nine Decades of Adventure, Espionage, and Diplomacy in Asia* (New York: Public Affairs, 2004).

Carnes Lord, *The Modern Prince: What Leaders Need to Know Now* (New Haven: Yale University Press, 2003).

Douglas J. MacEachin, *Predicting the Soviet Invasion of Afghanistan: The Intelligence Community's Record* (Washington, DC: Center for the Study of Intelligence, Central Intelligence Agency, April 2002).

Douglas J. MacEachin, *U.S. Intelligence and the Confrontation in Poland, 1980–1981* (University Park: Pennsylvania State University Press, 2002).

Douglas J. MacEachin, *CIA Assessments of the Soviet Union: The Record versus the Charges* (Washington, DC: Center for the Study of Intelligence, Central Intelligence Agency, May 1996).

Melissa Boyle Mahle, *Denial and Deception: An Insider's View of the CIA from Iran-Contra to 9/11* (New York: Nation Books, 2004).

Earnest R. May (ed.), *Knowing One's Enemies: Intelligence Assessment before the Two World Wars* (Princeton: Princeton University Press, 1984).

Anthony D. McIvor (ed.), *Rethinking Principles of War* (Annapolis, MD: Naval Institute Press, 2005).

Judith Miller, Stephen Engelberg, and William Broad, *Germs: Biological Weapons and America's Secret War* (New York: Touchstone, 2002).

Richard Miniter, *Losing Bin Laden: How Bill Clinton's Failures Unleashed Global Terror* (Washington, DC: Regnery Publishing, Inc., 2003).

Lindsay Moran, *Blowing My Cover: My Life as a CIA Spy* (New York: G. P. Putnam's Sons, 2005).

The New American Bible, Saint Joseph edition (New York: Catholic Book Publishing, 1992).

Don Oberdorfer, *From the Cold War to a New Era: The United States and the Soviet Union, 1983–1991* (Baltimore, MD: Johns Hopkins University Press, 1998).

William E. Odom, *Fixing Intelligence for a More Secure America*, 2d ed. (New Haven: Yale University Press, 2004).

Richard A. Posner, *Uncertain Shield: The U.S. Intelligence System in the Throes of Reform* (New York: Rowman & Littlefield, 2006).

Richard A. Posner, *Preventing Surprise Attacks: Intelligence Reform in the Wake of 9/11* (New York: Rowman & Littlefield, 2005).

John Prados, *The Soviet Estimate: U.S. Intelligence Analysis and Soviet Strategic Forces* (Princeton: Princeton University Press, 1986).

John Ranelagh, *The Agency: The Rise and Decline of the CIA* (New York: Simon & Schuster, 1986).

Mitchell Reiss, *Bridled Ambition: Why Countries Constrain Their Nuclear Capabilities* (Baltimore, MD: Johns Hopkins University Press, 1995).

Jeffrey T. Richelson, *The U.S. Intelligence Community*, 4th ed. (Boulder, CO: Westview Press, 1999).

James Risen, *State of War: The Secret History of the CIA and the Bush Administration* (New York: Free Press, 2006).

Barry Rubin, *Paved with Good Intentions: The American Experience and Iran* (New York: Penguin Books, 1981).

Richard L. Russell, *Weapons Proliferation and War in the Greater Middle East: Strategic Contest* (New York: Routledge, 2005).

H. Norman Schwarzkopf and Peter Petre, *It Doesn't Take a Hero* (New York: Bantam Books, 1992).

George P. Shultz, *Turmoil and Triumph: My Years as Secretary of State* (New York: Charles Scribner's Sons, 1993).

Richard Shultz, Roy Godson, and Ted Greenwood (eds.), *Security Studies for the 1990s* (New York: Brassey's, 1993).

Gary Sick, *All Fall Down: America's Tragic Encounter with Iran* (New York: Random House, 1985).

Jennifer E. Sims and Burton Gerber (eds.), *Transforming U.S. Intelligence* (Washington, DC: Georgetown University Press, 2005).

L. Britt Snider, *Sharing Secrets with Lawmakers: Congress as a User of Intelligence* (Washington, DC: Center for the Study of Intelligence, Central Intelligence Agency, February 1997).

James E. Steiner, *Challenging the Red Line between Intelligence and Policy* (Washington, DC: Institute for the Study of Diplomacy, Georgetown University, n.d.).

Gregory F. Treverton, *Reshaping National Intelligence for an Age of Information* (Cambridge: Cambridge University Press, 2003).

George Weigel, *Witness to Hope: The Biography of Pope John Paul II, 1920–2005* (New York: HarperPerennial, 2005).

James J. Wirtz, *The Tet Offensive: Intelligence Failure in War* (Ithaca: Cornell University Press, 1991).

David Wise, *Nightmover: How Aldrich Ames Sold the CIA to the KGB for $4.6 Million* (New York: HarperCollins Publishers, 1995).

Markus Wolf with Anne McElvoy, *Man without a Face: The Autobiography of Communism's Greatest Spymaster* (New York: Random House, 1997).

Bob Woodward, *Plan of Attack* (New York: Simon & Schuster, 2004).

Bob Woodward, *Bush at War* (New York: Simon & Schuster, 2002)

JOURNAL ARTICLES AND CASE STUDIES

David Albright and Corey Hinderstein, "Unraveling the A. Q. Khan and Future Proliferation Networks," *The Washington Quarterly* 28, no. 2 (spring 2005).

Robert Baer, "Wanted: Spies Unlike Us," *Foreign Policy* (March/April 2005).

Bruce D. Berkowitz and Jeffrey T. Richelson, "The CIA Vindicated," *The National Interest* 41 (fall 1995).

Richard K. Betts, "Fixing Intelligence," *Foreign Affairs* 81, no. 1 (January/February 2002).

Richard K. Betts, "Intelligence Warning: Old Problems, New Agendas," *Parameters* (spring 1998).

Richard K. Betts, "Should Strategic Studies Survive?," *World Politics* 50, no. 1 (October 1997).

Richard K. Betts, "Analysis, War, and Decision: Why Intelligence Failures are Inevitable," *World Politics* 31, no. 1 (October 1978).

James G. Blight and David A. Welch, "What Can Intelligence Tell Us about the Cuban Missile Crisis, and What Can the Cuban Missile Crisis Tell us about Intelligence?" *Intelligence and National Security* 13, no. 3 (autumn 1998).

Daniel Byman, "Strategic Surprise and the September 11 Attacks," *Annual Review of Political Science* 8, no. 1 (2005).

Ashton B. Carter, "How to Counter WMD," *Foreign Affairs* 83, no. 5 (September/October 2004).

Eliot Cohen, "'Only Half the Battle': American Intelligence and the Chinese Intervention in Korea, 1950," *Intelligence and National Security* 5, no. 1 (January 1990).

William J. Daugherty, "Behind the Intelligence Failure in Iran," *International Journal of Intelligence and CounterIntelligence* 14, no. 4 (winter 2001).

Lawrence Freedman, "War in Iraq: Selling the Threat," *Survival* 46, no. 2 (summer 2004).

Lawrence Freedman, "The CIA and the Soviet Threat: The Politicization of Estimates, 1966–1977," *Intelligence and National Security* 12, no. 1 (January 1997).

Robert M. Gates, "An Opportunity Unfulfilled: The Use and Perceptions of Intelligence at the White House," *Washington Quarterly* 12, no. 1 (winter 1989).

Robert M. Gates, "The CIA and Foreign Policy," *Foreign Affairs* 66, no. 2 (winter 1987/88).

Michael I. Handel, "Intelligence and the Problem of Strategic Surprise," *Journal of Strategic Studies* 7, no. 3 (September 1984).

Robert Jervis, "Reports, Politics, and Intelligence Failures: The Case of Iraq," *Journal of Strategic Studies*, 29, no. 1 (February 2006).

Robert Jervis, "What's Wrong with the Intelligence Process?," *International Journal of Intelligence and CounterIntelligence* 1, no. 1 (spring 1986).

Richard Kerr, Thomas Wolfe, Rebecca Donegan, and Aris Pappas, "Issues for the US Intelligence Community," *Studies in Intelligence* 49, no. 3 (2005).

Klaus Knorr, "Failures in National Intelligence Estimates: The Case of the Cuban Missile Crisis," *World Politics* 16, 3 (fall 1964).

Joseph S. Nye, Jr., "Peering into the Future," *Foreign Affairs* 77, no. 4 (July/August 1994).

Paul R. Pillar, "Intelligence, Policy, and the War in Iraq," *Foreign Affairs* 85, no. 2 (March/April 2006).

Jonathan D. Pollack, "The United States, North Korea, and the End of the Agreed Framework," *Naval War College Review* LVI, no. 3 (summer 2003).

David S. Robarge, "A Look Back: Directors of Central Intelligence, 1946–2005," *Studies in Intelligence* 49, no. 3 (2005).

David S. Robarge, "Getting It Right: CIA Analysis of the 1967 Arab-Israeli War," *Studies in Intelligence* 49, no. 1 (2005).

Richard L. Russell, "Iraq's Chemical Weapons Legacy: What Others Might Learn from Saddam," *Middle East Journal* 59, no. 2 (spring 2005).

Richard L. Russell, "Iran in Iraq's Shadow: Dealing with Tehran's Nuclear Weapons Bid," *Parameters* XXXIV, no. 3 (autumn 2004).

Richard L. Russell, "Spies Like Them," *National Interest* 77 (fall 2004).

Richard L. Russell, "Intelligence Failures: The Wrong Model for the War on Terror," *Policy Review* 123 (February & March 2004).

Richard L. Russell, "CIA's Strategic Intelligence in Iraq," *Political Science Quarterly* 117, no. 2 (summer 2002).

Richard L. Russell, "Tug of War: The CIA's Uneasy Relationship with the Military," *SAIS Review* XXII, no. 2 (summer–fall 2002).

Richard L. Russell, "The Fog of War: NATO's Bombing of the Chinese Embassy in Belgrade," Pew Case Study, no. 253 (Washington, DC: Institute for the Study of Diplomacy, Georgetown University, 2002).

Richard L. Russell, "A Saudi Nuclear Option?" *Survival* 43, no. 2 (summer 2001).

Richard L. Russell, "American Military Retaliation for Terrorism: Judging the Merits of the 1998 Cruise Missile Strikes in Afghanistan and Sudan," Pew Case Study, no. 238 (Washington, DC: Institute for the Study of Diplomacy, Georgetown University, 2000).

Daniel Yankelovich, "Poll Positions: What Americans Really Think about U.S. Foreign Policy," *Foreign Affairs* 84, no. 5 (September/October 2005).

NEWSPAPER AND MAGAZINE ARTICLES

John Barry and Evan Thomas, "The Kosovo Cover-Up," *Newsweek*, 15 May 2000.

David Barstow, "Who the White House Embraced Disputed Arms Intelligence," *New York Times*, 3 October 2004.

William J. Broad and David E. Sanger, "The Bomb Merchant," *New York Times*, 26 December 2004, A1.

Barbara Demick, "North Korea's Ace in the Hole," *Los Angeles Times*, 14 November 2003.

John Diamond and Judy Keen, "Bush's Daily Intel Briefing Revamped," *USA Today*, 25 August 2005, A1.

John Diamond, "CIA's Spy Network Thin," *USA Today*, 22 September 2004, 13A.

Bob Drogin, "Spy Work in Iraq Riddled by Failures," *Los Angeles Times*, 17 June 2004, A1.

Thomas Fingar, "Questionable Intelligence," Correspondence, *The New Republic*, 10 July 2006.

Douglas Frantz, "A High-Risk Nuclear Stakeout," *Los Angeles Times*, 27 February 2005.

Douglas Frantz, "Iran Moving Methodically toward Nuclear Capability," *Los Angeles Times*, 21 October 2004, A1.

Douglas Franz and William C. Rempel, "New Find in a Nuclear World," *Los Angeles Times*, 28 November 2004, A1.

Barton Gellman, "Iraq's Arsenal of Ambitions," *Washington Post*, 7 January 2004.

Reuel Marc Gerecht, "I Spy with My Little Eye...," *Wall Street Journal*, 9 November 2005.

Reuel Marc Gerecht, "The Sorry State of the CIA," *The Weekly Standard*, 19 July 2004.

Jeffrey Goldberg, "The Unknown," *The New Yorker* 78, no. 46 (10 February 2003).

Stephen Grey and Don VanNatta, "In Italy, Anger at U.S. Tactics Colors Spy Case," *New York Times*, 26 June 2005, A1.

David Ignatius, "Spying: Time to Think Outside the Box," *Washington Post*, 29 August 2004, B7.

Douglas Jehl, "Qaeda-Iraq Link U.S. Cited Is Tied to Coercion Claim," *New York Times*, 9 December 2005, A1.

Douglas Jehl, "Bush's Arms Intelligence Panel Works in Secret," *New York Times*, 6 December 2004.

David E. Kaplan, "Playing Offense: The Inside Story of How U.S. Terrorist Hunters are Going after al Qaeda," *U.S. News & World Report*, 2 June 2003.

George F. Kennan, "Spy and Counterspy," *New York Times*, 18 May 1997, A17.

Jim Mann, "Threat to Mideast Military Balance: US Caught Napping by Sino-Saudi Missile Deal," *Los Angeles Times*, 4 May 1988.

Mark Mazzetti, "Spymaster Tells Secret of Size of Spy Force," *New York Times*, 21 April 2006.

Josh Meyer, "CIA Expands Use of Drones in Terror War," *Los Angeles Times*, 29 January 2006, A1.

Steven Lee Myers, "Chinese Embassy Bombing: A Wide Net of Blame," *New York Times*, 17 April 2000, A1 and A10.

Greg Miller, "CIA Operation in Iran Failed When Spies Were Exposed," *Los Angeles Times*, 12 February 2005.

Daniel P. Moynihan, "Do We Still Need the CIA?" *New York Times*, 19 May 1991, E17.

Walter Pincus, "CIA Morale on Hayden's Menu," *Washington Post*, 18 May 2006.

Walter Pincus, "Intelligence Director's Budget May Near $1 Billion, Report Finds," *Washington Post*, 20 April 2006, A11.

Walter Pincus, "CIA Spies Get a New Home Base," *Washington Post*, 14 October 2005, A6.

Walter Pincus, "Goss Plan to Strengthen CIA Is Ready," *Washington Post*, 16 February 2005, A2.

Walter Pincus, "Bush's Intelligence Panel Gains Stature," *Washington Post*, 7 February 2005, A19.

Walter Pincus, "Intelligence Efforts Get Boost: Undercover Officers to Keep Salaries from Civilian Jobs Abroad," *Washington Post*, 10 December 2004, A6.

Walter Pincus, "Bush Orders the CIA to Hire More Spies," *Washington Post*, 24 November 2004, A4.

Walter Pincus, "Spy Agencies Faulted for Missing Indian Tests," *Washington Post*, 3 June 1998, A18.

Dana Priest, "Covert CIA Program Withstands New Furor," *Washington Post*, 30 December 2005.

Dana Priest, "CIA Holds Terror Suspects in Secret Prisons," *Washington Post*, 2 November 2005, A1.

Dana Priest, "CIA Feels Strain of Iraq and Al Qaeda," *Washington Post*, 17 November 2002, A26.

James Risen, "To Bomb Sudan Plant, or Not: A Year Later, Debate Rankle," *New York Times*, 27 October 1999, A12.

Steve Rodan, "All in the Family," *Jerusalem Post*, 13 June 1997.

Richard L. Russell, "Saudi Nukes: A Looming Intelligence Failure," *Washington Times*, 5 January 2004.

David E. Sanger, "Pakistan Found to Aid Iran Nuclear Efforts," *New York Times*, 2 September 2004.

David E. Sanger and William J. Broad, "Pakistan's Nuclear Earnings," *New York Times*, 16 March 2004.

David E. Sanger and William J. Broad, "From Rogue Nuclear Programs, Web of Trails Leads to Pakistan," *New York Times*, 4 January 2004, A1.

Scott Shane, "Iraqi Official, Paid by CIA, Gave Account of Weapons," *New York Times*, 22 March 2006.

Scott Shane, "Intelligence Center Is Created for Unclassified Information," *New York Times*, 9 November 2005.

Scott Shane, "Official Reveals Budget for U.S. Intelligence," *New York Times*, 8 November 2005.

Scott Shane and Neil A. Lewis, "At Sept. 11 Trial, Tale of Missteps and Management," *New York Times*, 31 March 2006, A1.

Scott Shane and David E. Sanger, "Daily Intelligence Briefings are Vague, Officials Say," *New York Times*, 3 April 2005

Edward G. Shirley [Reuel Marc Gerecht], "Can't Anybody Here Play This Game?" *Atlantic Monthly* 281, no. 2 (February 1998).

Richard H. Shultz, Jr., "Showstoppers: Nine Reasons Why We Never Sent Our Special Operations Forces after al Qaeda Before 9/11," *The Weekly Standard*, 26 January 2004.

Phillip van Niekerk, "South Africa Had Six A-Bombs," *Washington Post*, 25 March 1993.

John Walcott and Brian Duffy, "The CIA's Darkest Secrets," *U.S. News & World Report*, 4 July 1994.

Joby Warrick and Glenn Kessler, "Iran's Nuclear Program Speeds Ahead," *Washington Post*, 10 March 2003, A1.

Shaun Waterman, "Goss Says CIA Ban Excludes Terrorists," *Washington Times*, 25 March 2005, A5.

GOVERNMENT DOCUMENTS

George W. Bush, *The National Security Strategy of the United States of America* (Washington, DC: The White House, September 2002). Available at http://www.whitehouse.gov/nsc/nss.pdf.

Central Intelligence Agency, *Intelligence and Policy: The Evolving Relationship* (Washington, DC: Center for the Study of Intelligence, June 2004). Available at http://www.cia.gov/csi/books/Roundtable_june2004/IntelandPolicyRelationship_Internet.pdf.

Central Intelligence Agency Report, "Further Comments on Iraqi Weapons of Mass Destruction," August 1995, Gulf Link Declassified Document. Available at http://www.gulflink.osd.mil/declassdocs/cia/19960705.

Commission on the Intelligence Capabilities of the United States Regarding Weapons of Mass Destruction, *Report to the President* (Washington, DC: U.S. Government Printing Office, 31 March 2005). Available at http://www.wmd.gov/ report.

Commission on the Roles and Capabilities of the United States Intelligence Community, *Preparing for the 21st Century: An Appraisal of U.S. Intelligence* (Washington, DC: U.S. Government Printing Office, 1 March 1996). Available at http://www.access.gpo.gov/su_docs/dpos/epubs/int/pdf/report.html.

Committee of Privy Counsellors, *Review of Intelligence on Weapons of Mass Destruction* (Norwich, UK: Her Majesty's Stationery Office, 14 July 2004). Available at http://www.butlerreview.org.uk/report/index.asp.

House Armed Services Committee, Subcommittee on Oversight and Investigations, *Intelligence Successes and Failures in Operations Desert Shield/ Storm* (Washington, DC: U.S. Government Printing Office, August 1993).

House Permanent Select Committee on Intelligence, *Intelligence Authorization Act for Fiscal Year 2005* (Washington, DC: U.S. Government Printing Office, 21 June 2004). Available at http://intelligence.house.gov/Reports.aspx?Section=56).

House Permanent Select Committee on Intelligence and Senate Select Committee on Intelligence, *Joint Inquiry into Intelligence Community Activities before and after the Terrorist Attacks of September 11, 2001* (Washington, DC: U.S. Government Printing Office, December 2002). Available at http://www.gpoaccess.gov/serialset/creports/911.html.

National Commission on Terrorist Attacks upon the United States, *The 9/11 Commission Report* (Washington, DC: U.S. Government Printing Office, July 2004). Available at http://www.9–11commission.gov/report/index.htm.

National Intelligence Estimate, *Iraq's Continuing Programs for Weapons of Mass Destruction* (Washington, DC: National Intelligence Council, October 2002). Available at http://www.fas.org/irp/cia/product/iraq-wmd.html.

National Intelligence Estimate, *Yugoslavia Transformed* (Washington, DC: National Intelligence Council, 18 October 1990). Available at http://www.foia.cia.gov/nic_collection.asp.

National Intelligence Estimate, *Trends in South Africa's Nuclear Security Policies and Programs* (Washington, DC: National Intelligence Council, 5 October 1984). Available at http://www.foia.cia.gov/nic_collection.asp.

Colin Powell, "Iraq's Failure to Disarm," Remarks to the United Nations Security Council (Washington, DC: Bureau of Public Affairs, Department of State, 5 February 2003). Available at http://www.state.gov/p/nea/disarm/.

Senate Select Committee on Intelligence, *Postwar Findings about Iraq's WMD Programs and Links to Terrorism and How They Compare with Prewar Assessments* (Washington, DC: U.S. Government Printing Office, 8 September 2006). Available at http://intelligence.senate.gov.

Senate Select Committee on Intelligence, *Report on the U.S. Intelligence Community's Prewar Intelligence Assessments on Iraq* (Washington, DC: U.S. Government Printing Office, 7 July 2004). Available at http://www. gpoaccess. gov/serialset/creports/iraq.html.

Special Advisor to the Director of Central Intelligence on Iraq's WMD, *Comprehensive Report*, Volumes 1, 2, and 3 (Washington, DC: Central Intelligence Agency, 30 September 2004). Available at http://www.cia.gov/cia/reports/iraq_wmd_2004/.

Index